HEFFO

A Brilliant Mind

www.**transworldbooks**.co.uk

Also by Liam Hayes

Out of Our Skins

HEFFO

A Brilliant Mind

LIAM HAYES

TRANSWORLD IRELAND

TRANSWORLD IRELAND
an imprint of The Random House Group Limited
20 Vauxhall Bridge Road, London SW1V 2SA
www.transworldbooks.co.uk

First published in 2013 by Transworld Ireland,
a division of Transworld Publishers

A CIP catalogue record for this book
is available from the British Library.

ISBN 9781848271852

Addresses for Random House Group Ltd companies outside the UK
can be found at: www.randomhouse.co.uk
The Random House Group Ltd Reg. No. 954009

The Random House Group Limited supports the Forest Stewardship Council® (FSC®),
the leading international forest-certification organisation. Our books carrying the
FSC label are printed on FSC®-certified paper. FSC is the only forest-certification
scheme supported by the leading environmental organisations, including
Greenpeace. Our paper procurement policy can be found at
www.randomhouse.co.uk/environment

Typeset in 11.5/15pt Minion by
Falcon Oast Graphic Art Ltd.
Printed and bound in Great Britain by
CPI Group (UK) Ltd, Croydon CR0 4YY

2 4 6 8 10 9 7 5 3 1

To all those men who went to war with Kevin Heffernan on
hundreds of football fields . . . and all of us
who stood in his way.

CONTENTS

Acknowledgements

Kevin Heffernan stood, and strode across, the Irish sporting land-scape as a colossus. He was an emperor and a genius. For forty years he was viewed, and admired and feared. And even though he subsequently, for over a quarter of a century, remained in 'retirement' as a national figure, Heffo never surrendered the mystical quality that had first presented itself in him as a young man heading out in search of adventure on GAA fields, looking for an All-Ireland title he could call his own.

A great many people, Dublin footballers and opposing managers and footballers, and sports fans, and sports writers and broadcasters, viewed Heffo for so long. All, without exception, remained forever enthralled.

Some writers came to brilliantly capture the man in words. Foremost amongst those from this present generation are Tom Humphries and David Walsh, and their writings and their works are acknowledged at different times in this publication, and again in detail in this book's notes and bibliography. But there are others too. RTÉ's Brian Carthy, in his broadcasting and writing, has done the life and times of Kevin Heffernan, and so many of his teammates and opponents (and the footballers on Heffo's Dublin teams) so proud. Equally, Radio Kerry's Weeshie Fogarty has brilliantly captured, forever more in print and broadcast, the wonders of the Dublin versus Kerry years.

However, before this present generation, there were men like Mick Dunne, who secured for Gaelic football and hurling fans the most intimate details of the greatest teams and greatest heroes from the 1950s and 1960s and 1970s. In the pages of the *Irish Press*, and later in his new working life in RTÉ, Dunne especially was a most trustworthy guide and chronicler for GAA people.

Other men and women from generations past, and from the heart of Dublin GAA – from the strong and visionary St Vincents GAA club – also afforded me the opportunity of tracking every step taken by Kevin Heffernan from his earliest years. The St Vincents members who compiled such a thorough history of their club to celebrate its fiftieth anniversary (1931–81) aided me in seeking to make this story of Heffo the story of the man's whole GAA life – and not just his life as the legendary manager of the Dublin football team in the crazy and unbelievable 1970s.

These men from different generations of journalists, in particular, but also so many other excellent writers and broadcasters whom I will not mention in these acknowledgements (at the risk of omitting even one name) enabled GAA people, and sports fans of all hues throughout the country, to see the deeds of Kevin Heffernan in their most astonishing magnificence. These men also enabled me to attempt to the best of my ability to write this first biography of Kevin Heffernan. I owe them all a thank you.

I would also like to thank so many other people who generously, and kindly, helped me through the course of the last two years as I built this book. The book was a work in progress long before 2011 when I sat down with Kevin Heffernan and informed him that I was about to attempt to capture the fullness of his public life in a biography. For many years, as a journalist and a footballer, I had spoken to so many people about the great man. Therefore, I wish to formally thank everybody who ever gave me even the tiniest glimpse into Heffo's actions and his thinking – and I must thank especially those, again, whom I will not mention by name, who gave me their time and hearty support.

If I mention one person, it must be Dessie Ferguson. Dessie and his wife, Maura, welcomed me into their home, and shared with me their cherished memories, and also shared with me their great store of newspaper articles and books which told the story of Dublin football and hurling teams over many decades. The Fergusons' 'treasure-trove' was almost the equal of the Mick Dunne Archive in Croke Park, which was so kindly opened to me by Joanne Clarke and Mark Reynolds.

With the support of those I have mentioned by name, and so many others, I set out to make an unbelievable story, believable.

Heffo was more than some magical 'grey' or 'white' wizard from the pages or the film set of *Lord of the Rings*! However, too often that was all we saw of him. That's how he was captured and presented by too many writers, far too often. We got too much of Heffo in a grey or white cape, and a big pointy hat, and not half enough of Kevin Heffernan, the man.

Or the boy and the young man who existed for and played the game, and won fifteen Dublin football titles and six Dublin hurling titles, before the rest of Ireland first got to meet him, in the early seventies, as 'the Great and Amazing Heffo'.

I wanted to write a book which told the story of the boy, man and wizard – and I sincerely hope that *Heffo: a Brilliant Mind* allows people to sec all three persons.

Prologue

'No . . . I don't think anybody would be interested in reading about me!'

KH

Thursday, 5 May 2011

There was no point in waiting.

As soon as the large pot of tea arrived and a nice plate of brack, with two slices already buttered, each kindly cut into two smaller pieces, I said what I had come to say.

'Kevin . . .'

We had already chatted for about fifteen minutes.

About his health, and mostly my ill health, and my continuing battle to get back fully on my feet after four months of chemotherapy and radiotherapy, though less than two years later, after his own longer fight, Kevin Heffernan would die from cancer at 83 years of age, after a lifetime of pulling and dragging forever on Sweet Afton and half a dozen other famous brands of fags.

We were in one of Heffo's homes from home, sitting at a quiet corner table in the old clubhouse in Clontarf filled with its stories.

Heffo's golf club, just across the Malahide Road from St Vincents GAA club.

Heffo's GAA club.

Parnell Park just around the corner, no longer the dingy little field where he completed his greatest piece of work as a football man, but now looking quite pristine, and floodlit.

His own house on the Howth Road, which he had built for himself and his wife, Mary, and their only child, Orla, just around the next corner.

All told, a small enough plot of land in a large city which, simply put, became the 'Kingdom of Kevin Heffernan' a long time ago. In the early seventies?

Longer than that, right back to the early fifties.

'Kevin ... I'm writing your story ... I'm writing your biography!'

I said it twice because I wanted to make sure that he had heard me, and that he knew exactly why I had asked him to meet with me.

Before saying what I had come to say, I felt a gnawing sense of dread. That's the way it usually was when half-strangers with pens and jotters approached Heffo and, often enough, like everyone else who looked to speak with him, I was nearly always filled with a tidy amount of terror.

One look from Heffo could make most men, tall or plump, shut up and think of quickly turning on their heels.

Scalded cats, all of them, before they had even opened their mouths. 'It's a story that has to be told ... just your story. And I'm here with complete respect to let you know ... that ...' It was time not to talk any more.

Kevin Heffernan, the mighty and amazing Heffo, even at his great age, had put both of his hands up to his face. He did so with an extra dash of drama. I had not expected that.

Neither did I expect him to lower his head, his hands still covering his face, towards the table. He stayed down for several seconds.

His head bowed in my direction.

I looked at the top of his head, and I took an extra deep breath as my uncertainty now definitely catapulted itself in the direction of genuine dread.

He had looked old, so frail.

I didn't expect him to be using a stick when he walked into the clubhouse but when I stood up and walked over to him, and held his hand, he was more Heffo than ever before. He sometimes had a look that could be as hard as nails and, on occasion, he had another look that was extraordinarily detailed in its open affection.

This morning there was no mistaking the warmth in his sunken face. His handshake was firm. He knew why I wanted to see him.

I had no doubt about that.

He respected me enough to make the time to get himself over to the golf club and talk, enough to sit in front of me and thank me for thinking about him. But, then he was going to say . . .

'No . . . I'd rather not.'

Or . . .

'No . . . who'd care to read about all of that now?'

He'd said it to me before. It was sure to be a definite 'No!' again. If I was to ask his permission, which I had no intention of doing.

It was almost twenty years since we had last met.

We had spoken on only a handful of occasions in our lives.

The first time was in the spring of 1986 when, in my first week working on a national newspaper, I decided to jump into the deepest end of journalism in Ireland. Chasing down either Heffo or Charlie Haughey dared journalists to that place. I was going to call Kevin Heffernan and ask him for an interview. I knew Heffo didn't do interviews, and I knew that he had no time for journalists, and that if he ever made time it was usually a few minutes filled mostly with barely concealed contempt. The phone call was pleasant, even welcoming. The next morning Heffo was waiting for me in the foyer of the Burlington Hotel and we shared a light breakfast.

I'd played against Heffo's new Dublin team in the eighties a few times. Twice in the first round of the Leinster Championship in 1983, again in the Leinster final the following year, and there were a handful of league and challenge matches sprinkled here and there, including a 'warm-up' game against Dublin, in St Margaret's on the northside of the county, one wet evening a few weeks before the 1985 All-Ireland final. I'd scored four or five points from mid-field, and had completely outplayed two of Heffo's first-choice men.

I'd walked off the field thinking, more than anything else, that I had shown Heffo something. But, I hadn't.

Through the summer of 1986 I was also part of a large Irish squad managed by him, and every Saturday morning for two months I turned up in O'Toole Park on the southside of Heffo's city. In the autumn Ireland were due to fly 'down under' and everybody was about to take their lives in their hands by playing against the big, bad men of Australian Rules all dressed up in their tight little ballerina numbers.

All dressed up and ready to knock our heads off once again, as they had two years earlier. Then do a dainty little dance on our graves.

I was quite sure I wanted to be on Heffo's plane.

Heffo, however, had no intention of letting me anywhere near his plane. I knew he didn't like me all that much as a footballer. He knew I was good enough, but he didn't believe I was good enough to do the job when it most needed to be done on the football field.

He had said just five words to me in those two months in O'Toole Park, and one week later he kicked me off his squad without another word being uttered.

Heffo had us all on one end-line, and he was standing out in front of us, about 20 or 30 yards in front, looking the same as he always looked, in the same jumper and shirt, same casual slacks he had worn on the sideline all his adult life.

'Take a deep breath . . .' he had ordered.

'And . . . hold it, and jog out to the "fifty"!'

There must have been forty of us on the end-line, and we all jogged towards Heffo, but when we arrived at the 50-yard line I found Heffo standing right in front of me.

'You didn't hold your breath!'

That's all he said.

Five words which meant nothing much to me.

But it was Heffo saying goodbye.

Almost twenty years skipped by since I had called him, and met him, in his offices in the Labour Court, where he was chairman, and where he said 'No . . . I don't think anybody would be interested in reading about me!' in reply to my second request to work with him on his autobiography.

Twenty years, unbelievably.

When I had called him at home a week earlier and an old man's voice answered, I decided to be sure I had taken the correct number from the telephone book.

'This is Liam Hayes calling . . . I'm wondering . . . ahem . . . is this Kevin Heffernan the former Dublin manager?'

I'd kept my voice light, informal.

'Is this Liam Hayes . . . the former Meath footballer?' the hoarse, raspy voice replied at the other end of the line.

Heffo seemed happy enough to hear my voice.

I took a soothing, deep breath.

'It is, Kevin . . . how are you?'

Finally, he lifted his head.

Heffo had a half-smile on his face, which was a nice surprise. It was a massive surprise, in truth.

'You know I have always wanted to write your story,' I informed him, unnecessarily, and waited.

No words were spoken for the next five seconds, six seconds.

'You're going to do it?' he asked.

'I am, Kevin.'

He lifted his cup to his lips and took the tiniest sip.

'Well . . . I can't stop you!' he said.

'I wish you weren't doing it . . . but . . . I know you'll do a fair job on me.

'And . . . I wish you well with it!'

Our conversation was still just beginning.

The hard part was done.

For both of us, I felt.

We had brack to eat, which Heffo promised me was very good, and we had teacups to be refilled.

We stayed talking until shortly before lunchtime, about every-body. Managers in the old days and managers today, and footballers we knew and loved. There were certainly footballers that Heffo genuinely loved as wholeheartedly as a man might love the most beautiful woman he had happened upon in his entire life.

Most of those footballers were some of his own Vincents lads: Keaveney and Hanahoe, and Mullins. Especially Brian Mullins. Two or three of them were Kerry lads. And then there was Mick Lyons, one Meathman.

An hour and a half skipped by.

This book was never mentioned again.

Part One

A Farewell to Heff

'I always wanted men who would die for one another . . . die to win.'

KH

Monday, 28 January 2013

Kevin Heffernan was in their hands now.

A little earlier in the evening his hearse began its short journey from St Francis' Hospice in Raheny to his parish church in Marino. The cortège had travelled down the Howth Road on the cold, drizzly Monday night, before turning on to Collins Avenue and stopping outside Parnell Park.

There, in Parnell, on that bumpy field that was turned up at one corner, and in the dingy old hut with the galvanized roof in another corner of the ground, Kevin Heffernan had built one of the greatest football teams there has ever been.

Out of nothing.

That was 1974. And by September of that year, Kevin Heffernan had become the bewildering, the miraculous, the stupendous 'Heffo', after taking his team from A to B, and then the whole damned way to Z.

From a putrefied group of footballers!

To white tracksuited celebrities and the dandiest of All-Ireland champs ever beheld by the trusty old game!

Until '75 that is, when Mick O'Dwyer's giddy young bucks from Kerry sent Heff and his team and his entire army of supporters high in the air with a devastating, surprising punch which, crazily, also came from nowhere.

*

The next twelve months, until September '76, were the longest of his life. The pressure and the torment, from all sides, and the demands massively self-induced in the Dublin manager's head, nearly finished him off. But Kerry were put down in the 1976 All-Ireland football final.

He had waited twenty-one years to defeat Kerry just once, when nothing else mattered, on the biggest day and last day of the entire season. That single victory in September of '76, however, would have to last him through the remainder of his life.

Even if that victory in '76 was very personal for Kevin Heffernan, and the most precious day of all in his GAA life, it still would be listed down the running order and behind the semi-final meeting of the two teams the next year, in 1977, when Dublin and Kerry came head-to-head one more time to decide, for good, who owned the decade.

The game in '77 quickly became titled for good as the greatest Gaelic football match ever played. However, as it was teased out to its conclusion, Heff was not in the Dublin dug-out or standing on the sideline with a cigarette almost squeezed to death between his right thumb and index finger.

He was in the Hogan Stand.

Retired.

Gone, and gone too early from the Dublin job for his own good. He'd be back, too late, in 1978. Then, once again, Dublin would lose to Kerry in the All-Ireland final. They'd lose again in '79 to Kerry.

Heff would stay even longer.

He'd lose to Kerry again with a new Dublin team in the 1984 All-Ireland final. Lose again in the '85 final to Kerry. Then, and only then, Heff would leave a second time. Get out for good, and stay out, officially. Unofficially, Kevin Heffernan never stopped guiding, and being consulted, and offering direction, and helping in every little way he could.

Tony Hanahoe managed Dublin in '77, and on the field he brilliantly orchestrated everything, right down to the final two late match-winning goals.

Only 1974 and '76 were Heff's.

Though '76 was outrageous and overwhelming in its own way.

Starting 20 seconds in when Kevin Moran immediately made nonsense of the No.6 on his back and careered forward with the ball, played a one-two with Bernard Brogan, and thundered the ball wide of the Kerry goal with a breathtaking drop-kick. When Dublin did score the first point of the game, another drop-kick, this time a neater and more exquisite drop-kick was at its heart.

Jimmy Keaveney took a short pass from David Hickey. He was nearly 50 yards from the Kerry goal, and was within range, but the full-forward chose to float the ball to the edge of the Kerry large square where Tony Hanahoe popped up, unannounced, exactly where Keaveney himself should have been found. Hanahoe curled his kick over the bar.

That was how '76 began.

The match ended with Dublin defeating Kerry for the first time in a championship game of football since 1934. A forty-two-year wait for the people of Dublin, in which time there had been six defeats and one draw. That untidy list of disappointments at Kerry's feet included the All-Ireland final of 1955 in which Heff struggled with a slight injury, but mainly found himself entirely suffocated by the momentous importance of the day itself.

It was a day, and a defeat, for which he could never forgive himself. Often he would openly admit to feeling shamed by his own failure. He felt he had given in to the day and given up on himself in '55, and he had waited, and waited, and when the final whistle sounded in the final in '76 he found himself marching across the field and grabbing Kevin Moran around the neck.

'I've waited twenty-one years for this!' Heff shouted into the ear of his centre-back, who was born seven months after the clock had started ticking on his manager's wait for a day of redemption.

The cortège moved back on to the Malahide Road, stopping outside St Vincents GAA club for a few good minutes, stopping again outside Clontarf Golf Club on the other side of the road. Gardai had the traffic halted in all directions as the hearse turned on to magnificent Griffith Avenue.

It inched its way slowly up the avenue. The car came to a final stop outside St Vincent de Paul church. The door was opened.

A folded Dublin flag lay on Heff's coffin.

So many of the men whom he had hand-picked through his days as the boss of all bosses in Dublin football awaited him.

Truly, they now had him in their hands.

It was only a short journey into the church, but there were so many hands available, beginning with the oldest hands in the churchyard belonging to the longest standing members of Clontarf Golf Club.

The next oldest hands belonged to his footballers from the seventies.

Anton O'Toole and Jimmy Keaveney.

Kevin Moran and Robbie Kelleher.

Bobby Doyle and Gay O'Driscoll.

The Blue Panther and Mr Dainty Feet. The Marauding Defender and the Deepest Thinker. The Galloping Gourmet of the forward line and the Enforcer in the deepest line of Kevin Heffernan's defence.

The coffin then passed to hands ten years younger, the property of the Dublin team that Heffo had redesigned and sent out to win his third and most defying All-Ireland title of all as manager in 1983.

Joe McNally and John O'Leary and Tommy Conroy.

Tommy Drumm and Barney Rock and John Caffrey.

Still waiting . . . there were still younger hands.

Young men from St Vincents who were also present-day Dublin footballers with All-Irelands still in front of them. They brought Heff the last few yards to the church door.

2

'I had so many satisfying things happen to me but in retrospect the thing about the game is the people you meet and the friendships you make.'

KH

Tuesday, 29 January 2013

If he had thought that they were going to applaud him, and his whole extraordinary life, he would certainly have given someone fairly sharpish orders to have his coffin, unceremoniously, hurried out one of the back doors of the church of St Vincent de Paul.

There were more and more pairs of hands awaiting Heff after his funeral mass on Tuesday morning.

Even bigger hands.

Brian Mullins was one of the easiest of all Heff's choices in all his days and nights managing football teams, and the once long-haired blond giant, who now had little hair at all, but whose shoulders now looked as wide as two medium-sized men, caressed the wood before taking a big step back from the coffin.

Goodbye Heff.

To Mullins, and to everyone who knew Kevin Heffernan as a young friend in the first half of his life, and an old friend and tormentor thereafter, there was no Heffo.

There was only Heff.

'They did him proud,' said Mickey Whelan quietly, in the church-yard that had hushed itself again at the end of the lengthy and spontaneous round of applause that had greeted Kevin Heffernan's coffin at the door.

Whelan, the mastermind behind the incredible levels of fitness which Heff sought from his team, from the very beginning in 1974, was speaking principally of Tony Hanahoe and Pat Gilroy, Vincents men both of them, and both of whom led Dublin to All-Ireland titles, in 1977 and 2011, in Heff's lifetime.

Both had spoken from the altar during the funeral mass.

Gilroy took just three minutes, deciding upon brevity in honour of a man who always had a preference for a message delivered short and sweet, even if it had blood-curdling intent. Especially short, actually, if such intent was being stamped and addressed.

'He created a very healthy legacy, such as how to carry success,' Gilroy reminded both friends, and foe, from olden days.

'He was very humble.

'He never sought the limelight or accolades.

'For him, it was always about the team.'

Hanahoe, a man more used to rich eloquence after almost half a lifetime representing others in the courts of the land, mentioned most precisely '. . . tea, Marietta biscuits and sheer determination'. He listed each as the three improbable, but chief ingredients of Dublin's march to six All-Ireland finals in succession in the seventies.

Three days earlier, Hanahoe had visited Heff in St Francis' Hospice. Hanahoe had looked at a man, he revealed, who seemed to be wondering where he was going and who he was going to select on his team when he got there.

'I could see him saying . . .' said Hanahoe.

'I'll have Lar Foley, Paddy Bawn Brosnan, Enda Colleran, Páidí, Ó Sé, Tim Kennelly . . . they're the backs.

'Des Foley, John Timmons, Purcell, Freaney . . .

'Dermot Earley, Frankie Stockwell . . . I'll build around the rest.'

Three of Heff's 'Team of the Heavens' were Vincents men.

Hanahoe may have short-changed his dear friend in that selection as Heff's life experience had left him in no doubt whatsoever that if enough Vincents men bandied together anything was possible.

Fourteen of them dressed up in the all-white of Vincents, with only one six-inch blue band wrapped around their chests, had played the reigning All-Ireland champions in April of 1953. It was a National League final. The Vincents players appeared in front of 37,605 paying customers accompanied only by Paddy O'Grady of the Air Corps who manned the goals.

A club team which did not even have a football field it could call its own property, and would have to wait another six years before doing so, was seated in the large cavernous tiled dressing-rooms underneath the Cusack Stand, waiting.

Waiting for them was Cavan in the persons of the Gunner Brady and his most famous bosom buddies, including Simon Duignan and Mick Higgins, who had earned themselves three All-Irelands in the previous six years.

It was all so improbable.

Or most likely a probable humiliation.

The thought of defeat never entered the head of a single Vincents man. Dessie Ferguson looked around him and nothing looked unusual. Nobody looked out of place. Everything was normal.

Perfectly so, right up to the last minute when they left the dressing-room.

'It's a fact,' he remembers to this day. 'We never thought for a second that we might get a bad beating . . . that would never have entered our minds.'

Right from the throw-up, the blond heads of Dessie Ferguson and Ollie and Cyril Freaney caused mayhem in the Cavan defence. Bernie Atkins scored Dublin's first goal after five minutes, Kevin Heffernan scored a second after eight minutes, and Ollie Freaney set up his brother Cyril for a third goal on ten minutes.

By the end of the afternoon St Vincents had scored 4–6. The All-Ireland champions had managed 0–9.

Two of the goals were Heff's. Two of the points as well. The No.15 had, most people in the club calmly reckoned on their way out of Croker, just played the greatest game he had ever played for the club or the county.

All in one short afternoon.

In the same churchyard of St Vincent de Paul, where they now all waited to see Heff off on his final journey, Kevin Heffernan had also waved off too many of the men who had once sat either side of him, and opposite him, in dressing-rooms in so many grounds on so many unforgettable Sundays.

With his dearest friends of all, he'd won fifteen Dublin senior football titles, including a seven-in-a-row, and six more Dublin senior hurling titles. The Vincents fellas had more than enough medals between them to share around the entire parish and, halfway through that haul, in the club's jubilee year of 1956, it was agreed by the players to get their medals smelted down and made into a gold chalice, which was presented to one of the two 'black cloths' who had founded St Vincents.

The Reverend Dr William Fitzpatrick, or 'the Doc' to all and sundry who lined out under his eye in the blue and white, was the recipient of the perfectly made chalice. His younger co-founder, Reverend Brother Ernest Fitzgerald, pulled the shorter straw from the same group of fellas. He was handed a golden pen and pencil set.

Over half a century later, Heff's funeral mass was celebrated by the Doc's nephew, Fr John Fitzpatrick. The chalice took pride of place on the altar. Built by so many men, by Heff and others gone too early before him.

Two years younger than Heff, Noel Drumgoole had been taken from the St Vincent de Paul church on a cold, bleak January afternoon in 1995. A footballer and a hurler, and captain of the Dublin team that went down to Tipperary in the All-Ireland final in 1961 by a single point. His medals were part of that chalice.

Before Drumgoole's funeral mass, Heff remarked that his friend was the 'most honest Vincents man ever'. The most loved Vincents man, however, may have been Ollie Freaney. He'd died four years before Drumgoole.

Freaney had died suddenly, twenty-two years earlier, back in

September of 1991, during a family holiday in Donegal. And Freaney, with his socks down around his ankles and his jersey flowing over his shorts, was the first man they all had ever known to embark on open psychological warfare on GAA fields. Particularly, Ollie's motley choice of amusing and light-hearted remarks was usually aimed at the opponents of other Vincents players. They chaired him off the field when he captained Vincents, in his last game, to victory over UCD in the Dublin senior final in 1959.

Ollie, the original Tony Hanahoe.

All movement, all the time running defenders around the field like dummies, and all the time leaving wide open spaces behind him in the middle of the opposing defence. Ollie was brought back home from Donegal to the same church. He was 62 years old when they said goodbye to him.

Ollie Freaney's medals were in the chalice.

Too young to have their medals on the altar, the famous Foley brothers were also long gone, though Heff and the fellas had to see them off from a different church than St Vincent de Paul, closer to the Foleys' birthplace in Kinsealy. The once tall, blond Adonis, Des Foley, had passed away at the age of just 54, in 1995. Des was empowered with such athleticism and raw power in the middle of the football field and the hurling field, but his stout, older brother Lar was a rock of muscle and common sense in the centre or the corner of those same Vincents and Dublin defences.

Lar was 65 when he went. He was right corner-back on the Dublin team that Heff captained to the 1958 All-Ireland title, beating Derry on the same day that Des Foley captained the Dublin minor footballers to All-Ireland victory also.

Heff and Des had the two trophies back home in Scoil Mhuire and Joey's the following day, commencing one of the happiest weeks the people of Marino, and the members in St Vincents would ever remember.

Before 1974.

After '74? Oh, after 1974 it was never the same for Dublin and for the GAA folk who lived in every nook and cranny in the city, not just Marino and Fairview and Donnycarney. After '74, and after

Dublin and Kerry had formally commenced the most pulsating duel in the history of Gaelic football the following year, life was never going to be the same again.

In the churchyard, they lingered awhile.

It was not a day to rush home. It was a day to feed one another memories of all the days, the bad days and the good days. All were equally enriching.

Young and old, and politicians and footballers and hurlers, they talked and they listened. They shook their heads and smiled. Laughter could also be heard. They knew that Heff would not want them to take the business of his funeral mass with a deathly seriousness.

In the middle of them all, maybe not as tall as everyone had remembered him, but wider, even wider than Mullins, was 'the Bomber' himself.

It was the Bomber, also known as Eoin Liston to his mother and father, who had begun the process of pounding Heff's beautiful, mesmerizing Dublin team into the dust in the final two years of that long duel in the seventies.

The Bomber chatted about great battles that ended all too quickly in the end, especially after the All-Ireland final in 1978 when he plundered three goals and Dublin were obliterated long before the final whistle. Kerry had five goals and 11 points that afternoon, making it not just an unholy rout in the second half, but the biggest winning margin in an All-Ireland final since 1936, when Mayo beat Laois by 18 points. Dublin managed just nine points after, weirdly enough, leading by 0–6 to 0–1 in the middle of the first half.

Tears had flowed down Hill 16 that day. And into the night not enough of the hardest stuff could flow down the throat of a Dublin man or woman to lighten memories still only hours old. The dream of three All-Ireland titles in a row had not perished. It had been pulverized.

Five maddening goals.

John Egan getting the first with an immaculate pair of hands at work. Mikey Sheehy, the second, chipping a free-kick over the head of the frantic, panicked figure of Paddy Cullen trying to scramble back on to his line. Then the Bomber, one, two, three . . . Boom, Boom, Boom!

Five of the best.

Now, thirty-five years later, everyone chatted, and huddled up against the chill wind as they slowly followed the hearse out on to Griffith Avenue, remembering only the joy of living through those six exhilarating years.

They remembered those gone from those games in the seventies.

Egan went twelve months earlier. He was 59. Tim Kennelly was only 51 when he went, in 2005. Mick Holden in 2007, went at 52.

The Horse . . . Egan . . . Holden . . . and then, six weeks before Heff passed, Páidí Ó Sé had also died suddenly at 57 years of age.

All of them too young. All suddenly.

Heff, at the end, was the fine age of 83 years old.

He was always a man to do his own thing, and decide on his own timing, on his arrival and, more importantly, his departure.

And, coming or going, Heff never wanted any fuss.

He hated that.

No fuss fellas . . . you hear me?

Part Two

A Parish Built of Stone

'In a football sense Vincents was always my home. That's how I view it. And like all homes and like all families, you have squabbles and arguments, but it's when some outside influence tries to upset things that you really see unity and purpose.'

KH

Thursday, 10 August 1893

'The Doc' was born.

The building of the parish of Marino on the northside of Dublin was a long way off. So too, the creation of St Vincents GAA club. Thirty, forty years, the pair of them. Meanwhile, a few miles outside Mountrath, in County Laois, Michael Fitzpatrick and Mary Phelan brought three sons into the world, two of whom would give distinguished service in the Archdiocese of Dublin.

One of the pair, Willie, would himself bring into the world, with the help of another religious figure, or 'black cloth' as Willie preferred to call the two of them, a GAA club which would do more than offer distinguished service and do whatever was asked of it.

They concocted St Vincents.

And St Vincents would very quickly be leading the way for Dublin football and hurling folk and, more than that, St Vincents would be moulding a whole different Dublin than anyone thought possible.

Willie Fitzpatrick.

A man of prayer. But never long-winded, never tripping over himself to sound extra important or impressively eloquent. His sermons were simple, they ran in straight lines, direct, and to the point. In the net, and on to the consecration! Off the altar, always a sense of humour, always a good chuckle, but never a riotous laugh. By nature quiet, retiring, humble, but with charisma to burn on a daily basis.

A hurler more than a footballer.

A GAA man and a rugby man, who was dispatched from the family's large enough farm in his earliest teens and was sent firstly to St Kieran's College in Kilkenny, and secondly to Rockwell College in Tipperary, and did not care about 'the ban' whenever he arrived at the turnstiles on Lansdowne Road.

He would pass away peacefully, sitting in his favourite armchair in the 'priest's house' in Raheny on a Friday, on a cold January evening in 1972. He was then fully titled the Right Reverend Monsignor William Fitzpatrick MA, DD. He was 79 years old.

Kevin Heffernan and the young men from Marino, and Donnycarney and Fairview, and other bolt holes close by, had a shorter name for him.

They called him 'the Doc'.

Or 'Doctor Fitz'.

One day, Kevin Heffernan and thirteen others squeezed themselves into the Doc's car. Though, in truth, not everyone was in the car.

Two boys were half-standing and half-sitting on the big strong mudguards which were bolted either side of the baby Austin. That was four outside in total, ten inside, not including the man of the cloth behind the wheel who drove right through the centre of the city as he made his way out to the Fifteen Acres in the Phoenix Park.

Fourteen was a record.

Others said they'd seen more fellas on the inside and the outside of the Doc's car on one or two occasions, but nobody pushed it. Fourteen was a good record, and there was nobody more proud of it, or of his boys, than Willie Fitzpatrick, who could be a shy man, until something had to be done fast.

Then he would be defiant, and bloody-minded. And if a guard

was to stop him on his way to a football or hurling match, as he whisked three-quarters of the team to their destination, then the Doc would let the officer of the law know in no uncertain terms that he was, amongst other things, taking on the Wrath of God.

'Cowboy stuff,' remembered Snitchie, affectionately.

If Kevin Heffernan was always simply 'Heff', then Des Ferguson was always, from the very beginning, 'Snitchie'. Respectively, each would power the St Vincents senior football and senior hurling teams for two full decades, and each would also play starring roles for the other man's team on a regular basis for good measure. Each was irrepressible.

'It was like . . .' explains Snitchie, 'the Doc's car . . . it was like something you'd see in the silent movies . . . fellas hanging on for dear life.'

But, Willie Fitzpatrick and his God made sure that nobody ever fell out of, or off, the baby Austin, ever, not once.

Doctor Fitz was a Doctor of Divinity after studying for three years in Rome during the Great War, and was ordained to the priesthood in the Basilica of St John Lateran in 1919.

The Archbishop of Dublin had Doctor Fitz in Terenure to begin with, then Dún Laoghaire, and then Portland Row, but his first curacy was in Fairview parish. It was good timing. Dublin Corporation was about to build one of the first dormitory suburbs in the city. The Church was in the building business too, in the same neck of the woods.

Marino was on its way, stretching into the adjoining country-side. And St Vincent de Paul church was also on its way, stretching heavenwards. Doctor Fitz would keep the same name in mind when it was time, later on, to build his GAA club.

Schools were called for. Two of them, able to take in 1,500 children each morning. In the middle, befitting a place called Marino, was Griffith Avenue, a road dressed up as a grand and magnificent boulevard that was as formidable as any in any European city.

All in all, a whole new parish was being built of stone.

*

Even when he was made Monsignor, Doctor Fitz stayed Doctor Fitz, or 'the Doc', and it was just as well that he carried a quick and easy name. Doctor Fitz was a fast one when it came to hitting places and people's lives.

They could easily remember him.

He would never forget all of them.

Once Doctor Fitz whizzed through either of the new schools that were built, Scoil Mhuire primary school or St Joseph's CBS, he would never forget a boy's name. He whizzed twice daily, before and after lunch. Tuesdays, Thursdays and Saturdays he had the boys in 'The Circle' in Marino, one of the two giant greens in the centre of the parish, which spawned smaller greens all around them.

Marino was named a parish in 1942.

It needed to be, because another large bunch of houses north of Marino, called the Donnycarney building scheme, had also sprouted up using the old Puckstown Road, which would become Collins Avenue, as its axis. Parishes made of stone were appearing all around the city, following the huge success of Marino, and Doctor Fitz was transferred to the new parish of Coolock, for a short while, in 1949.

Doctor Fitz would have new parishes in Marino, Donnycarney, Coolock, Killester and Raheny on his CV, and he would add to them more new parishes in Grange, Donaghmeade and Edenmore.

When it came to shaping a place and its people, Archbishop McQuaid thought that Willie Fitzpatrick had an especially brilliant touch.

4

'Location is extremely important. And we came to live in Marino very early on. I went to school in Scoil Mhuire, where football and hurling was next to religion.'

KH

Wednesday, 2 September 1931

The boys trooped in and sat down, and behaved themselves. There were two 'black cloths' at the top of the room already sitting down.

One was the Doc.

The other was their old teacher.

The boys were 13 and 14 years old, and most of them were in their first week back in school after their brilliant, never-ending summer holidays. There was homework to be done that Wednesday evening. But, when the boys asked at home about going to a meeting, and quickly informed their mam or dad who had called the meeting, there was no big inquisition at the kitchen table.

Kevin Heffernan had not been allowed out from the Heffernans' house on Turlough Parade that Wednesday evening. Heff hadn't asked his mam or dad.

He was only two years old.

They were all in the Richmond Hall, on Richmond Avenue, by 7.30 p.m. They were chatty and excited, but keeping a lid on things. None of the boys had ever been to a meeting in the hall at night-time before, and none of them knew what an agenda was like. All they knew was that there was something, and only one thing, to be talked about.

'Boys,' began their old teacher, who was happier than the Doc to get up on his feet on occasions such as this. 'Boys . . .' he continued, 'I've spoken to nearly all of you these past few weeks . . . and you all seem to believe it is a good idea to form our own Gaelic club here in the parish.'

The second 'black cloth' who would shape the lives of Kevin Heffernan, Des Ferguson and the whole gang, and who believed that a GAA club was needed if all of the young lads playing mostly hurling up and down the newly built roads were not to be lost to the devils in their imaginations, was a smaller, though equally thin man called Ernest Fitzgerald.

Reverend Brother Ernest Fitzgerald, supremo of Scoil Mhuire National School, and President and co-founder of St Vincents GAA club, to correctly present him in all of his finery.

He caught the Doc on one of his quick visits to the school a couple of weeks earlier, called him into an office, and put it to him that it was time to build a club for the boys, especially those boys who had left his school.

To begin with, the Doc was dubious.

That hesitation lasted about ten minutes.

Ernest Fitzgerald was thirteen years younger than Willie Fitzpatrick and he was a city boy himself. Waterford city. He knew city boys. His parents had no farmland to keep him busy morning and night, either side of school. His father, William, had been a farmer, but was now an ironmonger. Margaret Power, his mother, managed the family meat shop and public house that was sited in the centre of the city.

He had options in life.

In July 1921, however, Ernest opted to get the train up to Dublin, and the bus out to Baldoyle, keeping close enough to the water's edge as he had done all his life in the south-east of the country, and there he joined the Juniorate of the Christian Brothers. A year later he received the habit at the Novitiate of St Mary's, Marino.

Four years after leaving his home in Waterford, he found himself on the staff of St Joseph's in Fairview, teaching boys from third class up to sixth class. Three years later, in 1928, the year before Kevin Heffernan was born, Brother Fitzgerald was appointed to the newly opened Scoil Mhuire National School.

Sixth class and games, that was the Brother's day job.

He was quickly named school principal. Brother Fitzgerald was not a complete GAA man and nothing else. He loved the noble art, and formed a boxing club, and took charge of contests himself as an accredited referee. He loved music, and formed a musical society, and with his sleeves rolled up honoured two of his favourite composers, Gilbert and Sullivan, staging *The Mikado* and *The Pirates of Penzance*. All of Brother Fitzgerald's great loves in life, however, did not come to full colour on the northside of Dublin.

He had been 'moved' in the late summer of 1939 out of Dublin, and his devotion to the boxing ring and the great stage was enacted in front of the peoples of Cork, Mayo and Louth, before he was summoned back after twenty-seven years. In 1952 he commenced teaching the Leaving Certificate class at O'Connell Schools on North Richmond Street, the 'working man's Belvedere College' as locals liked to consider it, in a side-quip at the nearby fee-paying school, and Brother Fitzgerald would remain in that other great GAA nursery for the remaining days of his working life.

There were distractions for the boys in Marino.

Greater were the distractions, and temptations, however, for the boys up the road in Donnycarney. They had it all. A city at their backs, and a whole flowing countryside at their front doors.

It was a prized opportunity for young boys more than young girls. There was all the room in the world to play hurling and football, and nothing to stop them. Unless the man selling coal came by. When his horse and cart had moved on, the milkman might get in the way, an hour or two later.

There were no interruptions, no cars. People would walk by and cycle by at the side of the cement GAA pitches. There was nothing to stop a right good game once it got up and running on any of the streets which all had lovely new names. When the Fergusons moved to Donnycarney, from Castlewellan in County Down, they found themselves a nice new home on Elm Street.

Other Vincents boys were on Oak Road, and other streets named after all of the trees that could be found in the woods on the opposite side of Collins Avenue. Across the avenue, 300 yards on the other side of it, first of all, there was a stream, but after that it was open countryside.

Not so much for the boys from Marino like Heff and his like. 'Marino was a little more upmarket,' explains Des Ferguson, purposely with a sense of mischief at work. 'The Heffernans and the families from Vincents living in Marino thought the likes of us in Donnycarney were eating our young.'

Tuppence halfpenny looking down on tuppence, perhaps. The boys in Marino had their 'circles' of green in the middle of their housing estates, but the boys in Donnycarney had the real thing. And they'd dig up potatoes and other bits of vegetables from gardens and allotments, without disturbing any neighbours by asking permission or anything like that, and off into the country they'd go.

And disappear.

'Across Collins Avenue, over the stream,' declares Snitchie, 'and you were in the heart of the country. Nothing more . . . until you hit Monaghan . . . or Down!'

Their pockets would be filled.

Fires would be lit in the woods, and feasts would be set out. The thrill of cooking their own spuds over a fire in the middle of the woods usually lessened, considerably, once the first couple of boys tried to bite into their pitch-black bounty, still muddied, and hard and raw.

5

'I'm not going to tell you why Des Ferguson was called "Snitchie" . . . but, like everything else, I probably got blamed for it.'

KH

Sunday, 11 September 1955

It was the time of a young man's life.

The young men in St Vincents GAA club were about to win their seventh senior football championships by the end of '55. Each one grabbed straight after the other. And, also, they were into their first All-Ireland final.

Two semi-final replays, for the first time ever, were played in Croke Park, and on a nice balmy Sunday twelve of the Vincents men made up the Dublin team that fought out the last couple of minutes against Mayo with their backs firmly to the wall. They won by a single point, 1–8 to 1–7, and were into the 1955 All-Ireland final where they'd meet Kerry.

They would also meet Kerry as the hottest of favourites.

The first half of the 1950s were about winning everything in hurling and football. Hopefully winning one of the big ones soon for Dublin. Getting married. Starting families. Buying houses, or building them.

Kevin and Mary Heffernan would live on the Howth Road.

Des and Maura Ferguson would start out their lives, next door, on the same road. As would Jimmy Lavin and Joe Duffy from Vincents, and two fellas from Civil Service, Jimmy Shaughnessy and John Fay.

Six young couples.

Some married, and some waiting to get married.

Six houses to be built.

The sites on the Howth Road were picturesque. Charlie Haughey, an accountant who went to Joey's too, but was four years older than Heff, lived across the road. He had played a bit of football with the enemy, Parnell's, and wasn't having much better luck trying to become a TD. It was a nice wide part of the road, and a lay-road divided the sites from the bigger road. Further dividing the sites from the lay-road was a lovely belt of strong, mature oak trees.

It had been an easy agreement.

Everyone thought it a grand spot, with an easy quick run into the city on one side, and a nice handy walk down to Dollymount on the other side. The decision for each couple to put two hundred pounds into one kitty, making the principal sum of £1,200 to begin with, was a bigger step. But it was done.

The job of building the six houses lay with Des Ferguson. His father, Liam, had been a builder in County Down, and the Ferguson family stayed in the building trade when they came down south. The job of looking after the money side of things, and all the bookwork, lay with Jimmy Shaughnessy.

Des Ferguson had to keep things tight.

The houses had to be built on budget. And they were, and life for the first generation of young Dublin northsiders, nearly all of them raised where they now lived, if not all born and bred in Fairview and Marino and Donnycarney and Raheny, was up and running.

Building, and more building.

One hundred years earlier, in 1855, the Church of the Visitation in Fairview was completed and opened for worship after a build of eight long years. Dublin city had a population of 200,000, give or take, and the city was on the move. Slowly. Too slowly. Roads and houses were constructed at snail's pace given the needs of the people, and that would not change for the next half a century.

When the church was built, there were only twenty-one houses on Fairview Strand, one of them a police barracks. On tight, stringy

Philipsburgh Avenue there were another forty-one houses. There were two houses on Windsor Avenue, though most of the little avenues breaking away from Philipsburgh Avenue were built by a proud Scotsman who left trailing in his wake avenues by the names of Melrose, Waverly, Inverness and Lomond.

Before all these little roads and avenues and their small houses, there was only one real house built in Marino. This was a further one hundred years back, in the mid-eighteenth century, when James Caulfeild, the 1st Earl of Charlemont, enjoyed life in the splendour of Marino House. He lived to the grand old age, in that century, of 71 years. He was 26 years old when he arrived in Dublin in 1753. He was an interesting man, with a cultivated taste for the artistic and the literary and, surprisingly enough, politics.

Charlemont's quest for classical art and culture took him, in his early adulthood, on a nine-year tour of Italy, Greece, Turkey and Egypt. Marino House was duly named after his lengthy experience of living it up in Lazio, in the little city of Marino in the Alban Hills just south of Rome.

He nearly crippled his estate building Marino House, but then insisted on building another 'little house' in his grounds, linked to his main residence by a tunnel. It was his Casino, his 'casa', his 'playhouse', which became the most talked about neo-classical building in the entire country. From the outside it looked like a house made up of one large room. Inside, Charlemont had a base-ment and a main floor, servants' quarters, reception rooms, and a state bedroom, naturally.

The big house would have to give itself up.

On its lands, in 1924, the Free State Government of Ireland began its own biggest and finest build, the Marino housing scheme.

Charlemont's house would be levelled. The house which had been built in the south-eastern corner of the vast estate, and had such an exquisite view of Dublin bay once upon a time, was soon gone. Charlemont's Casino would be untouched, but his lands would become covered by new houses, hundreds and hundreds of them. A 'Garden City' of 1,300 houses would be built on

Charlemont's once private patch of Ireland. Such city builds were the dream of the son of a London shopkeeper, Ebenezer Howard, who had gained considerable attention for his publication *Garden Cities of To-morrow*, which planted the utopian idea of people living hand in hand with nature, and still living in great big cities.

It would take five years.

Five years of ingenious planning and layout. Two estates, Charlemont and Croydon. Two huge circular greens in the centre of each estate. Avenues of houses fanning in all directions like the spokes of a wheel from each expansive green. And more rectangular greens, smaller in size, but big enough for any pursuit dreamt up in the head of a boy or a girl.

All of these patches of green would be scuffed and dug up in winter and spring, and worn down and hardened in summer and autumn, as games of football and hurling matches turned them all into screeching battlegrounds. Reputations were gained and lost on these patches of green by some of the greatest footballers and hurlers in the history of St Vincents GAA club.

'I did not want strong dummies. At that time intelligent guys were available and that is a very rare happening in sport.'

KH

Monday, 23 November 1931
8.30 p.m.

Sixty-eight mostly boys, and a handful of men, attended the first general meeting of the proposed new St Vincents GAA club in Richmond Hall in Fairview. In his little black notebook, the Doc recorded the names, addresses and dates of birth of all of those who looked any way fit for duty on a hurling field or a football field.

Then, the hard work had to start.

The primary venue for this work was 'The Circle', one of the great-sized greens built under the housing scheme.

It was one of Scoil Mhuire's homes to begin with, 'The Circle', and also Dolan's field at the top of Philipsburgh Avenue, but the Doc had made 'The Circle' even more of a home by inveigling the corporation to build one communal dressing-room.

The building was constructed at the north end of the green, and while they were at it, the Doc also talked the corporation into putting an iron railing around the whole blessed thing.

In the decade before the coming of St Vincents, Scoil Mhuire had afforded the young fellas the opportunity of winning more games than they ever lost. There were happy days, and sad days, and then there was the day when Scoil Mhuire won the 'Kerry medals'.

At the tail end of the 1920s, into the early thirties, Kerry and Kildare were the two giants in Gaelic football. They would meet in four All-Ireland finals. Kerry would win three of them. They were two busy teams, but the Doc marched up to the pair of them with the idea of getting together in Croke Park, for one more Sunday, and helping reduce the onerous debt being carried by the new church in Marino.

Discussions of this nature normally weaved their way, to begin with, through the homes of men of the cloth in all of the necessary counties. When the men of the cloth were satisfied that the idea was worthy, and could make a good few bob, then the men who ran the GAA in the same counties were usually told what was about to happen. Kerry and Kildare were duly informed of what was happening.

Financially, the match was a huge success.

Kerry won, but either they snubbed their noses at the set of gold medals about to be handed out, due to the fact that they had been purchased in England, or so the story has been retold, or else they were asked by the men of the cloth, would they consider leaving the set behind them, in Dublin?

Kerry went home empty-handed.

The gold medals were put up for a new tournament, for all of the primary schools in Dublin. The final of the competition was held in Croke Park. Westland Row met Scoil Mhuire. Westland Row worked everything around Jackie Carey. A few years later Carey would be snapped up by Manchester United for a breathtaking £250 and commence a brilliant career at inside-left for club and country. Scoil Mhuire did very well to draw with Westland Row.

The Doc turned down the offer of extra-time. Scoil Mhuire had more work to do in Dolan's field. They reappeared for the replay, neutralized young Jackie Carey as much as they possibly could, and won the match by a handsome margin. The 'Kerry medals' were theirs.

So, gold medals were already on display on the sideboards of a large number of the boys who attended the first general meeting of St Vincents GAA club. Hard work was no problem to them. They had already done their sums. They knew exactly what hard work nearly always equalled.

*

This was the nursery awaiting Kevin Heffernan.

The club colours were agreed. All white, with a blue band six inches wide across the chest. The first playing kit was bought. The date was set for the first game of football to be played by the new St Vincents GAA club. It was six days after the general meeting. Sunday, 29 November 1931. Fingallians were the opposition.

Except Fingallians did not turn up on their bikes in sufficient numbers, even though the game was only a few miles down the road in Finglas. However, the local team from Erin's Isle were hanging around that afternoon, and the two played a friendly match.

St Vincents won by two points.

St Vincents 1–5, Erin's Isle 1–3.

Trouble would brew.

St Vincents, a young club with underage teams only, and no adult team of their own, were about to sail into a storm that would blow hard and often, and trouble the club for the guts of a decade.

Parnell's GAA club was nearly forty years older than St Vincents, and all of its life Parnell's had first call on the best hurlers and foot-ballers in the growing parishes of Donnycarney, Artane and Coolock. What's more, all of the best hurlers and footballers answered that call.

When the young men from St Vincents were grown men, they became Parnell's men, it was as simple an arrangement as that.

St Vincents had more than enough young lads. More than enough success too, winning all four titles in 1936, minor football league and championship and minor hurling league and champion-ship. Sharing the lads around was not a problem, and watching them grow further still as hurlers and footballers with Parnell's was part of the natural order of things at the beginning of the 1930s. And Parnell's were getting stronger and stronger through the decade, with former Vincents men celebrating in the green and black jerseys when Parnell's closed out the decade as reigning senior football champions.

In the mid-1930s, however, not everybody thought this such a great idea any more. Meetings were ruffled every so often with protracted discussions about the whole deal. Some, still, considered it decent. Some thought it a damned arrangement. General meetings saw men get to their feet, and discussions sometimes ceased, and physical exchanges commenced.

It was time to vote.

Really, every man voted privately with his own conscience, and his future wishes for himself and his young family. St Vincents ended up divided, if not wholly bisected right down the middle.

Schoolmates went in opposite directions.

Teammates played their last games.

The Doc grieved.

7

'Hurling is a great game, a better game ... unfortunately, I was a better footballer.'

KH

Sunday, 14 December 1941

On the Sunday morning a large gang of hurlers gathered, as usual, on the corner of Griffith Avenue and prepared to set off by car and bicycle. Some supporters would follow on foot.

The junior hurlers had qualified for the junior A final, and a win would see St Vincents land one foot into the county's senior ranks for the first time in the club's history. Con Colbert's, made up greatly of Limerickmen, and named after their countyman who worked as a clerk in Kennedy's bakery in Dublin and bravely gave his life in 1916, were the opponents. It was always good to cycle and walk out to Coolock for a match on a nice summer's morning.

The middle of winter was a different matter.

But it was a big day.

St Vincents won, and topped the junior A table at the year's end, two points ahead of Con Colbert's and four points in front of Fontenoy's.

The hurlers were senior.

The hurlers were up.

This did not surprise too many people in the club. The Brothers teaching in the schools in Marino were largely Munster men, and if not from Cork and Tipperary and Limerick, they were coming up to Dublin from Leinster's hurling superpowers, Kilkenny and

Wexford. As a result, hurling became number one in the local schools.

It would take a little time longer for St Vincents footballers to also arrive, safely, as a senior team. Though the clock was ticking industriously with many dozens of fine young footballers leaving Scoil Mhuire every year, and most of them heading into Joey's and O'Connells to further finesse their abilities, and sharpen their ambitions.

The conveyor belt was speeding up every single year.

Sitting on that belt was the young fella by the name of Kevin Heffernan, who was a footballer first of all. Hurling was very much his second love.

The Doc kept his baby Austin for match day.

When he was visiting the schools and calling to the houses of his players, he preferred his trusty, double-crossbar, black Raleigh bike. And the bike would make its way up Turlough Parade and visit the Heffernans to keep them up to date of what would be required of their talented young fella.

The older Kevin became the busier he was, and as a young man leaving Joey's – now officially 'The Heff' to his friends – he was as busy as the rest of them. Football and hurling matches were played on the same Sundays through the 1940s, and fellas who were playing a football match way out in the west of the county, as far away as Ballydowd in Lucan, might have to cycle like hell to get to Crumlin, or head all the way back over to Balbriggan, for a hurling match two or three hours later.

The sandwiches would have to be packed that morning. Often or not, there was no time to be running home or stopping off.

The footballers from St Vincents never did win their way out of the intermediate ranks. In the end, the footballers were sent up to senior with a bit of a leg-up, and a heave-ho, having to be enacted.

In 1946 the footballers were elected to go up.

There was no silverware, no great night of celebration like that enjoyed by the hurlers. The club had to apply to the Dublin county board. Nobody considered St Vincents any kind of threat. They got the nod.

Everybody knew that Vincents were young and inexperienced, and in all their innocence they played the ball more with their fist than their boot. It was not a tactical recipe which seemed suited to the Dublin senior football championship, but, in 1946, in their first attempt as a senior team, Vincents beat St Mary's from Saggart in round one of the championship, really surprised the mighty Geraldines in round two, and made their way to the semi-finals where the reigning county champions, Parnell's, awaited.

It was a match that had everyone talking.

In the end, there was not one explosion of violence on the field, only skirmishes. Nobody got hurt, and Parnell's won by two points.

What hurt Vincents more, when they arrived back to their homes in Marino, however, was the fact that they were properly undone on the day by Quinner.

Brendan Quinn.

One of the Vincents underage stars.

It was true. Vincents did play the ball around so fast that onlookers wondered, did the lads in blue and white all think that the feckin' ball was red hot? Nevertheless, the innocent young group of footballers would serve a short apprenticeship as a senior football team.

Three years later, they would win the Dublin senior football championship for the first time. There were some great names on that team. Names that would remain great for Vincents and Dublin for the next decade and beyond, and at No.15 was Kevin Heffernan.

The Heff.

He was in the full-forward line to stay, unless of course he decided to wander and bring his man on a bewildering run down to the halfway line. Heff would stay in that full-forward line for the next two decades.

Heff and Vincents would win fifteen Dublin senior football championships before they were finished.

8

'I think in the end he took pride in not being interested. I'd come home and he'd want to know what happened for when he got asked in the station. Sometimes he would be on duty outside Croke Park when we would be playing. He'd make a point of not going in.'

KH

Sunday, 6 October 1946

For the final three years of the Second World War, the All-Ireland minor football and hurling championships were seen as being of little importance. They were not staged. In the autumn of 1945, at the war's end, Dublin won both.

Both teams were chock-a-block with Vincents lads.

In 1946, there was again no stopping the teenagers from Vincents and Dublin, and the minor hurlers handled Tipperary in the All-Ireland final with assuredness for the second year on the trot, winning by two points. There were ten Vincents lads on the Dublin team in the All-Ireland football final on the first Sunday in October in 1946. They looked sure to beat Kerry. Paddy Lawlor was No.3, Jimmy Lavin No.6, Sean Guina and Nicky Maher Nos. 8 and 9, Ollie Freaney No.11, Tony Clohessy No.14.

And Kevin Heffernan No.15. They formed the spine of the team and had the team's star customer in the top left corner. Nobody in Marino could see them losing. They lost by seven points. Never really played in the second half.

They folded.

Young Heff never got out of the traps.

Kerry 3–7, Dublin 2–3.

42

Ciarraí.

The Kingdom.

All of their aul' guff.

Their absolute and total brilliance, on top of that guff.

Heff had found his greatest enemy.

That Sunday evening in 1946 was the beginning of a long war that Heff would wage ... no, completely and agonizingly rage against Kerry until, at last, finally, he said enough was enough, forty years later.

Turlough Parade was never much of a parade to begin with. The street comprised just four houses on either side, and the entire parade was tucked snugly away to one side off Griffith Avenue.

But, between the eight houses, there were footballers and hurlers, soccer and rugby players, and a hammer thrower. The Lawlors answered to almost all of those callings, and Paddy would play in the second row for Ireland, and John would stand his ground in the steel cage at the Olympic Games in Rome and Tokyo and let rip with the round lump of steel.

Two doors down from the Lawlors lived John and May Heffernan, an Offalyman and a Kilkenny woman.

Their son, Kevin, with the thatch of blond hair, would show the other families on Turlough Parade that he might make a name for himself at something. Though he was on his own in that mission in his life. May Heffernan had strong maternal, supportive instincts, but John Heffernan didn't push, shove, or pull his son back. He didn't get involved at all.

John Heffernan was not a sportsman. He was a garda. He was a fisherman, and ran dogs, and went shooting. In the summer months he might spend some evenings high above the Featherbeds in the Dublin Mountains cutting turf. Other evenings he'd be in Beaumont, working his allotment, tending to his prized plot of vegetables.

The Heffernans' was the corner house on Turlough Parade. The one with the cherry tree in the centre of the small front garden. The garden with the immaculately presented and tended flowers. That was John Heffernan's life outside his family home.

No hurling.

No football, and not an ounce of interest in either.

None.

St Vincents second shot at the senior football championship was short and wide of the mark in 1947, losing to St Mary's of Saggart in the first round. In 1948, they were a little older, and some of the lads from the Dublin minors of '46 were now coming through on the team, including Heff.

Vincents got on a bit of a roll in '48, and trundled into a semi-final where they accounted for their closest of neighbours, Parnell's. In the final they came up against Garda.

It was close all through.

Garda had plenty of big guns. Tom Langan of Mayo, who would be named with Kevin Heffernan on the GAA football Team of the Century, was in at full-forward for starters. Kerry's Teddy O'Sullivan was also in the forwards. In the half-back line they had the formidable pair from Roscommon, Brendan Lynch and Bill Carlos, who had won two All-Irelands in 1943 and '44.

There was one point in it.

Garda 2–8, St Vincents 2–7.

The defeat was painful for Vincents, but the still young Heff was off the field and had other things on his mind by then. The pain at the side of his jaw was unbelievable every time he moved his mouth. His jaw had been broken by the fist of a garda, but despite his pain Heff had to get his head down.

He was starting his Leaving Cert exams that same week.

In July of 1949 Heff was back, standing in the middle of the back row, as Vincents posed for their team photograph in Croke Park before another Dublin championship final.

There was sweltering heat in Croker that Sunday afternoon. It was midway through the longest, hottest of summers. Vincents had defeated Banba in the first round, and they took UCD out by 2–12 to 1–7, as Maurice Whelan completely controlled Mayo's war horse

Padraig Carney in an epic midfield tussle. A replay was needed to get past O'Toole's in the semi-final, but there was seven points in it the second day. Vincents were back in their second final in succession.

In Croke Park, the main event of the day was Meath and Louth. The 'afters' was the Dublin senior football final. Meath and Louth had just completed their epic battle over three Sundays in the Leinster championship minutes earlier, and Meath would win the Leinster championship, and the All-Ireland title for the first time, by the end of the year.

Before the last of the Meath and Louth footballers had dragged themselves into the shade, however, the Vincents team had raced on to the field. And they never stopped running on a pitch that had been whitened and baked hard as bricks by several weeks of glorious and continuous sunshine.

They had Clanna Gael completely over-run by half-time. Eight points was the difference between the teams. Long before the very end, Clann had officially thrown in the towel. Three of their men were sent off. Vincents energetic, maddening running game had got the better of them. Roasted them physically, tortured them mentally. The Freaneys and Snitchie Ferguson were unstoppable.

Heff scored a goal and eight points. He left nothing to chance any time he got the ball into his hands, and Vincents finished up, pretty much pulling up.

St Vincents 4–11, Clann na Gael 2–5.

Twelve whopping points.

A first senior title.

A day to be celebrated like no other in Marino, though with fourteen titles following in the next two decades that day of triumph in July of '49 was soon swallowed up, and almost forgotten.

Part Three

A Time of Triumph and Terrible Regret

9

'It has to start with the defence . . . if it doesn't start there, then it doesn't start at all. I found that out early enough.'

KH

Sunday, 6 December 1953

Poggy Lillis accepted one last slap on the back.

There were about a dozen and a half of them since the game had ended. Des Ferguson, Norman Allen and Liam Donnelly, Terry Jennings, they all slapped him good and hard, or grabbed him in one shape or another.

'Poggy,' came one cry, 'save of the century!'

'UNBELIEVABLE,' someone else roared from the other side of the dressing-room. And, indeed, Paddy Lillis, employed by Tayto crisps most of his life, who would have four of his sons play for Vincents, and who remained Poggy right up to his funeral notice in May of 2011, had no reason not to believe that he had pulled off one of the greatest saves anyone had seen in Croke Park in maybe a decade.

He hadn't seen much of it, but everybody else had. They told him he'd made the save of all saves, so why wouldn't he believe them?

He'd saved a sure-fire goal and St Vincents had beaten the mightiest hurling team in the whole country by a single goal, 3–11 to 2–11, in an absolute thriller. They'd beaten Glen Rovers. Des Ferguson might have been the hero of the hour, if not for Poggy.

St Vincents v Glen Rovers was encapsulated from beginning to end by Des Ferguson v Christy Ring.

Two contests in one, really.

Ferguson lined out at centre-back. Not a big man, and needing to get up on his tippy-toes to hit the six-foot mark, Snitchie at the same time always properly filled out the No.6 shirt for Vincents' hurlers.

Snitchie was in control of Ring, but in the crucial moments coming up to half-time Ring, for once, got away from his man.

Ring got up a head of steam and was bearing down on Poggy, coming in from the right-hand side of the Canal End goal. Fifteen yards out, Ring let off a rasper, in the most classic Christy Ring style.

The ball was bound for the top corner of the net. Every Vincents defender had stopped in his tracks. Everybody stilled themselves. Croke Park was momentarily frozen in time. There was just the ball on the move.

The ball, and Poggy, who was also on the move, hurtling himself across his goalmouth. His stick touched the ball on to the post, as far as everybody witnessed. The ball bounced back into play. It was cleared down the field.

The next morning, one newspaper in particular decided to take a closer look at the save, and duly upended Poggy's personal celebrations. The newspaper reproduced the 'save', and minutely followed the progress of the sliotar with a white dotted line. The ball had struck the post about two or three feet above the tip of Poggy's outstretched hurley.

That victory on that dry, mild December afternoon in 1953 brought to an end a year that Kevin Heffernan, even Heff, who preferred to aim for the stars rather than the ceiling, never even dreamed of.

He ended the year with a stick in his hand, in the full-forward line with Mark Wilson and Budger Keely. The three of them could be proud of themselves. Keely and Heff each hit the back of the net and, incredibly, Vincents had seen off half of the Cork team that had won the All-Ireland title in 1952 and again in '53. Glen Rovers were back-boned by Ring, John Lyons, Vincent Twomey, Josie Hartnett, Johnny Clifford and Eamonn Goulding. With the rest of his mates in Vincents, Heff once again had the church to thank for the opportunity.

A crowd of just below 20,000 also thanked the men of the cloth for providing them with the greatest game of hurling between two clubs anyone had ever seen. The new Bishop of Cork, Con Lucey, had asked for the game. He wanted it included in his fundraising efforts aimed at a massive church-building programme in and around Cork city.

Nobody had forecast 1953.

For five years, St Vincents had been on a journey that started out into the unknown, with everybody wondering what might become of the club.

The journey quickly became an exciting, enthralling adventure. The years slipped by, and the adventure became part and parcel of everyday life for hurlers and footballers living in Marino. By 1953, St Vincents was the single most powerful force in Dublin GAA. The club had led the county.

In many respects, so often, the club had become the county.

In '53 St Vincents won the Dublin senior football and senior hurling championships. St Vincents won the Dublin intermediate football and intermediate hurling championships. To keep the conveyor belt of future talent ticking along nicely, they'd also lifted the Dublin juvenile football championship.

The year was also book-ended with sensational victories over the greatest teams outside of Dublin.

In April of '53, fourteen St Vincents men had taken on the reigning All-Ireland football champions, Cavan, in the National League final and won by nine points. And, in December of '53, St Vincents had taken on Glen Rovers and half of the Cork team that was reigning All-Ireland hurling champions and beaten them by three points.

But it was not totally flabbergasting.

The road, and the long journey to 1953, had been taken in a courageous and utterly defiant manner.

Ourselves, and ourselves alone.

That's how St Vincents decided it should be, in their very own 'Sinn Fein' view of Dublin GAA life, five years earlier.

It was time to build high walls around the club.

Build them high around the county too.

Make sure that men wearing the Vincents white and blue jersey, and the men wearing the Dublin sky blue jersey, were Vincents men and Dublin men, and did not belong to anyone else.

Since the very founding of the GAA, club jerseys and county jerseys in Dublin had been used and abused. Accepted one week, thrown back on the floor the following week. Too many Dublin clubs had too many important players on 'loan' from clubs all over the country.

Too many Dublin clubs, in fact, were created by country folk. Geraldines took in the Kerry lads. Westerners took in the lads from Mayo and Galway. Faughs had lads from Kilkenny and Tipperary, a great many of them working as barmen, and it was always good to get them early on a Sunday morning when half the Faughs team was usually still in need of a few hours' sleep. Though caution was always needed if a Vincents man took a swig out of a Faughs' water bottle as, occasionally, the contents included some extra fortification.

Civil Service had lads from everywhere. There were other clubs too that were all founded for many good reasons, but reasons that did not have the continued or improved health and welfare of Dublin written down in anyone's blood.

And with men from different counties wearing the Dublin jersey, and some of them happy to wear the Dublin jersey over their own county jersey, GAA people in the city couldn't be bothered paying good money to watch or support their own county. It was as personal as watching wandering minstrels.

When Dublin had won the All-Ireland football championship in 1942 the attendance was 37,105. There were twice as many people in Croke Park to see Roscommon win the 1943 final, and 79,245 turned up to see Roscommon win two in a row in '44.

Bobby Beggs from Skerries wore the Dublin jersey when Dublin lost the 1934 All-Ireland football final to Galway. Four years later he won an All-Ireland with Galway. Four years after that, he was back on the Dublin team which defeated Galway in the All-Ireland final in '42.

In that final in 1942 Joe Fitzgerald captained Dublin. He played with Geraldines. He was a Kerryman, from Dingle, as was his mid-field partner that day, Mick Falvey. Joe was a guard working in Rathmines, and only lived in Dublin for a short period of his adult life. Back home in Kerry he remained a loyal Dublin supporter, even though he never did find out why he was chosen as Dublin captain in '42.

In 1943, Dublin lost to Louth in the first round of the Leinster championship. It was a completely changed team. Joe Fitzgerald, who had been at home in Kerry on holiday a year earlier when he had first received a letter from the Dublin county secretary asking him to turn up for a training session, saw for himself in '43 what was so wrong with the county.

'There were a lot of players from other counties who declared for Dublin right away after we won the All-Ireland final,' he remembered in Brian Carthy's *Football Captains: the All-Ireland Winners*. 'Many of them were picked for the Dublin side and a good deal of the players who were part of the All-Ireland winning team were left out.'

St Vincents put an end to all of that.

In their own club first of all, and later in agitated meetings of the Dublin county board, Vincents men stood and explained, and argued, for a whole different future.

Finally they were believed that Dublin should be Dublin. And that Dublin football and hurling teams should be made of Dublin men only.

The 1950s were in full swing.

The Vincents' journey, after winning their first Dublin senior football championship title in 1949, was getting up to full speed.

Vincents won their second Dublin football title in 1950. They retained their title by beating Peadar Mackin, Garda, Sean McDermott's and, in the final, Parnell's. Heff scored three points. Cathal O'Leary grabbed the goal.

In '51, it was down to Sean McDermott's to stop Vincents winning a hat-trick of Dublin senior football championship titles. Sean

McDermott's had Paddy O'Brien and Christo Hand from Meath, Cecil Manning from Galway, Batt Lynch from Roscommon, Noel Crowley from Clare, and they had so many countymen coming and going in the club that two of them were unable to play in the Dublin county final, having to turn up, instead, for the county finals in their native counties. But Heff scored one goal and three points from Vincents' winning tally of 1–6. And he was back in the No.15 shirt, one week later, for the county hurling final.

The thought of doing the double had magnified itself when Young Irelands were defeated in the county hurling semi-final. Irelands had Bill Walsh of Kilkenny on board, and the fine total of five Tipperary countymen, Pat Stakelum, Seán and Paddy Kenny, Seamus Bannon and Phil Shanahan. Vincents brought this galaxy of countymen down to earth.

The final, however, was a disaster. Neighbours, Eoghan Ruadh scored six goals and six points, in a ten-point victory. Neither did Vincents accept their defeat with grace or dignity. Vincents completely cracked. They lost it, and let themselves down and their club down in front of 22,000 paying customers, by provoking a series of ugly punch-ups.

And they knew it.

Vincents' men were sickened by what happened on the field that day. Sickened in particular by the bloodied state of Seán Óg Ó Ceallacháin, a Fairview native and a former Scoil Mhuire boy, who had transferred from Vincents to Eoghan Ruadh while still in his teens. Seán Óg took the direct impact of his former club's uncontrolled fury. He suffered a serious facial wound, but refused utterly to take any action outside the remit of the Dublin county board.

Everyone wanted to stop Vincents winning every single football match they ever seemed to play. Peadar Mackin tried everything they could, on and off the field in the 1952 football championship quarter-final. The game was summed up, in the pages of the *Irish Times* as 'a mixture of spasmodic football, frequent wrestling matches and occasional fisticuffs with many deliberate fouls and some interference by sideline supporters.' Vincents won most of the contests that transpired on the field during the hour.

Sean McDermott's had 'mobilized' an even stronger army of big named footballers for the '52 football championship. Sean Quinn from Armagh and Mick Furlong from Offaly were now also lining up against Vincents to make it a round dozen of county men.

The teams met in the semi-final.

Four calmly pointed frees from Heff kept the champions in a game that looked like extending itself from their reach, and a late, late goal saw Vincents edge their way into the final by two points. On two Sundays in succession in Croke Park St Vincents and Garda made the 1952 county football final especially nerve-racking and Garda had chances aplenty to win the second day, right down to a 21-yard free in the final minute of the game, and stop Vincents. The cool, composed Kerryman Teddy O'Sullivan lined himself up to tip over the winner. However, O'Sullivan scuffed the ball into the arms of Nicky Maher on the Vincents goal-line.

There were two periods of extra-time before Vincents secured their fourth title in succession, winning 0–13 to 1–8.

However, the chance of the double, for Heff and Snitchie, was ruined in the county hurling final, once again. This time it was Faughs, who ensured that all the barmen on their team did not work on the Saturday night before the county final.

It looked like the footballers from St Vincents were tiring. It also looked like the hurlers from St Vincents, most of them footballers as well, were coming up short in their search for a first Dublin senior title.

Nobody, nobody, nobody forecast 1953.

Though when Vincents gained some sweet revenge over Faughs, beating them in the '53 hurling semi-final, 2–11 to 3–4, the year had a freshening appearance. In the final, Civil Service called on hurlers from Cork, Clare, Waterford, Laois, Wicklow and Dublin.

Vincents showed not a moment of doubt in the final, and from Poggy Lillis in between the sticks, to Kevin Heffernan in the furthest corner of the field, they were businesslike, winning 4–10 to 3–5. Heff got three of the points, though the hero was Norman Allen, who equalled and finally controlled Cork's Con Murphy in the centre of the field.

Heff and the Vincents footballers made it five senior football championships in a row a month later when, on a wet Friday evening, 12,000 paid in to Croke Park to see if Clanna Gael could cause an upset.

Clann opened the scoring with a point after three minutes.

Heff lined up a free to level the game, but his kick from 35 yards came back off the crossbar. Cathal O'Leary punched the ball to the net.

Heff lined up another free, this time 25 yards out, and again failed to connect properly. The Clann men on the goal-line were half asleep. The ball hit the back of the net.

It was 2–0 to 0–1 at half-time, and hardly a classic in the making. Points from Ollie and Cyril Freaney, Des Ferguson and two from Heff finished off the game.

St Vincents 2–5, Clanna Gael 0–4.

The 'double' was done and dusted.

Finally.

'Paddy was an outstanding player ... he was a big man with a brilliant pair of hands on him. If I stood beside him and jumped for a high ball, I wouldn't catch very many of them.'

KH

Sunday, 24 July 1955

Paddy O'Brien was in trouble.

His right knee had been causing him problems since the beginning of the summer. Now he felt it might buckle under him at any moment. He was OK standing in and around his own goal-mouth in games, but running out the field, and turning, was tricky. Now, with ten minutes still to go to half-time in the Leinster foot-ball final, O'Brien knew he was in bigger trouble than he had ever been in his whole glorious life as a Gaelic footballer.

The prince of all full-backs.

The only footballer in the country honoured with the title of 'Hands'. A man who would carry his fame with him into old age, landing himself the No.3 shirt on the GAA's two greatest selections of all, the 1984 'Team of the Century' and 1999 'Team of the Millennium'.

Paddy 'Hands' O'Brien.

On each of those mystical teams he would have Kevin Heffernan as one of his teammates. But now, in Croke Park, on a savagely hot Sunday in July, Heff was killing him. Heff had started the Leinster final at full-forward.

O'Brien had only marked Heff once before, in the National League final a couple of months earlier when Dublin ran rings around the reigning All-Ireland champions. It was an unbelievable 2–12 to 1–3 at the end. Any time before '55, whenever Meath played Dublin, Heff would be in the left corner, where Paddy O'Brien's first cousin, Michael O'Brien, attended to matters with a sticky relish. 'I'd never played on Kevin before that year,' Paddy remembered. 'I'd been playing in the centre of the field most of my club career in Dublin with Sean McDermott's, and with Meath I had never seen very much of him, to be honest.'

Now . . . !

Now, Heff was racing out the field, and looking for the ball outside the 50-yard line. He didn't care about leaving the best full-back in the game alone, in front of the Meath goalmouth, in his own large square. Every two or three minutes Heff chased down the field.

Paddy O'Brien didn't give chase.

Not once.

Twice in the first half he had shouted over at the sideline.

He knew he needed to come off the field.

But nobody was listening to him, no other Meathman at any rate. Meathmen on the field were in a state of heightened confusion. Meathmen on the sideline were in a state of complete panic.

But Heff could hear him. Des Ferguson, as well, and any other Dublin forward who roamed across the Meath goalmouth knew that Paddy 'Hands' O'Brien was finished with a Leinster final that was not yet even half over.

Something had to happen. O'Brien had to be taken off. Either that, or O'Brien had to catch Heff by the collar, and wring his neck without anyone noticing. Actually, it didn't matter whether anyone noticed or not.

It was way past time for O'Brien to bury Heff.

He never did.

More than anything else, really, Paddy O'Brien was a gentleman. He was strong and brave, and it would take an exceptionally brave and foolish man to declare war on the full-back, whether he was wearing the No.8 shirt for Sean McDermott's or the No.3 shirt for his county of birth.

O'Brien was also rare amongst full-backs. He was a midfielder for the first half of his career, so he possessed a fine athleticism and had power in his legs. Unlike the standard-sized gorilla chosen at full-back by most counties, O'Brien was civilized, courteous even, and he was a man who never betrayed the influence of Brian Smyth, his headmaster in Skryne National School in the heart of his home county. Paddy O'Brien always and forever walked tall with his shoulders back. And when Paddy O'Brien spoke, he did so clearly and eloquently.

Foul language was not his thing.

Besides, O'Brien was in business in the city. He had opened his own large grocery store on Drumcondra Road some years earlier upon moving from the country to Dublin. He was admired and liked, as a footballer and a businessman.

Burying the blond young fella whom everyone in Dublin was talking about was not in his nature. Burying Kevin Heffernan anywhere in Croke Park, in front of 48,860 people, the biggest crowd ever to attend a Leinster final, was never on Paddy O'Brien's agenda.

The first ball Heff took into his arms he quickly turned and saw that O'Brien was ten yards off him. Heff ran straight at his man, aiming to jink to his right as O'Brien lunged into the tackle. O'Brien lunged too heavily, lost his balance and ended up grabbing his opponent with both hands. Dublin scored from the free. Less than five minutes later, Heff was on the ball again. O'Brien, once again, was holding back, lying deeper into his own defence.

Heff ran at him a second time.

O'Brien knew he could not pull his man to the ground again. Heff jinked inside. O'Brien had his back to goal, and took an age to turn. Heff was gone. Inside the first fifteen minutes of the Leinster final the scheming, chasing blond figure in the No.14 shirt had two goals. He rocked Meath a third time, and left the champs traumatized in their own dressing-room, by setting up a third goal for Cathal O'Leary before half-time. Snitchie and Johnny Boyle had two more goals in the second half. Meath's humiliation had hardly a moment's respite. The biggest ever beating received by defending All-Ireland champions was furiously handed out.

Dublin 5–12, Meath 0–7.

*

It was all over for Paddy O'Brien and Meath.

They had won four Leinster titles in the previous six years, sharing complete dominance of the province with Louth. And Meath had also won All-Ireland titles in 1949 and '54. But, now, they had been twice beaten by Dublin in a three-month period. They had been destroyed. First by 12 points in the League final. Then by 20 points in the Leinster final.

And, in that Leinster final, Kevin Heffernan had been joined by ten St Vincents men, by his captain Denis Mahony and Snitchie, and by Jim Lavin, Mick Moylan, Norman Allen, Nicky Maher, Jim Crowley, Ollie Freaney, Cathal O'Leary, and Pádraic 'Jock' Haughey. The summer of '55 had landed Dublin their first Leinster football title in thirteen years.

It had taken St Vincents seven years!

Seven years to largely conquer Dublin and Leinster on their own, and seven years to finally prove that St Vincents' meddling ways might change the face of the old game for ever, and perhaps call a halt to seventy years of catching and kicking the ball. There were many hands at work in that meddling.

But the two pairs of hands that mostly directed proceedings, and served out the instructions from Sunday to Sunday, belonged to Ollie Freaney and Kevin Heffernan. Others had their say as well. Every player was invited to plot something new and surprising. But Freaney and Heff were the master craftsmen.

Both men were GAA men to the core. Gaelic football and hurling came first. There was no second. However, Freaney liked to learn from other sportsmen. Heff, most especially, devoured smart ideas. As a student in Trinity College he discovered the basketball court to be a place where winning and losing was never left in the lap of the gods, but was usually determined by hours of plotting on paper and breaking the game down into the tiniest little pieces.

Heff also looked at what was happening in even more 'foreign' games, like the game of soccer. The game was the GAA's 'public enemy no.1' and Heff had neither the time nor the inclination to give it a go himself. But he was not blind either. Across the water, things were changing in English football. Young lads like himself, in many instances, were effecting that change.

Two years older than Heff, and playing for Manchester City, was a centre-forward called Don Revie, who would become one of the game's greatest player-managers, and would make Leeds United one of the most successful and controversial teams in the history of the English game. In 1974, Revie and Heff would both lead Leeds United and Dublin to their most talked about championship successes.

Heff fancied himself as a player-manager too. Unofficially he was Dublin's player-manager for long spells in the fifties, and he heard and read extensively about how Don Revie was revolutionizing English football by playing centre-forward in a deeper-lying role than anybody else had ever imagined possible. In 1955, Revie published his autobiography, *Soccer's Happy Wanderer*. He was British Footballer of the Year, and led Manchester City to the Cup final for the first time in twenty years. A man would want to be blind, and mad, in Kevin Heffernan's estimation, not to see how Don Revie's battle plan could be fitted to Gaelic football.

Heff had waited a long time.

All his adult life.

He'd had seven wonderful years with St Vincents. The club had won the Dublin senior football championship six years on the trot, and would claim a seventh title by the end of 1955. The club would also win the Dublin senior hurling championship in '55, making it a hat-trick of triumphs.

By the close of 1955, and at 26 years of age, Kevin Heffernan would hold ten Dublin senior championship medals. And his career with St Vincents would not yet be even half done.

There were so many great days of triumph with St Vincents. And there were occasional days, like the 1953 National League final when St Vincents presented themselves in the sky blue jersey of Dublin, and defeated the reigning All-Ireland champions Cavan by nine points.

The same football team, dressed for St Vincents or Dublin duty, was on the go every single Sunday, some of them twice on Sundays. Heff and a dozen others from the club were regularly starting for Dublin, and by the time of the '53 League final victory over Cavan that number would be increased to fourteen.

In '53, the fourteen Vincents men on the field, and Paddy O'Grady of the Air Corps in goals, were all men who had been schooled in Dublin, and were products of the Dublin Primary Schools' League. There were no imports. No chosen ones. No fly-by-nights from the country. The job of producing one Dublin football team, all of them bred, if not born and bred in the city, was completed. A year earlier, in '52, Dublin had lost by one point to Cork in the League final.

In the fifth minute of the 1953 League final a Cavan attack was stopped in its tracks and a free awarded to Dublin. Jim Lavin struck it quick and long to Heff. He slipped it to Bernie Atkins, who shot to the net.

Three minutes later, Heff nipped in, gained possession and rounded his man with a standard jink, and scored the second goal.

Jim Crowley struck a fine point.

Ten minutes in, the Cavan defence was still trying to calm itself down when Ollie Freaney broke down the middle. He slipped it to his brother. Cyril Freaney blasted home the third goal.

Dublin were seven points up at half-time.

Heff would score two goals and two points by the end, when the final scoreline announced itself.

Dublin 4–6, Cavan 0–9.

St Vincents + one 4–6, All-Ireland champions Cavan 0–9.

St Vincents' new and bold brand of football, all about running with the ball and movement off the ball, was invigorating. It was tantalizing to watch. Mouthwatering for the team's supporters.

But St Vincents and Dublin, brilliantly and forever intertwined, had done nothing in the Leinster and All-Ireland championships.

The fifties were fast becoming a time of triumph and terrible regret. Heff and his teammates had to wait until 1955 for their very first Leinster football title. It had taken seven years to walk on to the greatest stage of all.

There, in the All-Ireland final, Dublin would meet Kerry. Both teams made it to the last day of the championship by winning semi-final replays that were played on the same afternoon, on a balmy Sunday in the middle of September. Kerry tore through Cavan at the second attempt, winning by four goals. Dublin were backed up in a fierce rearguard fight right to the last minute against Mayo before earning a one-point win.

There was one book published in Ireland in the 1950s that explained to everybody in the country how to play Gaelic football. Unlike Don Revie's story that explained to English football coaches and fans alike how to break all the rules, this book informed GAA folk that by sticking to the rudiments of the game, staying with the known and trusted, success was in anyone's hands. It was published at the end of the decade, in 1958, and its author was the greatest and most celebrated trainer that Gaelic football had ever seen.

Dr Eamonn O'Sullivan's *The Art and Science of Gaelic Football,* however, was not a publication that was destined to ever be picked up by Kevin Heffernan or Ollie Freaney, or leafed through by any of the other freethinkers who populated the St Vincents dressing-room.

The 1955 All-Ireland final was sure to be a clash of beliefs and tastes, a clattering meeting. Old-style country against the city boys with the fanciest of new ideas.

Dr Eamonn O'Sullivan, who had guided Kerry to his first All-Ireland title as manager thirty-one years earlier, beating Dublin by a single point, 0–4 to 0–3 . . .

Versus

. . . Heff, Freaney, Snitchie and the Vincents crew who believed that Dr Eamonn's theories on the game were outdated, and ready for debunking.

The doctor was the purest football man.

He was also a man with many great responsibilities.

In Killarney, St Finian's was known only as the 'mental hospital' through the first half of the twentieth century, and when Dr Eamonn O'Sullivan arrived there and began rearing his family in his own quarters in the hospital overlooking the beautiful town, built at the hospital's feet, there were over one thousand patients on its books, kept within its cold, Victorian stone walls.

Dr Eamonn was a dignified, imposing figure, but not at all a rabid disciplinarian. He was a loving figure to his own family, and calm and kindly whenever possible with his patients. With footballers, however, he occasionally let loose. But only now and again, preferring to keep matters in the dressing-room, and out on the training field, open to thoughtful debate.

Like Kevin Heffernan, Dr Eamonn was a man who liked his round of golf, and like Heff he found an adequate amount of time to bring his handicap down to a very respectable nine. The tranquillity and silence of the golf course often allowed both men to think more clearly about a football game the following Sunday.

But, more than anything else, Dr Eamonn was a builder. He built up troubled people, and he built football teams. He even built places.

He saw to it that Killarney Golf Club was built. He drove through with the building of Fitzgerald Stadium. And, for five decades, off and on, he would have eight All-Ireland winning football teams in his hands, building his last team in 1962, the year he resigned from St Finian's as Resident Medical Superintendent, four years before his death.

When his teams practised in Fitzgerald Stadium, Dr Eamonn kept the gates open at all times. Always in the middle of the field, always tall and stately, dressed in a good suit, and with a stopwatch in his hand, Dr Eamonn attended to his team after he attended to his patients all day long.

He had his stopwatch and whistle in either hand. He never arrived out on to the field in a tracksuit, and never wore football boots. Some evenings, however, he would take a golf stick which doubled as a leathered seat with him, and he would actually 'take a seat' as he put his players through their paces, up and down the field, running flat out for 14 yards, stopping to a fast walk, and running and walking, up and down the field, until he felt that everyone's reactions were quickened up, especially those of his defenders.

He'd have the boys piggyback, skip rope, and spend long hours over the summer months kicking the ball and punching the ball, with the right and left foot, and the right and left hand. Dr Eamonn was entirely a catch and kick football coach. But he still believed that every footballer in his care should be the purest footballer he could possibly become.

In the language of every man and woman, in every part of Ireland, Dublin were the hottest of favourites to win the 1955 All-Ireland football final.

It was their style of play.

Their speed.

Those blond heads, belonging to Heff and Snitchie, and Ollie and Cyril Freaney, which darted in and out of position on both forward lines.

Peculiarly or not, as he waited for the final, and as he heard people talk about Dublin's new-fangled game plans, Dr Eamonn O'Sullivan decided to change very little, if anything at all, about his view of how a game of football should be won.

'In my memory ... the hour compacts. I only remember small incidents. I remember putting a ball over the bar instead of giving it on to Johnny Boyle. Then later ... not taking the points ... being closed out.'

KH

Sunday, 25 September 1955

John Dowling of Kerins O'Rahillys was absolutely bursting with excitement as he planted his right foot on the rich green grass of Croke Park. He had run on to the field, without looking over his shoulder. He was Kerry captain. He was leading the team on to the field in the All-Ireland final.

There was a small problem, however.

The Kerry team was not behind him, and Dowling had taken several strides out on to the pitch before he was aware of being a lonely figure in green and gold. He stood with his hands on hips for a few seconds.

Dowling was mad to get going. He'd missed Kerry's win over Armagh two years before, after he'd been slapped with a fifteen-month long suspension for playing illegally with a club in Cork. He'd played illegally all right, but they'd no evidence that he'd played at all, the feckers! He'd never really forgiven the GAA. He'd bought himself a shotgun, and most Sundays he passed his afternoons by going out shooting, at animals, not at GAA officials.

Where were they?

John Dowling was out on the edge of the field on his own.

Dowling had no idea, not yet, that the stewards guarding the

30-yard passage between the door of the Kerry dressing-room and the gate out on to the field, had met with all sorts of bother once the Kerry captain had bolted. There were so many people milling around, and filling up the passage, that it was impossible to let the rest of the Kerry team follow their captain.

A few seconds passed, before John Dowling spotted John Savage, one of his friends in Tralee, sitting in his coat and hat on his sideline seat. Dowling made his way back off the field, and squeezed himself into the seat beside his neighbour. They chatted for thirty, forty, fifty seconds until, finally, the Kerry midfielder and captain saw other green and gold jerseys run out the gate to his left.

He said goodbye to John.

The sideline seats in Croke Park had been closed by eleven o'clock that morning, four hours earlier. That's how long John Savage had been waiting.

All gates into the ground were finally slammed shut twenty minutes into the minor final, in which Dublin proved too good for Tipperary, winning by six points in the end. There were two small breakthroughs by supporters, twice in the minor game, but gardai and stewards piled in together to make sure that the field was kept clear. Nobody was at all surprised at the pandemonium inside the ground, and outside on the adjoining streets where disappointed fans were still numbered in their thousands.

Officially, it was announced later in the day that there were 87,102 people in Croke Park on Sunday, 25 September 1955, but the GAA also issued a disclaimer with this number, stating that counting had stopped at an early stage in the afternoon. Two gates had been broken down by agitated supporters. Nobody really knew how many people were in the place. Not a clue.

It was a day when a Dublin football team was, for the first time, received by its own supporters on Hill 16. It was the first Sunday that Dublin people claimed the hill as theirs, and the noise coming from that end of the ground had both the Kerry and the Dublin players equally shocked.

When the game was ready to start, and the ball was about to be thrown up, the President of the GAA, Seamus McFerran, was joined in the middle of the field by two men of the cloth. On his right was His Lordship Dr Moynihan, Bishop of Kerry. And, on his left, was the Doc.

Willie Fitzpatrick.

The Reverend Dr Fitzpatrick was chosen as Dublin's official 'holy man' for the day. The Doc was surrounded by his boys from Scoil Mhuire and Joey's as he waited in the middle of Croke Park on All-Ireland final day. Here they all were, and he could have pinched himself and still hardly believed it.

He was a proud man.

Despite himself, he'd prayed hard that morning for all the Dublin boys. Norman Allen was missing. He'd been into hospital to get his appendix out a few weeks earlier, and Allen's replacement for the semi-final replay, Mark Wilson, was also gone from the final with a leg injury. In the middle of the field, Jim McGuinness was carrying a leg injury into the game. He'd play. But neither the Doc nor anybody else knew how he'd go. Prayers were needed all right.

And then there was Heff.

The Doc knew that Heff wasn't one hundred per cent right. The little blond fella, who had caught his eye the first time he'd ever seen him solo the ball twenty-one years earlier, in the circle in Marino. The boy he'd told everyone would be the one to watch. And here he was, still blond, still a sight to behold every time he got the ball into his hands. Here was young Heffernan in an All-Ireland final with all of these people watching him, and shouting encouragement at him, and cursing him.

The Doc knew that Heff needed a prayer or two as well.

Heff had a bad ankle.

He'd gone over on it in the replay against Mayo. There were mornings he could hardly walk. He'd finally gone to a doctor in Clontarf, who had emptied a syringe filled with Novocaine that looked fit for a racehorse into Heff's ankle, and then told him to stand up. The doctor ordered Heff to walk to Howth every evening without fail.

Every day Heff returned to the doctor's surgery.

Every day he looked at what he was sure must have been a needle measured for a horse or a rhinoceros, filled to the brim with Novocaine.

Every evening he walked to Howth.

In the Dublin dressing-room, before he got to put on his nicely polished boots and lace them up, just tightly, but not too tightly, another last needle had Heff's name on it.

From the throw-in, John Dowling won the ball and drove it out to Tadhgie Lyne on the wing. Lyne was moving diagonally towards the Dublin goal, and there was nothing stopping him. He lobbed the ball over the bar.

Kerry had scored in the first minute of the game.

In the early minutes, Dublin might have had three goals. The first shot skimmed past the left post. The second the right post. Then, Cyril Freaney, who had taken the place of the injured Wilson, had space to get in his kick. He belted the ball. It cannoned back off the crossbar.

But Kerry never fretted. Dr Eamonn's team soon found its rhythm, and his wing-forwards, Lyne and Paudie Sheehy, were winning lots of ball and sending it in to the full-forward line time and again.

Dublin were playing against a stiff breeze, but they levelled the scores after three minutes when Heff placed Pádraic Haughey who managed an overhead kick. Both defences tightened up after such a blistering start. Ollie Freaney put Dublin in front for the first time after 15 minutes from a free. Lyne levelled the game once again with a free at the other end. A goal could have come at either end, but, slowly, surely, goal chances were drying up in a supremely tight, physical battle.

Lyne scored his third point, and Dowling kicked a '50' in the 25th minute. Kerry led 0–4 to 0–2. It wasn't a big lead. The wind was still strong, and Dublin's defence had settled into a stubborn shape.

In a fluid movement, Ollie Freaney gained possession just inside the Kerry half and soloed the ball. He found Snitchie, and Snitchie passed inside to Johnny Boyle, who kicked the best score of the game. At the other end, Kerry needed scores before half-time. They were wide with three good chances before, finally, they won a free on the 21-yard line and Lyne knocked over his fourth score.

Kerry led by five points to three at half-time.

Heff had never really got out of the traps. He would only score one point by the game's end. He never left the edge of the square in the first half, and in the second half he would continue to stay put, trying to go shoulder to shoulder with Ned Roche. That was a mistake. Ned Roche had the finest pair of shoulders in the entire Kerry dressing-room. Undoubtedly, the Kerry full-back looked slow, but he had a razor-sharp knowledge of when to make a move for the ball.

He was also keen as mustard.

Roche was born in Knocknagoshel in the north-east of the county, but his football career had seemed lost and forgotten until a couple of years earlier. He'd joined the army as a young man. Found himself stationed in Clonmel, and played in the blue and gold of Tipperary for a few years. In 1953, however, with Tom Moriarty and John Cronin, who both lined out in the half-back line in front of him in the '55 All-Ireland final, he 'declared' for his home county.

The three were welcomed with open arms by Dr Eamonn, who had warned Roche not to move out of his square at all costs, and not to even think of following Kevin Heffernan out the field. Dr Eamonn wanted every man in every position in his defence present and correct at all times. The ball would come their way, Dr Eamonn believed. And their Dublin opponents would also have to journey back in the same direction if they were to get the scores they wanted.

Heff had never managed to get inside Ned Roche once in the first half. Everybody felt that Heff would have too much pace for the Kerry full-back, that he'd burn him or round him, or both, quite possibly.

It still remained to be seen.

Back in the Dublin dressing-room it was obvious to everybody that Jim McGuinness was in no condition to continue playing. In the second half, without McGuinness, John Dowling and Denis O'Shea started winning twice as much ball as they had won in the first half, and piled it all into the full-forward line. For twenty minutes in the second half, Dublin were backed up in their own defence.

John Cronin was ruling Ollie Freaney, after a testy first half. Kerry were commanding the middle of the field. Dublin could not get the ball out of their own defence fast enough, but it kept coming back in just as quickly.

Kerry were 0–12 to 0–6 in front when the siege on the Dublin goal was finally lifted. There were ten minutes left.

'Kevin Heffernan's point in Dublin's first excursion up-field looked a bad omen for the immediate future of the Kerry defence,' Mick Dunne would inform his readers in Monday morning's *Irish Press* newspaper. 'But the Metropolitans forward line, so often the heroes of the same Croke Park sod, could do nothing right when the All-Ireland medals seemed right within their grasp.'

Dublin's All-Ireland hopes looked lost.

Everybody in a blue jersey started looking for the goal that might bring them some hope. Heff was as big a culprit as the rest. Four times he had tried to work out a shot at goal when he might have taken his points. He was included in the general panic that had descended upon the entire team.

With five minutes left, Ollie Freaney placed the ball and took a long run back. Dublin had won a free directly in front of the Kerry goal. Freaney had only one thing on his mind. He blasted the ball low and hard and, somehow, it pierced a hole through all of the legs gathered on the Kerry goal-line.

The last precious minutes flew by on Dublin. For Kerry, they crawled. But there were no more scores.

Kerry 0–12, Dublin 1–6.

The day would end up being called 'Tadhgie Lyne's Final'.

Lyne was Kerry's answer to Kevin Heffernan. Lyne was born and raised just a half a mile from the football ground in Killarney that would be built by Dr Eamonn and called after the great Kerry maestro.

Lyne had already won and lost All-Ireland finals in the previous two years, and early in '55 he had turned down the offer of a contract with Glasgow Celtic. He would end the day with six points, half of Kerry's total. He would score five goals and 42 points in the championship, and there was nobody to doubt his right in being named 'Footballer of the Year'.

All of that awaited Tadhgie Lyne.

For Kevin Heffernan, on the evening of the lost final, the lost opportunity of a lifetime, perhaps, a drive out to Skerries on his own, as far away from Croke Park and Marino as he could go, before heading back into the city for the team's All-Ireland dinner, was all that was in store.

He spent as long as he could in the country town, looking out to sea.

He felt sick with utter disbelief.

12

'I felt ashamed ... the team was spiritless ... I became very, very determined that we would right that one way or another.'

KH

Sunday, 19 August 1956
UCD 2–3, St Vincents 0–6.

Two months short of a full eight years without a defeat in either the league or the championship, it happened.

Vincents lost.

They lost to UCD, who selected eleven county players on the day, for a Dublin senior football league game in Parnell Park, and after the game the Vincents captain, Danno Mahoney, walked into the students' dressing-room to congratulate them on their historic achievement.

It didn't matter to Danno, or anybody else in his own dressing-room, that Vincents had been 'down' men, that Mark Wilson, Mick Moylan, Norman Allen and Moss Whelan were missing, and that Des Ferguson was playing a game of hurling elsewhere and only made it over to Parnell Park at half-time.

It didn't matter that with numbers low, Danno had started in the more adventurous position of centre-back rather than the corner, and that Lar Foley, who was still a minor, was given a run in the No.8 shirt.

There were no excuses.

Des Ferguson had lined out in Croke Park a little earlier, for Dublin hurlers against Waterford in the National League. Dublin lost 2–8 to 1–8, but he'd been told that morning by

Heff to make it out to Parnell Park as quickly as he could.

By then, with Snitchie back in the half-forward line, and with Ollie Freaney and Kevin Heffernan present in the No.11 and No.14 shirts, it looked perilous for the students who led only by 1–1 to 0–2. With five minutes left, the teams were level. Vincents threw everything at the UCD defence.

It was a defence that had Armagh's Felix and John McKnight, Monaghan's Eddie Duffy and Cavan's Jim McDonnell, and that had Longford's Pat Gearty in goal. Vincents surged forward in numbers. But, in a breakaway attack by the students, the champions were short in numbers at the back all of a sudden. The ball was dispatched down the field where it reached Limerick's John O'Donovan, who had come in as a substitute. He blasted the winning goal, giving Noel Drumgoole no chance whatsoever.

Life as a Vincents and Dublin footballer had become one without any real worries, apart from one thing. One item. They'd won everything, except an All-Ireland. That was the only big worry.

Otherwise, life had been good to them. Most were still not married. Only three of them in the dressing-room took a drink of the hard stuff. Nobody else touched a drop of alcohol. What money there was to be had, was being saved. Houses were being built or bought.

All they did was talk football.

And hurling.

Think and talk, and play.

Full-back Jim Lavin would fill his car with as many men as the Doc might have fitted into his Baby Austin a decade or two earlier, when he held the record of bringing fourteen young boys off to a game in the Fifteen Acres. As grown men they'd spend more than one evening each week, when there was no training, fitted like sardines into Lavin's car. It was only a short spin out to Howth.

They'd walk the Head of Howth only the once if everyone was happy enough. If there was more to talk about, they'd take it in a second time.

There were no cares.

No wives as yet in the vast majority of cases.

And no pubs to go to.

Only three wives were amongst the Dublin travelling party that had jetted off to the United States, less than three months earlier, in May of 1956. Joan Mahoney, Kathleen Freaney and Margaret Maher were the only ladies amongst the Dublin party that comprised mostly Vincents footballers. Also travelling were Kerry, who had defeated them the previous September in the All-Ireland final.

The reigning All-Ireland champions would play the reigning National League champions in the Polo Grounds in New York City. On 3 June, in the Bronx, Dublin extracted a small but interesting measure of revenge against Kerry. They beat their opponents up a stick, 3–12 to 1–4. They enjoyed it too. Norman Allen dominated in the centre of defence, and Jim Crowley lorded it in the middle of the field. Though victory came at a price.

The Dublin team returned home with some walking wounded. Chief amongst these was Heff, who had damaged ankle ligaments. Jim McGuinness had a broken nose. Crowley was worse off than the pair of them, after breaking his ankle. He was on crutches. Kerry's Mick Murphy had a broken arm in a plaster cast.

When a special KLM charter plane from New York landed in Shannon airport on 13 June a denial that anything 'unpleasant' had occurred in the Polo Grounds was made by GAA President, Seamus McFerran, on behalf of the Dublin and Kerry teams.

'I deny emphatically such reports, as the most harmonious relations existed between the teams at all times during the tour,' stated McFerran, adding, perhaps unnecessarily, 'The games of course were keenly contested and reporters lacking specialized knowledge of the game may have mistaken keenness for rough play.'

Dublin were out in the championship ten days later.

One week before travelling out to New York they had defeated Westmeath in a first-round championship game in Carlow. It was a routine enough 2–11 to 1–5 victory. The same again against

Wexford, back in Carlow, was fully expected even without Crowley and Heff.

Dublin slumped!

Wexford 2–7, Dublin 0–7.

The Dublin senior football championship was delayed until the autumn in '56. Vincents defeated UCD in the first round, putting the students back in their place double quick after the impertinence of breaking a winning streak two months short of eight years. Garda had Gerry Daly from the All-Ireland winning Galway team on board, but they were soundly beaten by six points in the semi-final. In the final, Vincents were meeting more students.

There was a tiny amount of uncertainty creeping through the team in the week before the game. Everybody knew that the team was not hitting any great heights in '56, though Vincents had fought their way through more than one championship season without having everyone flying. Erin's Hope were formed from the trainee teachers from St Patrick's in Drumcondra. The club had not won a Dublin senior title since 1887. But the Erin's Hope selection in '56 was a particularly good vintage, as it included Fintan Walsh from Laois, Mattie McDonagh of Galway, and Kerry's Tom Long.

On 16 December, in Croke Park, Vincents assembled for their team photograph before looking to win an eighth senior football title in succession. What followed was as difficult and un-compromising as everyone in Marino expected, and in the crucial few minutes after half-time the students broke through for a goal. They were already four points ahead by that time and now looked strong, holding tight to a 1–7 to 0–3 advantage.

Vincents never clawed their way back.

Heff and his footballers had to accept a second defeat in '56, and had to live with just seven Dublin senior football championships in a row.

Des Ferguson and his hurlers had lost their way much earlier in the year.

*

Heff was almost 28 years old.

He had won seven Dublin senior football championships, one after another, and in 1957 he would win the first of another eight senior football championships. He was on his way to winning six Dublin senior hurling championships. But, if it had not been complete heresy to even think of such an unforgivable act, Heff might have handed back half of that number for one All-Ireland.

Them all, maybe?

Heff was growing desperate. All of the lads were feeling the pressure of not being able to push through and become, on the All-Ireland stage, the footballers they had repeatedly shown themselves to be on countless Sundays in Croke Park for St Vincents.

Worse was to come, a feeling of almost complete dejection.

In the summer of '57 Dublin were gutless.

Heff saw no hiding place from that.

He looked at himself first.

He felt ashamed.

Dublin were four points up, five minutes into the second half of the 1957 Leinster football final. The game was theirs.

Louth had given their all before half-time, and especially in an intense opening twenty minutes which had skin and hair flying, at the same time as the heavens opened above Croke Park with a thundery downpour. On top of all that, twice there were lengthy enough bouts of fisticuffs.

But Dublin had put manners on their opponents in those off-the-ball exchanges and, when it really mattered, they had taken the game by the scruff of the neck. The same could not be said of Heff. He never got into his stride. He never broke free from Louth full-back Tom Conlon. He was out-fielded every time.

He didn't manage a single point all afternoon.

The teams were level 1–2 to 0–5 at the interval. Ardee's Jim Roe had broken down the left wing, and struck the ball hard and low, but when his shot was blocked by Paddy O'Flaherty in the Dublin goal, Jim McDonnell was first to react and blast the ball to the net. That goal had spurred Louth to half-time.

They needed it, as Dublin were completely on top in the middle of the field, and with so much plentiful possession coming their way too many men up front were looking for goals. Heff amongst them. His lob came back off the post. Next Johnny Boyle struck the crossbar, and then Boyle had a point-blank goal chance saved.

Dublin resumed with all guns still blazing in the second half. Midfielder Paddy Downey put them in the lead. Then Cathal O'Leary swung a high centre across the Louth goalmouth and Snitchie finished the ball to the net. Dublin were four points clear.

It was time to finish off Louth.

Dublin stalled.

Three pointed frees in quick succession brought Louth within a point. Two minutes later, Dermot O'Brien fielded a Dublin kickout and McDonnell broke through a confused Dublin defence to win possession and whack home Louth's second goal. And Louth stayed that much in front.

With five minutes to go, drenched spectators started heading to the exit gates. There was no spark in Dublin. They were lifeless, completely spiritless. They looked weary. In defence they lacked bite. Up front they lacked hunger. Only Snitchie was spared in the press reports the following morning, when it was suggested that the long and brilliant road that had been travelled by St Vincents and Dublin appeared to be at an end.

Ollie Freaney was called out.

Heff too.

In the Dublin dressing-room, nobody wished to be spared. Heff had walked off the field with his head low. He felt desolate.

He knew that he had let everybody down.

There was no hiding.

One week before the Leinster final, Heff had played fleetingly for Dublin in the semi-final of the Leinster hurling championship. He came on as a sub against Kilkenny and scored the crucial goal shortly after half-time that set up Dublin for a rousing second-half performance.

The game ended in a draw.

Kilkenny won the replay. They won the All-Ireland too.

For the remainder of the summer and into the autumn, as Louth went the whole way to the All-Ireland football final, and won the damn thing with two points to spare over Cork, Heff was still unable to spare himself.

He was now, officially, all of 28 years old.

He knew that soon, very soon, when it was all over, all the triumphs in his life as a footballer might be unforgivably balanced by a terrible regret.

He had the ravaging disappointment of '55 and the shame of '57 to contend with, and understand. And do something about.

Heff decided to quit hurling.

It was a big decision to make. He knew he would be letting the lads down. Snitchie especially. They had always been there for one another. But Heff felt he had no choice.

It was time to put everything he knew, and everything he ever possessed as a footballer, into winning one All-Ireland.

Or maybe two, or three?

Heff had to wonder that if so many of the Vincents lads had not worked so hard to win everything as footballers and hurlers, if they had not tirelessly chased down every game, league and championship, chased all of them down as if each was the single most important game of the whole year, then what?

Had they foolishly, through high pride, and some greed that had to be forever nursed, left one or two All-Irelands behind them already?

Kevin Heffernan had to find out.

He would do so in 1958.

He was named team captain.

Heff would lead Dublin into '58 with no distractions.

13

'Building the right team should not be rocket science ... there are men you need, and places you need them.'

KH

Sunday, 17 August 1958

Cyril Freaney was on the run.

He was wearing his street clothes, and was running down the sideline in Croke Park towards the Railway End.

The All-Ireland football semi-final of '58 was into the second half and things were going OK for Dublin. But they could have been going better. Galway looked to be getting stronger. Their defence was letting nothing past.

Freaney was a Dublin selector.

As county champions, and as was their right, Vincents held the power on the Dublin 'selection committee', and Freaney was one of their men. Johnny Joyce was also a young Vincents man, but he wasn't playing well. His man was winning too much ball, too often.

The game was getting away from Dublin. The selectors had quickly huddled. They all decided it was time to take off 21-year-old Joyce. Cyril Freaney got the job. He had run down the sideline until he had young Joyce directly in his sights. He let out a first shout.

After that he let out two roars, but the old ground was now coming alive. The game had lifted itself to a higher notch, and the crowd, which included a big number from the west, was also raising its voice.

Freaney couldn't make himself heard.

He took off again, heading for the back of the Galway goals.

Freaney rounded the corner flag.

He was ten yards from the Galway goals when the ball was lobbed high into the square. The ball was broken down.

Johnny Joyce grabbed it.

He turned.

Nobody could get a hand on him.

Cyril Freaney was behind the goals. He had watched the centre sail towards the Galway goals. The ball looked to be going wide from John Timmons' free-kick. But Heff got up high on the end-line and knocked the ball back. Joyce nipped in between two Galway defenders. Joyce had the ball.

He saw Joyce shoot.

Freaney ducked.

Instinctively he fell to the ground, thinking that the ball would hit him in the face. There was a giant roar from behind him. When he looked back up the ball was tucked away in the back of the net.

Johnny Joyce had Dublin right back in the game with a brilliantly struck goal, and as Cyril Freaney remained at the Railway End, wondering what to do next, guessing whether he should fulfil the decision of the group of selectors, debating in his own head about running back to talk to them again, there was a second Dublin goal.

Johnny Joyce struck again.

Two goals.

The place was wild. Dublin had the smell of an All-Ireland final. The Dublin supporters were roaring and shouting their men on. They wanted more. Cyril Freaney was rounding the corner flag again, and heading back to the Dublin dug-out.

He had failed to do his job.

Thanks be to God.

In the final seconds of the final minute of the game, Heff grabbed the ball and turned for the Galway goal. He was pulled to the ground. Ollie Freaney had already twice missed with free-kicks from almost the exact same spot in the second half. Freaney was having one of his few off days with his frees.

Heff told him to take all the time in the world. With the last kick of the game, Freaney calmly popped over Dublin's winning point.

Dublin 2–7, Galway 1–9.

Heff had decided to get things done.

He started early in the year. By the end of the year he had the full-back line he wanted, made up of Lar Foley, Mark Wilson and Joe Timmons. They were all good footballers, but they were all tough customers first and foremost. They were a traditional full-back line. Old style.

Heff had felt it necessary to compromise. Reinventing the game of Gaelic football with a belief in 'total football' was fine and dandy, and had proved itself a smashing success for Vincents, but Dublin needed steel in front of their goal. It had to be done. And it could be done without interfering with the style of the team's play, as the half-back line had three of the best footballers in the whole damned dressing-room, Cathal O'Leary, Jim Crowley and Johnny Boyle.

Things were changed in the middle of the field too. There, John Timmons was now partnering Sean 'Yank' Murray. After that, the rest of the team was barely touched. Heff and Ollie Freaney had no intention of undoing the Vincents way of breaking down defences.

It was all about hardening up their own defence. After that it was all about upscuttling, as usual, the other team's defence.

Timmons and the 'Yank' in the middle of the field had not failed the team once all year. They were as strong as two horses. The 'Yank' Murray had never set foot in America in his life, but even before he became known as 'Yank' some in his own family had called him 'Manhattan'.

The family cottage in Skerries always had a few American flags on view, refusing to forget the ten years that Sean's mother had spent in the United States. She came home to Dublin in 1916. Her father stayed put. He'd jumped ship, or so the story was handed down in the Murray family, before reaching Ellis Island and had stayed on the water, working all his life on a coal barge on the East River. They called him 'Skipper'.

Heff and the Vincents crew liked the cut of 'Yank', and they especially liked that he had been reared on the GAA fields of north county Dublin, where he would last twenty years in the service of Skerries Harps which, in 'GAA years' in any other club in any other part of Dublin, was more like forty years of hard battling.

But Skerries doubled as a rugby town. The 'Yank' played in the back row with the local team when he felt like it. The rugby club had dressing-rooms, and showers. Most GAA fields had prickly shrubs in ditches for a man's clothes.

Heff's plans for 'Yank' Murray had nearly come undone twelve months earlier, when the 'Yank' arrived into Croke Park for a challenge game with Dublin and was informed not to bother togging out. He was told that he was on the 'banned list'. He was told, for good measure, that he had been spotted in Clonskeagh throwing a rugby ball around the place.

The 'ban' didn't stick, because people did not want 'Yank' banned. They also didn't want him wandering into more trouble by going to Lansdowne Road to watch the 'foreign' game, so next time 'Yank' marched up to the turnstiles at rugby HQ he wore a false moustache and a pair of thick-rimmed glasses.

Sean Murray was made of the right stuff, they'd no doubt about that. He'd seen it all in the north of the county. He'd played in matches that even had referees afraid for their lives. Before one club game had even started, he'd watched one referee call both teams together in the middle of the field, and he'd heard that referee ask all the players standing either side of him to please try to remember that their bodies were 'Temples of the Holy Ghost'.

Didn't work.

The year had started just about right.

If not perfectly.

There was nothing more that Heff could have asked for, and nothing that could have made him feel happier with his life, than getting Louth back into Croke Park and showing them exactly how the game should be played. Dublin killed off all possible notions Louth had of doing the 'double' when they wiped them off the field in the National League play-offs, winning 0–12 to 1–4. In fact, it was a game Dublin won everywhere on the field. Ollie Freaney kicked six points. Heff struck two from play. Johnny Joyce got two. Des Ferguson and Jock Haughey got one apiece.

Dublin might have kicked 24 points and, when tempers were let loose in the final ten minutes of the game, Louth got more than they had bargained for on that front as well.

The League champions from '57, Galway were next taken care of in the League quarter-final, and in the semi-final Dublin accounted for Mayo, 0–10 to 0–7. There was a record attendance of just over 50,000 in Croke Park for the final. Dublin remained unstoppable.

Dublin 3–13, Kildare 3–8.

Within sixty seconds of the ball being thrown in Heff had raced across the Kildare full-back line to take Jock Haughey's pass. He swerved past two defenders and shot from 15 yards out. The Kildare keeper, mesmerized like most of his defenders, barely raised an arm.

As captain in 1958, Heff was not one bit afraid to take things into his own hands. And when certain things were absolutely none of his business, he made them his business. Like getting the two Timmonses back 'home'.

That meant a couple of trips down to Wicklow.

John Timmons had lined out at full-forward against Dublin in an early National League game in '58, but Heff took little notice of that. The man wore a blue jersey. Heff's mission was to make sure it was a sky blue jersey and not a royal blue jersey. And he wanted his brother, Joe, as well.

The Timmons had been born in Dublin, in Charlemont Street. But Joe and John spent most of their adolescent years in Annacurra with their grandmother. Wicklow became their home from home, and the parish and county became their GAA home.

Heff didn't accept that.

He went after Joe first. Joe was Wicklow full-back. He'd played with the Wicklow minors for three years, and he was at No.3 when Wicklow found themselves playing nine minutes of added time against Meath in 1954 and losing to the eventual All-Ireland champs by a 'last minute' point. Heff drove to Joe's home and had the chat on behalf of the Dublin football team. Soon enough, Joe had joined St Mary's in Saggart.

John was next. Another drive into the country for Heff, and a harder conversation in front of him, he guessed. John Timmons was clearly acknowledged as Wicklow's greatest player of the decade.

He also said yes to Heff.

When Dublin defeated Kildare in the 1958 National League final, Joe Timmons was full-back. When the championship commenced in '58, John Timmons was in the middle of the field.

The championship had Dublin on the move.

A victory over Meath was enacted in Drogheda, and called for cool heads. The game also called early on for the Dublin defence to throw off the jitters, because Heff and his forward division found themselves two goals down in the first nine minutes. To begin with, Cathal O'Leary had fumbled a Dinny Donnelly shot in the fourth minute, and soon enough again Jim Crowley let a Dom O'Brien free slip through his hands. The ball deflected into the net off full-back Joe Timmons. Meath led 2–4 to 0–4 at half-time, but Heff then sounded out some fresh orders in the dressing-room.

Heff would end his day with two very valuable points.

Dublin 1–12, Meath 2–7.

For their Leinster semi-final meeting with Carlow, Dublin were dispatched to Portlaoise. This time Dublin struck early goals. Heff got one of them, Joyce two more, and Dublin led 3–3 to 0–4 at half-time.

Dublin 3–9, Carlow 2–7.

From Portlaoise, Dublin were told they were going to Navan for the Leinster final. And another meeting with All-Ireland champions Louth.

It was the first time in thirteen years that the provincial final was moved from Croke Park. Louth wanted the game in Navan, but it didn't make all that much difference, and for the second time in three months Dublin closed down the champions in defence, and Heff and Co. clinically took them apart up front. It was a business-like day. Des Foley's Dublin minors also beat Louth.

It was eight points to one at half-time. Dublin coasted thereafter as the rain came down in sprawling showers. Heff calmed everybody by fielding a long drive from John Timmons and getting Dublin's decisive goal.

Dublin 1–11, Louth 1–6.

Dublin finally landed in Croke Park in August and had their one-point win over Galway in the All-Ireland semi-final, thanks to the pondering of Cyril Freaney and the brilliance of Johnny Joyce. In the final they expected Kerry.

Heff and the fellas had been thinking about Kerry, and trying not to think about Kerry, all through the second half of the summer. There seemed no stopping Kerry. Nobody expected Derry to do so. It was, after all, Derry's first All-Ireland semi-final and everybody knew what happened to teams the first time they got on the big stage with Kerry.

But Kerry were sent hurtling out of sight after a one-point defeat, 2–6 to 2–5. All of a sudden, as they counted down the final weeks and days in Lorcan O'Toole Park, Dublin had to think all about Derry. Team trainer Peter O'Reilly, who had won his own All-Ireland medal in 1942, made sure to tell everyone who asked him, and even if they didn't ask him, just how quick and strong Derry were in '58. Chairman Danno Mahoney, the first and last Vincents man to hold the chair on the Dublin board, also liked to remind everyone in O'Toole Park that thirty-one counties were firmly in the Derry corner.

Heff also told his players that they were on their own.

As usual.

As Vincents and Dublin liked it.

For thirty minutes it was plain sailing.

Ollie Freaney kicked a point from a free in the fourth minute.

Heff shot over the bar two minutes later.

Derry immediately replied with their first point, but John Timmons kicked over a '50' after 19 minutes.

Dublin 0–3, Derry 0–1.

Sixty seconds later Freaney slotted over another free.

Thirty seconds later, Paddy Farnan had a point.

Dublin 0–5, Derry 0–1.

Derry pointed, Dublin pointed again from Freaney.

Heff pointed.

Derry pointed, and pointed again.

Heff pointed.

Dublin 0–8, Derry 0–4.

The difference between the sides was clear. Dublin were taking every decent chance that came their way. Derry were taking every second or third opportunity they gave themselves.

The ball was thrown in at 4.04 p.m. for the start of the second half, and everything changed. The orderly manner of the day was thrown up in the air. And, all of a sudden, Derry were winning everything in the air. Mainly Jim McKeever was grabbing every ball that sailed over the middle.

A boy wonder, a schoolteacher, a man they called 'Gentleman Jim', the Derry captain, and quite possibly the greatest fielder of the ball in the whole country, even though he was only five feet and ten inches tall, Ballymaguigan's Jim McKeever had decided to take complete control of the game.

Derry were pouring forward from the middle.

They had two points, one from McKeever, in the first six minutes of the second half, before Freaney kicked his third free of the day.

Then disaster.

Dublin conceded a goal which, if Croke Park had been hushed to complete silence, would have resembled a comic and manic ensemble from the earliest days of the silver screen. Goal chances and clearances were fluffed and fluffed again, and fluffed a third and fourth time, before Owen Gribben finally ended the mini-farce by smacking the ball into the back of the net.

The game was level.

Sean 'Yank' Murray could not do anything to stop McKeever. The 'Yank' was taken off the field and replaced by Vincents' Maurice Whelan.

Sean O'Connell kicked a bad wide for Derry.

McKeever also should have pointed.

Maurice Whelan had come in at right full-back when the 'Yank' was taken off, and he found himself up the field. Whelan lofted the ball into the middle. Des Ferguson grabbed it. He broke away, and then crossed the ball over to the right wing. Paddy Farnan beat Tommy Doherty to it.

Farnan was straight in.

He blasted the goal that would break Derry and win the All-Ireland title for Dublin. The second Dublin goal from Joyce, in the first of three minutes of added time, was also the result of sharp passing and incisive movement from Freaney and Haughey.

Joyce was on the go all the time. Heff was giving his man, Patsy McLarnon, a lesson in the modern game of Gaelic football. In Derry's historic semi-final, McLarnon had been one of the heroes, holding out manfully and repelling Kerry attack after Kerry attack.

In the final, McLarnon needed to get his hands on Kevin Heffernan, and on one man and one man only in the second half, and even though Heff did not get another score, McLarnon never quite managed that difficult feat.

Dublin 2–12, Derry 1–9.

Vincents had twelve men receiving All-Ireland senior medals at the end of 1958, and Vincents also had six young men receiving All-Ireland minor medals after victory over Mayo.

Heff and Des Foley, the captains of the two winning teams, were busy men the next day. They had to bring their two Cups to the Mansion House, and they had to bring them to schools and halls and houses all over Marino. On Tuesday they were in Balbriggan. On Wednesday they were in Tallaght. Thursday they were guests of the Dublin Men's Association at a dinner in Clery's Ballroom, and Friday the Dublin County Board had a céilí and presentation in the Irish Club on Parnell Square. And not a drop to drink for Heff or three-quarters of the team.

But, it was in Heff's house that the Cup was kept on the Sunday night of the game itself. Nobody slept. Half the team were looking for breakfast in Heff's kitchen the next morning.

*

In the front room, Heff threw the Sam Maguire into the arms of his goalkeeper, Paddy O'Flaherty. Heff and O'Flaherty were closer than most. The Dublin goalkeeper had been the centre of most discussion since the game had ended. Deep into the second half O'Flaherty had pounced on the ball in his own parallelogram. He'd stopped it, and punched it out of danger.

O'Flaherty hadn't picked the ball off the ground. No rule was broken but half of the attendance in the 73,000 who mostly stood, as only 10,000 were seated, shouted for a penalty that never was. Derry thought they were robbed of a massive half-time advantage.

Heff and O'Flaherty shared the same strange mixture of shock and relief in the hours after the game. O'Flaherty threw the Cup back to Heff.

'There it is!' he exclaimed.

'There it is,' agreed Heff, and tossed it back in the other man's direction just as quickly.

'All that trouble . . .' he added, 'just for that!'

'All for that . . .' laughed O'Flaherty. 'You can have it.'

Sam was in the air again.

14

'Just passing . . . and . . . said I'd drop in and say hello. How's Maura?
How's the kids? What are you doing tomorrow, then?'

KH

Saturday, 22 June 1963

Des Ferguson was cutting the grass in his front garden. It was a
garden deep in the country, over fifty miles from Dublin.

It was a Saturday. It would only take half an hour to polish the
garden off. Maura was cooking up a big fry-up for everyone.
The Fergusons already had a full table of mouths to feed. Eventually,
Des and Maura would have seven sons and two daughters, the vast
majority of them born and raised in County Meath, and in the
middle of the Ferguson gang was Terry, who'd win two All-Ireland
football titles with Meath in the late 1980s.

Des and Maura had sold their home on the Howth Road in
1959, and said their goodbyes to Heff and their friends living either
side of them.

They were moving to Meath.

North Meath, the whole way to Oldcastle. The famous Dublin
footballer and hurler was bringing, amongst other things, light and
water to one of his own county's oldest enemies. Ferguson had
moved out of the building business, and joined up with the rural
electrification scheme that, after stopping and starting in different
parts of the country due to budgets continually drying up, was being
pushed out hard from the beginning of the sixties. If a Meath farmer
wanted to build a septic tank, or get a kitchen in for his wife, Des
Ferguson overviewed the piece of work. Occasionally he would have

90

to take his coat off and do the job himself, even though he wasn't supposed to roll up his sleeves for any Meath man.

The job also meant living with the people of Meath.

Of course, Snitchie stayed a Vincents man.

Himself and Maura would get to seven o'clock mass on a Sunday morning, get something to eat afterwards, and load the gang into the car. Then belt up to Dublin. There was at least one game every Sunday, football or hurling, with the first game starting at eleven o'clock.

If Snitchie was late, he was never spared by anyone else.

'Where were you?' they'd ask him.

Or, typically, Heff would lay into him with the usual, 'What time do you think this is, Ferguson?!'

The Fergusons had no babysitters, nobody in Meath to mind the little ones or the big ones who were getting bigger every month. He'd hightail it to O'Toole Park for a hurling game. Des and Maura and the whole family. Then they'd race across the city to Parnell Park for a football game.

Or vice versa.

Vincents and Dublin, every single Sunday.

In 1958, Des Ferguson had decided it was time to retire from the Dublin football team. In his GAA career, that, at least, would leave him with one mouth less to feed. He kept playing football with Vincents.

Neither did he want to give up hurling with Dublin, and, in 1961, he helped backbone the team that lost by a single point to Tipperary in the All-Ireland final. But, by the summer of '63, he was 33 years of age. The family had moved thirteen miles closer to Dublin, and built a fine house one and a half miles outside Kells. He had the idea of giving it all up with Vincents very much in his mind, and joining the local club.

And he would end up his playing days giving five years' valuable service to Kells, winning Meath senior football championship titles in 1966 and '68, and after that he would one day find himself manager of the Meath senior football team.

But, there Snitchie was, on a Saturday morning in the summer of '63, cutting the grass, happy, and half-retired, when who drove in the gate?

Heff.

Snitchie stopped his cutting, his job half done.

'What are you doing way out here?' he enquired, walking over to Heff's car. They'd only seen one another a week earlier.

'I was passing . . .' replied Heff. 'Bit of business,' he added.

'On a Saturday?' asked Snitchie.

Kerry had taken the Sam Maguire Cup directly back from Dublin's hands in 1959, with Mick O'Connell presenting himself as someone who had the ability to become the greatest footballer the country had ever seen.

Even retaining the Leinster title had taken a lot out of Dublin, and two games against Louth in the provincial semi-final in Navan had turned into a bit more of an ordeal than anybody had wished. A last-minute point, once again, from Ollie Freaney's precious right boot, had kept Dublin alive in the first meeting between the teams, but in the replay it appeared that lives might genuinely be endangered. Especially John Timmons' life.

Heff had mostly been outsmarted by Ollie Reilly in the drawn game, and Louth still led at half-time in the second meeting, 1–7 to 1–6. Then Freaney pointed, Heff banged in a goal, Des Foley pointed, and Dublin eventually ran away with a 3–14 to 1–9 victory, that in turn led to a second Leinster title in succession when Laois did not prove too much bother in the final that was fixed for Tullamore.

Getting back to Croke Park at last, with the Leinster title in the bag, had been an achievement. Especially after the two visits to Navan, where Louth folk had become increasingly unhappy. Their anger was primarily directed at John Timmons, and the manner in which he tore into their hero, Kevin Beahan, in any clashes in the middle of the field.

Beahan had been only half-fit to play in the replay. And every time Timmons got the ball, the place was in uproar.

A bottle was thrown in the direction of the Dublin midfielder in the first half. Worse followed. 'His teammates honoured [Timmons] justly at the close when they carried him shoulder high from the field,' reported Mick Dunne, the GAA correspondent for the country's largest-selling daily newspaper, the *Irish Press*. 'But, even then, he had to jump down to defend himself against one implacable spectator.'

Dublin met Kerry in August.

Kerry defeated Dublin in the All-Ireland semi-final by two points, 1–10 to 2–5. And Dr Eamonn O'Sullivan went out of his way after the game to say that his boys were not flattered by just the two points margin.

'This was one of the hardest games ever played in Croke Park,' declared the Kerry trainer. 'We had only eight days' training. If we had another week, I'm sure we would have won by more.'

The scores had been level three times in the first half. Each time it was Kerry who equalized, but after making it 0–3 each in the 23rd minute, the challengers went one up through Paudie Sheehy in the 24th minute. And one minute later, disaster struck in the Dublin defence.

Actually, disaster had also struck a little earlier when their goalkeeper Paddy O'Flaherty had to go off injured, and Dublin had to put one of their sub forwards, Cyril Meehan, between the posts.

In the 25th minute, Sheehy broke through again, and he sent Dan McAuliffe racing goalwards. He beat an advancing Meehan very simply.

Kerry led 1–5 to 0–4 at half-time.

Heff had a point to his name, but he would not score after the change of ends, and by the 48th minute Kerry were eight points up. A Paddy Haughey goal gave Dublin hope. Seven minutes from the end, Heff got the ball on the end-line and swerved and weaved his way by three defenders before finding Ollie Freaney. He bagged the goal. It was a desperate finish, but Dublin were too late.

Kerry, with a few more weeks' training under Dr Eamonn, had six points to spare over Galway in the All-Ireland final.

*

In 1960 and '61 Offaly were Leinster champions, and twice narrowly lost to Down, in the All-Ireland semi-final, and then in the All-Ireland final.

Dublin handed over their Leinster title in the semi-final in 1960, when three goals stuffed them.

Offaly 3–9, Dublin 0–9.

Earlier, in their opening defence of their provincial crown that same summer, Dublin had been amongst the goals. Up to their necks in them, in fact, as they travelled to Mullingar and totted up ten goals against Longford. Johnny Joyce got five of them. Heff got three. It was an amusing 10–13 to 3–8 win that did not really do Dublin any good whatsoever.

In the 1961 Leinster final, Offaly were again stronger right down the centre and sorted out Dublin with the minimum of trouble.

Offaly 1–13, Dublin 1–8.

In '62, Heff was Dublin captain.

Heff was also ready to retire as a Dublin footballer.

He was going to give it everything, however, for one more summer. In the autumn he dreamed of a second All-Ireland.

Then he'd go.

Dublin took back control of Leinster once more, beating Louth by one point, and Laois by two points on an afternoon in Carlow when the number of fights in the crowd rivalled the number of fights on the field. Both reached double figures on a long, bad-tempered afternoon. In the Leinster final a total of 59,643 people turned up to see them put a stop to Offaly.

Dublin 2–8, Offaly 1–9.

Heff's last championship game as a Dublin footballer came one month later.

Dublin v Kerry.

Heff v Dr Eamonn.

Heff v Mick O'Connell and Mick O'Dwyer and the whole marvellous gang in green and gold. A second All-Ireland semi-final in four years, and a chance at a sizable portion of redemption.

The opportunity fizzled out in minutes.

Kerry full-forward Tom Long blasted a goal after four minutes. A Jerry O'Riordan free from the left corner had found Paudie Sheehy, and he let it into Long, who let it rip.

Cathal O'Leary beat O'Connell three times in the air in the first ten minutes, but after that O'Connell caught everything and anything high above his head. It was 2–9 to 0–3 at half-time.

Heff and the Dublin selectors sent John Timmons from full-forward to midfield for the second half. Des Foley was moved to the '40'. Heff ran his old legs off. Dr Eamonn O'Sullivan, meanwhile, decided on a watching brief for the whole second half. Kerry sat back and let Dublin come at them.

They were too far back.

Kerry 2–12, Dublin 0–10.

It was all over.

Kevin Heffernan knew it.

There would be a small re-think in the summer of 1963, and Heff would throw his name back into the pot for Dublin. But nothing would come of it.

It was time in the autumn of '62.

Heff would end his playing career with the simple, awful understanding that ever since he had first played against a Kerry team in 1946, in the losing All-Ireland minor final, he and everybody with him on every single Dublin team had looked second best.

Kerry had left him second best.

In November of 1962, after captaining St Vincents to their thirteenth senior football championship win, Kevin Heffernan retired as a Dublin footballer. He actually said he was finishing up completely, with everybody, Vincents and Dublin.

But, of course, that wasn't true.

When Vincents knocked on his door in '63, Heff said yes.

In the early summer of 1963 Kevin Heffernan had driven the whole way to Kells on business all right, football business.

He had something he needed Snitchie to do.

And Heff knew that rules were rules, and that the most unbreakable rule of all was that when a Vincents man asked another

Vincents man to do something, the answer could never be a 'no'.

Snitchie knew that rule as well.

The next day Dublin were playing Kildare in the semi-final of the Leinster football championship in Croke Park. Heff was a Dublin selector. He was one year older than Snitchie. They had soldiered for so long together, on football fields and hurling fields, that both men knew that they each well deserved a long and happy retirement.

Heff's retirement with Dublin had just formally commenced after he made the announcement, quietly, the autumn before.

Des Ferguson had retired from the Dublin football team four years before him, and when Heff trotted out his request as the two men stood in the middle of Snitchie's front garden, all he got in reply, to begin with, was stunned silence.

Des Ferguson gave him a look.

Then Ferguson got one word out.

'What?'

'Will you play for us tomorrow?' Heff asked a second time. 'We need you . . . I need you in the full-forward line!'

Snitchie felt like laughing, but he knew that Heff was quite serious. Heff didn't waste people's time by kidding around about football and hurling matters. He didn't like wasting his own time, for starters.

'Why don't . . . *you* play?' Snitchie, at last, replied.

'I'm gone . . . I'm a selector,' said Heff.

'But, sure, you're playing more football than me . . . you're fitter . . . you're playing better football than I am.' Snitchie was serious. Heff was playing great football with Vincents.

'I can't play,' stated Heff, emphatically, and explained to Snitchie what he wanted to do. He wanted to take Lar Foley out of the full-forward position and line Lar out at full-back, to fill a hole in that line left by an injury to Oliver Callaghan. And he wanted Snitchie to fill Lar's No. 14 jersey.

Heff knew how it would work.

In the first round of the championship against Meath a couple of weeks earlier, Dublin had struggled to move the ball around amongst their forwards. It was every man for himself in two games against Meath, a tightly drawn game, and then in the replay that Dublin had won by a single point. Against Kildare, Heff needed movement, and he especially needed the ball moving fast.

Des Ferguson had two things, at the very least, that would work perfectly in the full-forward line. He had fast hands, and he had not a selfish bone in his body whenever he got the ball. Snitchie would feed everybody. Even if he didn't get as much as a point, he'd make it work.

Des Ferguson had never played full-forward for Dublin in his life. Snitchie's jersey was always and forever the No.10. That would be one small problem, Snitchie thought to himself. The other problem was that he was training one of the local teams in Meath, Drumbaragh, and he had organized a game of hurling for them on Sunday afternoon in the tiny village of Wilkinstown, the same time as Dublin were going to be playing in Croke Park in the Leinster semi-final.

Snitchie didn't know what he could possibly do.

He told Heff they should get inside and have something to eat.

Heff sat down in the middle of the Ferguson gang and enjoyed his fry-up, and there was no more talk of football for twenty minutes. There were so many other things to talk about at the family table. Like life in the country, and life back on the Howth Road.

Finally, Heff thanked Maura for the food. Said a few friendly words to the kids, and told Snitchie he would need him in the ground a good hour before the game started. And he warned Snitchie not to be late.

'So, I have to play, then,' said Snitchie. 'Is that what you're saying?'

'Don't be late, Ferguson!'

Heff also had one last request.

'I'm not mentioning this to anyone, Des, OK?' he explained. 'Don't you open your mouth to anybody either. Let's keep it totally quiet. Nobody . . . right?'

Snitchie told Heff about the Drumbaragh lads.

'You can't say anything to them! We don't want anybody knowing,' insisted Heff.

'So I'm to tell them nothing?'

'Just leave them . . . not even show up?' added Snitchie.

Heff had that look on his face.

'Honestly . . . we can't tell a soul.'

Heff reversed his car in the driveway and, with the window down, gave a wave to Maura and Des.

As soon as he had disappeared out the gate Des Ferguson turned to his wife. 'Good God . . .' he said to Maura, and also to himself, remembering something, another small problem.

'I've got no laces in my boots . . .'

Heff had told Snitchie how he wanted it done.

He wanted Snitchie to appear in the dressing-room.

He didn't want Snitchie making a grand entrance into Croke Park with the rest of the Dublin lads through the players' entrance.

Heff wanted everything kept nice and quiet.

Snitchie had agreed to give Heff what he wanted.

He didn't say a word to the Drumbaragh lads, and felt awful about that, especially when he learned on Sunday evening that they were all sitting in the dressing-room, waiting for him, when some-one popped his head in the door and announced with a wild shout to the rest of the Drumbaragh team that Snitchie was up in Croke Park, playing for 'The Dubs'.

Snitchie had his boots in an old canvas bag.

He walked down Clonliffe Road with the Dublin supporters. Some said hello to him. Others asked him how he thought the game would go.

Snitchie said it would be close.

He queued at one of the turnstiles with the rest of them, and handed over his money to the man behind the grilled window. There was a good crowd already in the old ground, and as Snitchie made his way by the back of the Cusack Stand he was stopped in his tracks by Mick Dunne of the *Irish Press*.

'What do you think today?' asked Dunne.

'Close . . . it'll be close,' replied Snitchie. 'Kildare look good.'

'They look too good,' agreed Dunne.

Snitchie told the newspaperman that he had to run, he had some people to meet, and shook hands with Dunne.

'Any late changes on the Dublin team . . . did you hear at all?' shouted Dunne at the departing figure.

Snitchie had to tell his first big lie. 'No . . . not that I've heard of, Mick!' he said.

Snitchie didn't want to meet anyone else. He wanted to get to the dressing-room. When he did, he banged on the door.

The man on the door looked at him.

'Here to see Heff,' explained Snitchie, and he pushed his way in the door, and sat down as quickly as possible on one of very few spaces left on the wooden bench to his right. The Dublin team was already changing into their playing gear.

Snitchie pulled off his jacket and hung it up.

He opened up the top few buttons of his shirt, and the buttons on each sleeve, and then he sat down, and started taking off his shoes.

He knew that people were looking at him.

Snitchie was still tight-lipped.

He didn't speak to anyone, apart from a few quick hellos. But that's all. There was not one single conversation.

All of the fellas sitting down in the room were now looking at him, and wondering what the hell he was doing. Heff then walked in from the adjoining room, the one that had a huge tub sunken in the middle of the floor fit for two football teams or half a dozen small-sized hippopotamuses.

Heff stood in the middle of the floor, and asked for quietness for a minute. He told everyone he was ready to call out the team for the day.

He did so.

'You're back?' said John Timmons, standing beside him as Snitchie was bent over tying up his boots. '. . . You're playing?'

'I am!'

*

There were 38,470 people in Croke Park who were fairly shocked to hear over the public announcement system that Des Ferguson was on the Dublin starting team. That official number did not include the men in the press box, amongst them the *Irish Press*'s Mick Dunne. They too were disarmed.

For the first twenty minutes or so of the game, nobody in the Dublin full-forward line saw very much of the ball, apart from Snitchie in the opening sixty seconds. He fielded a Des Foley free-kick, turned his man and lobbed the ball over the bar. Simple enough from an old man.

The next twenty minutes were tough, and fierce tight.

Then Snitchie raced out to the corner flag to take a wild pass. He trapped the ball before it went out of play, took the ball up, looked up, and torpedoed a centre to the edge of the square. Brian McDonald held the ball and beat Des Marron in the Kildare goal.

That score settled Dublin. In the second half they had the wind at their backs. Kildare led 1–4 to 1–2. Snitchie scored a second point and the teams were level midway through the second half. With six and a half minutes to go, Mickey Whelan worked his way through from midfield with the ball and found Gerry Davey with a long pass.

The left half-forward crossed it in low and hard to Snitchie, who took it at the first time of asking on the 14-yard line and belted the ball to the net. It was 2–5 to 1–5 for Dublin.

Dublin 2–7, Kildare 1–5.

Dublin were back in the Leinster final, and they would hold on to their title, beating Laois by two points.

On the Monday before the 1963 All-Ireland final, Kevin Heffernan, one of the team's selectors, was named in Dublin's list of substitutes.

Nobody knew the full story.

Not even Des Ferguson.

Or the Dublin team captain, 23-year-old Des Foley, a Vincents man who was honoured with the job of leading the team directly because of Heff's sudden retirement less than twelve months earlier.

Dublin had been scintillating in the All-Ireland semi-final, and all systems fired all over the field against Ulster champions, Down. Dublin won by more than double scores, 2–11 to 0–7. In the final they were playing Galway, and a Galway team that was mighty dangerous and filled with footballers in their defence and in their forward lines who would, very soon, become some of the most famous names in the history of the game.

Galway would win the All-Ireland final in '64, beating Kerry by five points. They would beat Kerry again by three points in the '65 All-Ireland final. And, in the '66 All-Ireland final, they would beat Meath by six points.

As the weeks and days counted down to the 1963 All-Ireland final, it was felt in the Dublin camp that Heff's name should be thrown into the works. He was back playing with Vincents. His retirement had been ended within months as soon as Vincents had made a 'Vincents Request' of him.

At the beginning of September he had looked like his old self when he scored two goals and four points for Vincents in a tournament game in Newbridge. Yes, Heff was even helping out his club in tournament games.

Heff's name was now included on the Dublin panel for the All-Ireland final against Galway. Neither he nor the Dublin selectors made any comment.

They left everyone to work out for themselves what that really meant, though the vast majority of Dublin supporters concluded that if Dublin were struggling to break down the Galway defence, as a great many feared they might struggle, as they had when Galway had soundly beaten Dublin in their Divisional final in the National League five months earlier, then Heff would be thrown into the game.

Heff would join his old mate, Snitchie, in bringing some old craft, some old-style movement and pizzazz into the Dublin attack.

Lar Foley was still in the No.3 shirt for Dublin for the start of the All-Ireland final. Snitchie was still at No.14. In the middle of the field was Des Foley.

Foley was one of the most spectacular athletes, and probably the best-looking footballer, in the country. He was tall and blond, and fearless. And a nervous wreck if he did not stick exactly to his strictest routine the twenty-four hours before a big game. That meant getting confession in Malahide village on the Saturday evening. He was home by 9.15 p.m., and in bed by 10 o'clock. He'd read for half an hour. Then straight to sleep.

On Sunday morning he cycled to eight o'clock mass back in Malahide. He ate breakfast at the family table, and then went back to bed for a little sleep. When he got back out of bed, he washed himself in cold water to fully, completely feel awakened. He travelled in the family car up into Croker. In the dressing-room he sat just inside the door, on the left, right next to his brother, Lar.

Des Foley led twenty-two Dublin footballers out on to the field for the '63 All-Ireland final. First things first, it was necessary to get the team photograph out of the way. When twenty-three footballers formally posed for the cameras, and stood their ground in front of the eyes of over 87,000 people in the stadium, the third largest number ever to fit themselves in Croke Park, there was absolutely no sign of Kevin Heffernan.

From the very start, Galway looked smarter, and far more composed on the ball. Until the time came to shoot for points. Three or four early wides got the wind up everyone on the Galway team, and the wides count hit eight, nine, ten. In total Galway would shoot twelve wides in the 1963 All-Ireland final.

In that first half, Dublin lost their centre-back, Paddy Holden from Clanna Gael, who received a blow to the head that required eight stitches back in the Dublin dressing-room. If Galway had brought their shooting boots with them, then Heff and the entire Dublin dressing-room might have been in some disarray at half-time.

It was, instead, just 0–6 to 0–4.

Galway had their noses in front only.

Nine minutes after the restart Brian McDonald floated a sideline kick across the Galway goalmouth. Simon Behan rose highest. His blockdown was met by Gerry Davey, who fisted the ball to the back of the net.

Dublin hung on to a slim lead through the remainder of the half. With five minutes remaining there was two points in it. Galway were as nervy in front of goal at the end as they had been at the very beginning. Worse still, a late call for a penalty that had everyone in the ground in some doubt went against Galway.

Dublin 1–9, Galway 0–10.

Des Ferguson, the greatest hurler in Vincents, had a second All-Ireland medal. Two All-Ireland football medals. He had Heff to thank, but for the rest of his life, any time he was asked, Snitchie would always confess that he would hand over both for one All-Ireland hurling medal in return.

He had one medal more than his loyal friend Heff.

And Snitchie knew what Heff, the greatest footballer in Vincents, would have done for two All-Ireland football medals. He might have sold his own mother. He might have sold all of his old clubmates.

For one more All-Ireland?

For one more All-Ireland in which Dublin met Kerry, and Dublin made Kerry look second best?

Heff might have sold off the lot.

15

'It was always about the club.'

KH

Friday, 15 July 1966

At 36 years of age, Heff was in at full-forward for Vincents when they met Sean McDermott's in Croke Park, on a warm Friday evening in July, in one more county final.

It wasn't like the old days.

There were fewer than 7,000 people in the place, and all of them were confined to the Hogan Stand. Croke Park officials declined to open up the whole ground. They had less faith in the Dublin faithful than a decade earlier. And they were right.

Lar Foley was full-back for Vincents. A young Gay O'Driscoll was tucked in the corner beside him. Tony Hanahoe was in front of O'Driscoll on the half-back line. Jimmy Keaveney was centre-forward, and Heff was in front of him.

Vincents had a fair wind at their backs from the start, and they didn't waste time. They totted up four quick points. Heff took one of them. A goal killed off the fight in Sean McDermott's entirely. It was 2–6 to 1–2 at half-time.

The first half had been poor enough. The second was little better. It was nothing like the old days, when Sean McDermott's never rolled over for Vincents. Never, ever! This time, without John Timmons on the '40' and without his five points, Sean's might not have even bothered to come out for the second half.

Heff got himself into position for a second point before the end. Vincents won 3–9 to 2–6. That looked like the finishing point for

Kevin Heffernan's club career, but in '67 he was still there when Vincents beat Sean McDermott's again, 1–10 to 1–6.

It was the club's fifteenth Dublin football title.

Heff's too.

After that it was time, finally, to get off the field, with no fuss, no announcement of any retirement, just go.

After first announcing his retirement in 1962, Heff was soon requested to do an 'about-turn'. And, of course, Heff did as he was asked.

Heff had, finally and for ever, finished up his hurling career in '62, and by that time he had helped Vincents win their first six county titles.

On the football field things had dragged on, and every year the next championship battle looked more important and compelling than the last. Heff had stayed put until 1967.

He had played and personally directed Vincents ever since their seven-in-a-row of football titles had been achieved in 1955.

And after their foolishness of taking their eye off the ball in their important jubilee year in 1956 and winning nothing, Heff and Vincents brought home a further six county football titles on the trot.

In 1957 Vincents beat Clanna Gael, in '58 they beat Sean McDermott's, and in '59 they beat UCD. In 1960 Heff captained the club and sliced open the Air Corps defence twice to grab two goals and underpin a difficult 2–7 to 0–10 victory. In 1961 they beat Clanna Gael again, and in '62 they beat O'Tooles, 3–13 to 3–8, fighting back from a six-point deficit and finally getting on top of their opponents midway through the second half when Paddy Farnan intercepted a weak kickout and off-loaded the ball immediately to Heff, who feinted inside two defenders at top speed and cracked a rasping shot to the back of the net.

Heff had kept himself a busy man.

On the field, on the sideline, and far away from the field.

There were always things to be done in Vincents. Nobody got any marks in the club for dawdling. In addition to playing and managing teams, Heff was asked to hold down the position of club chairman for a couple of years.

Repeatedly, he took his place on large Dublin selection committees. For the full decade that followed the '63 All-Ireland win, Heff stepped in and out as a selector. He was always attracted to the job on the sideline. But, at the same time, he found it so damned frustrating when there were always so many other men, sometimes five or six other men, with an equal say in what should be done on the field.

Dublin lost their Leinster and All-Ireland titles in 1964, losing to Meath by eight points. They regained the Leinster title in '65, beating Longford by six points, but Dublin then ran straight into Kerry in the 1965 All-Ireland semi-final. There was another crushing eight-point defeat.

Dublin, indeed, were flattened by that experience.

In the next eight years, between 1966 and '73, despite Heff's presence on the sideline for four of those championship summers, Dublin never even got very close to a place in the Leinster final. They lost to Kildare, Westmeath, Longford, Kildare again, Longford again, Laois, Kildare a third time, and Louth.

Heff was there on the sideline for too many of them.

On the field were half a dozen of his own Vincents players, fellas who were winning a nice pile of Dublin county titles but never got even half a chance to prove their true worth as countymen.

Gay O'Driscoll was included in that number. Tony Hanahoe. And Jimmy Keaveney. All three had county careers that, to all intents and purposes, were destitute.

O'Driscoll played his first game for Dublin at 19 years of age, in 1965. He was a Scoil Mhuire boy, a Joey's boy, and like all of the boys who had sat at the dented and scribbled desks in those schools before him, he aimed high.

Hanahoe likewise. He got on to the Dublin team in '64, but two years later he left the Dublin team behind him. He was back in 1970 for more hard times. In '73 Hanahoe was gone again.

Jimmy Keaveney had had enough by then as well.

He'd given it the guts of a decade. He'd won a Leinster medal in

'65 with Dublin but, after that, zilch. It was zilch and a pair of crutches, as a matter of fact. In the All-Ireland semi-final against Kerry, Keaveney had broken his ankle in two places. But nobody knew that until the next day. Not Jimmy, and not anybody in the Dublin county board, who couldn't be bothered to ask.

On Monday morning, his ankle throbbing and swelling, Jimmy took the bus into town. He hopped down O'Connell Street, made a right, and hopped towards Jervis Street Hospital.

He left with a pair of crutches. Jimmy had no money for the bus home, and swung the whole way home on the crutches and one leg instead. That was Jimmy Keaveney's introduction to the 'big time'.

The craic and the magic which was always there in the Vincents dressing-room, before and after games, was never found in the Dublin dressing-room.

It wasn't like Heff's days.

It wasn't at all like the old days when the Vincents and Dublin dressing-rooms were nearly always the exact same room, save a handful of faces. The Vincents fellas who turned out for Dublin at the tail end of the sixties and the beginning of the seventies had no sense of a shared destiny.

O'Driscoll, Hanahoe and Keaveney, when they wore the white and blue, were living the lives of winning footballers.

And, whatever about Dublin, St Vincents were chasing an All-Ireland title all for themselves.

16

'In the seventies McGee and I would have spat at each other up and down sidelines, first when he was with UCD and I was with Vincents and then when he was with Offaly and I was with Dublin. We would have disliked each other intensely.'

KH

Sunday, 15 April 1973

St Vincents were the greatest football team in Dublin and Leinster.

It was official.

For well over two decades the club had dominated its own county, and in that time Vincents got dressed up as the Dublin team and defeated so many other counties, including teams that were parading themselves as All-Ireland champions. But it was not until April of '73 that Vincents' status was fully and formally recorded in the game's history book. In the Leinster club football final, in Navan's Páirc Tailteann, Vincents thundered past The Downs from Westmeath by 6–10 to 2–5.

Vincents were unbeatable, again, and Kevin Heffernan was enjoying building a football team which, of course, still played the game the Vincents way. He had steel right at the centre of his full-back line in Gay O'Driscoll, and more steel at No.6 in Dave Billings. Ollie Freaney was long gone from the field but Tony Hanahoe was now in Freaney's No.11 shirt and was constantly moving and making things happen for others. On Hanahoe's right was Bobby Doyle, and on his left a young kid with a mighty big frame, and possibly an even bigger future. It was Brian Mullins' first year as a Vincents senior footballer. Des Foley was playing his last few games for Vincents at full-forward. In the corner, Jimmy Keaveney had announced his retirement from Dublin after eight forlorn years, but was still the very man to nail critical points for the club.

Vincents had clinched a three-in-a-row of Dublin senior football titles the previous autumn, hammering down a mighty statement to all comers. In 1970 they had beaten Raheny. In '71 they beat Craobh Chiaráin, and by beating UCD 2–8 to 0–9 in '72, pummelling them 1–7 to 0–1 in a storming second half, they had once again launched themselves into the Leinster club championship, which they had just claimed for the first time by scalping the men from The Downs.

Heff was never enjoying himself more managing a football team. For the previous ten years he had been overseeing Vincents and Dublin teams in one form or another, and with mixed success. With Dublin, actually, he was meeting with zero success. And that made Vincents all the more important.

All the more personal too.

In the All-Ireland club final in '73, on the first weekend in June, Vincents went looking for the title of 'number one football team in Ireland'.

They drew with Nemo Rangers, 2–11 apiece. In the replay Nemo plundered four goals from the jaws of the steely Vincents defence, and that was the end of that.

Nemo Rangers 4–6, St Vincents 0–10.

Vincents would also lose their title in Dublin, a few months later, when UCD gained quick revenge for their loss in the previous year's final, and had four points to spare over Vincents, 1–11 to 0–10.

Heff and Vincents, suddenly, had a big fight on their hands.

Since 1970 there was often an equal amount of fighting and football every time the students from UCD and Vincents met up with one another. They would meet in the championship seven times in fast succession, five of them county finals. The games would become bloodthirsty extravaganzas for neutral football supporters from other clubs, but for Vincents and UCD there was no stepping back.

Heff wouldn't allow that. Neither would the man standing on the UCD sideline opposite him.

The blood feud between Vincents and UCD did not take much stirring.

And the students from the southside of Dublin and the proud men from Marino, on the northside of the city, would not confine their brilliant and sometimes shocking battles to championship football.

They'd fight anywhere. Anytime. Championship or league, and it was in a league game in the middle of the winter, in O'Toole Park, that one particularly spine-chilling encounter was enacted. That was the day that a student almost cut the entire ear off Vincents forward Eugene Mullins with a far-fetched but deadly punch.

Everyone stopped what they were doing.

One of the students on the field, who would later become one of Heff's best-loved footballers, was Pat O'Neill. He was finishing his medical examinations. He was in his final year, and he would not be around for the worst portions of the seven years' war between the two clubs. But that day O'Neill tended to Eugene Mullins.

Afterwards, O'Neill would tell his teammates that the blood flowing from Mullins' wound was freezing as soon as it exited the man's head. When the doctor-to-be finished up his piece of work on his opponent, the two teams got right back to the business of looking to half-kill one another, every time a man moved anywhere near the ball.

The '72 final between the teams in Parnell Park was deemed to be of particularly notorious quality. It was after that game that one of the big-time GAA officials in the county and future chairman, Phil Markey, announced at a county board meeting that Vincents were 'running Dublin football, and ruining it'.

Markey was training the Dublin team that same year. Once he had put on record his true feelings, all of the Vincents players on the county team quit Markey's dressing-room. When Markey became chairman a decade and a half later, Heff quit as team manager in the middle of the National League campaign.

*

Eugene McGee was a quiet one.

He was like Heff in that respect. He was never boisterous. Some considered him quite shy. But he was stubborn. He hated losing. He was so like Heff in every respect. Both men, also, made up their minds about players, and people in the GAA generally, in lightning fashion.

McGee was not a Dubliner. He was from the north-Longford village of Aughnacliffe, sixteen miles from Cavan town, sixteen miles from Longford town. He was the second youngest in a family of seven, and the son of the local National schoolteacher, Owen McGee.

Eugene McGee came to Dublin to be a National schoolteacher himself. After graduating from UCD, McGee lasted just one year in the classroom, however. He preferred to be a man of words, and the written word. He wrote for GAA publications, and soon became a respected writer on a variety of national newspapers.

McGee didn't hide his views on GAA matters. That made him quite different to Heff, who also happened to dislike most journalists, and refused to trust any of them for more than half a second. Heff felt he had lots of good reasons for not liking McGee, and on top of the lot was the fact that McGee had taken the UCD football team under his wing and was devoting every single spare hour he had to making UCD the best football team in Dublin.

He trained them harder than the students had ever been trained. And he trained them to be smarter. Once they were in his dressing-room, critically, McGee also made them forget that they had their own clubs 'back home' and their own counties. He made them proud, and he made them united.

Lastly, he made them all, every last student within earshot for those seven years, believe that Vincents were a crowd of tough guys and bully boys, and that UCD were doing everyone a big service by making Vincents look second best.

Heff knew what McGee was saying to his players.

McGee stuck in Heff's craw.

An immovable object.

It was like the bad old days, in Heff's private estimation, when footballers from all over the country would come together and show off at the expense of Dublin football. UCD had been around in those 'days' as well, and had won their first Dublin football title in 1943, six years before Vincents won their first, when Roscommon's Donal Keenan led them to victory.

The students in UCD were nearly all household names in their own counties of birth, and half a dozen of them, like John O'Keeffe from Kerry, Benny Gaughran from Louth, PJ O'Halloran from Meath, Eamonn O'Donoghue from Kildare and Kevin Kilmurray from Offaly, were some of the best young footballers in the whole country.

Together, they were too good for Vincents in 1973 and '74. The students won the county title by four points in '73 and six points in '74, and there was no stopping them. These victories propelled McGee and UCD into the All-Ireland club championship, which they won in '74 and '75, beating Armagh's Clanna Gael by seven points and Nemo Rangers by two points.

UCD were the best football team in Dublin, and they were also now the best football team in the country.

No.1.

No argument.

Beating UCD, and preferably destroying them, was now consuming Heff's life. He also had other things on his mind in 1974, '75 and '76, of course. In those three years he would win the All-Ireland with Dublin, lose the title to Mick O'Dwyer's Kerry, and then win it back again.

Heff had little or no time for O'Dwyer either.

Didn't much like him.

Didn't want to like him.

But through the mid-seventies, as everyone talked about the brilliant battle of wits and temperaments between Heff and O'Dwyer, the Dublin manager had a second fight on his hands, which would not go away.

Neither did he want it to go anywhere.

He had to handle Eugene McGee and Mick O'Dwyer at the same time. And that was fine by him. Hadn't Vincents men before him, ever since the club had started winning county championships in 1949, successfully handled all sorts of tricky customers at club level and county level, every single summer?

Fighting on two fronts was fine for a Vincents man.

Vincents were back on top in Dublin in 1975, and they stayed there in '76 and '77. Three county titles in a row. Though the first of the three, as ever when UCD were involved with Vincents, was highly controversial. In fact, in the estimation of most in Vincents it was not really a title at all.

The teams were due to meet in the 1975 final on 15 June.

But UCD refused to play because of college examinations. They argued that the previous year's championship was twice put back when Vincents requested it postponed because of the unavailability of their 'student', Brian Mullins.

The Dublin County Board Activities Committee stuck by their guns. If UCD did not show, the title would be handed to Vincents.

Eugene McGee had a motion passed at a county board meeting ordering the Activities Committee to refix a date. The Activities Committee appealed this decision to the Leinster Council. In November, the Leinster Council upheld the earlier decision. After all that kerfuffle Vincents were named Dublin champions without playing in a final.

However, neither team was very happy.

Heff, for starters, had no interest in having a title handed to him and his team. He wanted to win it on the field, and win it by throttling McGee and his students, not circumventing them and not even getting the chance to lay a hand on them.

Finally, Heff and his closest buddy, Vincents chairman Jack Gilroy, came to the decision to progress matters, and represent Dublin in the 1976 Leinster club championship as the 'nominee' of the Dublin county board.

Not as Dublin champions.

Heff might not have McGee's Dublin title, but he now went after McGee's All-Ireland title. That would have to do.

Vincents scraped past Carbury from Kildare, completely dismantled Wicklow's Newtownmountkennedy, and took the Leinster title when late goals from Mickey Whelan and Jimmy Keaveney finished off St Joseph's from Laois, 3–9 to 1–8.

In the semi-final, Vincents had Nemo Rangers to contend with. The same Nemo team that had beaten them three years earlier, but had been beaten by UCD only twelve months before. Nemo Rangers had three magnificent games against Kerry's Austin Stacks at their backs, and never looked better.

In the trickiest of windy conditions, Jimmy Keaveney kicked six points in outrageously difficult odds. Vincents scored five points in each half, for a ten points total. Nemo could only manage three points. Mullins' fetching in the middle of the field, and Keaveney's kicking, were the biggest difference between the two teams on a day when every other man on the field looked decidedly mortal.

In the All-Ireland final, it was more like 'God's v Mortals' as Roscommon Gaels slumped at Vincents' feet. Tony Hanahoe polished off the winning display with two classic late goals.

St Vincents 4–10, Roscommon Gaels 0–5.

That was something.

The club's first All-Ireland title.

At last, the official label of being the no.1 football team in the whole country! But, the remainder of '76 was just as good. Every bit, as the newly crowned All-Ireland champions came up against UCD for the fifth time in succession in the Dublin county final.

On paper, it stood at two-all in Dublin championship wins.

Heff stood on one sideline, McGee on the other. And neither man had much time for a piece of paper. Both men knew that it was not really two-all, that UCD were two-one up.

In the minds of all the Vincents players and the students, and in the continuing power struggle between the two defiant clubs, the 1975 Dublin county final did not count.

In 1976, Vincents beat UCD by three points, 3–12 to 1–15, in a game that brought a blistering feud to a conclusion, but left a war unfinished.

The final result unknown.

Part Four

A Brilliant Mind

'To start with, we wanted to make the players believe that they had an asset that nobody else had. We wanted to make them the fittest team in the country.'

KH

Sunday, 5 May 1974

There was no sign.

Of anything, seven months into Heff's reign.

Dublin beat Tipperary in the final of the foolish old Corn Na Cásca tournament. That was in Croke Park on Easter Sunday. Three weeks later, on 5 May, within a whisker of the first round of the championship, still nothing. Kildare were tidier and, after Dublin scored two early goals, tried that little harder to win a play-off game in Division Two of the National League. They succeeded.

Kildare 3–13, Dublin 2–9.

Dublin got to that play-off by beating Limerick, and then Carlow and Kilkenny before Christmas. They beat Waterford, lost to Clare, beat Antrim. All of them games in which, even if there had been a sign, it would have been best ignored.

A sign, in any of those matches, might have been a laughing matter. But, as they all sat in the dressing-room after their seven-point loss to Kildare, there was a mood lingering. They'd lost their first big match. They'd also lost a trip to London for the winners. They were angry with themselves.

They'd done enough to deserve a couple of days in London together. They didn't deserve anything more than that, but, a match in London, pints together in a few London pubs, that would have been very welcome.

Heff had been hard at work for those seven months, nearly eight, full months. He had been given all he wanted the previous September by his old chum, Jimmy Gray, who was now the county chairman. Gray was a rock of intelligence and common sense in the committee-trodden world of the GAA. Heff and he had talked the same language since they were much younger men.

Full control for Heff, and two selectors, in case he wished to talk to anybody. He would like talking with Lorcan Redmond and Donal Colfer, as it turned out.

They'd become his two watertight confidants.

Colfer and Redmond formally shook hands with Heff on a Tuesday evening, in Parnell Park, in September of 1973. They'd be together, in the Dublin dressing-room and in charge on the sideline, apart from Heff slipping out of the picture for one year, until January of 1986.

Heff and Redmond had played against one another. Redmond was a St Margarets man, from the far and northern reaches of the county. Heff once or twice mentioned that he carried scars to prove Redmond's presence on the football field. Colfer was a real city boy, a Synge Street footballer, whom both Heff and Redmond remembered as playing without a care in the world and with a pair of glasses kept firmly in place with a tight piece of elastic around his head.

The three men met their first group of Dublin footballers in Clontarf, in the Hollybrook Hotel. They laid it on the line. They asked a big group of footballers if they were in or out. Their first game was just a couple of weeks after that meeting. Dublin had to quickly play against Roscommon in a game left over from the 1972–73 league. The game was in Castlerea.

Two hours and fifty minutes.

Bad roads. Small towns. A long, and complete pain-in-the-backside two hours and fifty minutes, and Dublin had to win by eight points to avoid disappearing through the division's hatch door. Awaiting them were grey empty grounds in Division Two, for the first time in their history.

Roscommon 3–7, Dublin 0–11.

It was a bad sign.

Bernard Brogan heard Kevin Heffernan out.

Then he said, 'No . . . I can't'.

But thanks for asking. Brogan was a polite young man. A serious third-level student who had his final mechanical engineering exams just around the corner, after Christmas, who was busy in his young life and appreciated Heff and Donal Colfer taking time to ask him to come and try out for the Dublin senior football team. They'd even come to one of his games in hard-to-find Kinvara Avenue, off the Navan Road, to see him.

Waited afterwards.

Then popped the question.

Bernard Brogan didn't see how it would work, or how he could squeeze the Dublin team into his daily life. Other things would have to give. Was Dublin worth that? he quickly enough wondered. On the spot Brogan thought not. The Dublin football team was not even in Bernard Brogan's head.

Like Heff's dad, Bernard Brogan's father was a guard. And like Heff's father a couple of decades before, he'd be on duty in and mostly around Croke Park in summertime, but not many of his eight boys were bothered making the same journey into the city to see a game.

Their local club, Oliver Plunketts, was small and played in the junior leagues, but the club was all that really concerned Jim Brogan and his boys. Nevertheless, four of them would get asked in by Heff at different stages during the 1970s, Jim junior, Bernard, Ollie and Kevin.

Of the four, Bernard was the most athletic. He was a fine high-jumper, and bloody fast over 100 yards. He could run any distance, in fact he could run all day. And he could field the ball. He played basketball for Ireland in his middle teens. Heff liked the cut of him from day one. And Dublin managers long after Heff, would also like three of Bernard's sons, Alan, Bernard junior, and Paul.

Bernard Brogan didn't go to Castlerea.

He'd turned down Heff, but three weeks later he discovered Heff standing on the sideline again. Junior football, but there was Heff, and he wanted to talk a second time.

'I'll be there,' said Bernard Brogan this time.

He played for Dublin the next week against the Combined Universities. He marked the tight, muscular No.8 for the Universities, John O'Keeffe, a Kerryman whom they'd all come to know only too well within eighteen months.

Brogan did as well as Heff thought and hoped he would do. Heff had good ideas about Bernard Brogan being his full-forward for the summer. And Brogan would indeed wear the No.14 shirt when Heff named his team for the first round of the championship in 1974, against Wexford.

Too often, however, in those first seven and a half months, Bernard Brogan wondered why on earth he was bothering to squeeze Dublin into his life.

There was a huge crowd in Nowlan Park, the biggest crowd Heff and his car-loads of Dublin players had come across when they tried to get close to the ground, and park somewhere.

It was pretty much mayhem, however.

The rain was now belting down.

And it was a cold, miserable, son-of-a-bitch of a winter's day.

Nothing seemed to be organized. There was a hurling game on. When Heff asked, he was told that it was only after starting. It was half-past two. Dublin's game was down to start at three o'clock.

In the distance, Paddy Grace spotted Kevin Heffernan walking towards him. The Kilkenny county secretary had rarely spoken to Heff, but he admired the man. And felt a little sorry for him having to turn up in Nowlan Park for a game of football in the depths of winter. Dublin were playing Kilkenny.

'If you want the points,' grinned Grace, even before he said his hello, 'you can have them, Kevin!'

Heff asked him what was going on.

'Kevin,' continued Grace, 'it's a little bit early, but we'll have a team for you to play . . . don't worry a bit about that.'

Paddy Grace was more concerned with keeping an eye on the hurling game, and also keeping an eye on the day's takings.

Grace had been a corner-back for Kilkenny for over ten years, and was still playing in the corner when he took up the job of county secretary, a job he had held down for twenty-six years. He would remain county secretary for a further ten years, until his death in 1984.

On the second Sunday in December, in 1973, Paddy Grace did not have a Division Two National Football League game between Dublin and Kilkenny on page one of his list of 'concerns and worries' for the day. Besides, by the time the game would get under-way Nowlan Park would be virtually emptied. Almost 10,000 people would have gone home. He would only count three small clusters of people in the ground. But the last thing Grace wanted to do was to insult his guest.

Heff was being polite and not at all huffy in front of the Kilkennyman. It would be hard to create a bit of a scene in front of someone so good-humoured and happy with life. Besides, Paddy Grace was one of the greats. As a hurler, he was one of Heff's heroes. Grace had played in the famous 'thunder and lightning' All-Ireland final in 1939, which Heff remembered, as a boy, everyone talking about.

Kilkenny and Tipp at war with one another, and both fighting it out with the heavens! It was played the same weekend the Second World War kicked off. That was Paddy Grace's first All-Ireland medal, and he won a second in 1947, a game Heff watched in Croke Park, getting into the ground hours and hours before the minor match even got under way.

A Kilkenny team had appeared, as all the supporters disappeared.

Dublin would score six goals and 16 points against them, in a complete and total waste of a day. Kilkenny would score four points.

Paddy Grace knew it was a day with no upside for his guest, whom he wanted to say goodbye to, and to whom he would tell the biggest, fattest white lie he had told in a long time.

He felt he had to say something.

About a Kilkenny team that had appeared and had been half-useless? Or, about the 10,000 disappeared?

Which?

He chose to mention the latter.

'There was another big hurling game . . . over in Thomastown,' said Grace, as he shook hands with Heff, and wished him a safe journey home. 'That's where everyone had to head off, y'know . . . before your game started.'

Heff chose to half-believe him.

Heff had to wonder himself.

Nobody knew for sure what would become of the team he was building. That included Kevin Heffernan. Though Lorcan Redmond saw some progress.

Redmond had been a selector the year before when Phil Markey was in charge of proceedings, and he didn't think much of 1973.

But when Jimmy Gray had a chat with him, Lorcan Redmond thought the county chairman was talking complete sense at least. Gray wanted to guillotine the old way of getting a Dublin team out on to the field. That manner of business included five selectors, three picked by the county board, and two presented by the county champions. And the county chairman and secretary, like most other counties in football and hurling, also sat down in the room when teams were being selected.

Gray wanted three men.

Total. And he wanted one man, more or less, in total command. Gray wanted Heff to be the boss. But first he got Lorcan Redmond on board with his big idea. Then Donal Colfer. Both were happy with what they heard.

Getting Heff was going to be the hard part, and harder than Jimmy Gray thought. Heff had brought St Vincents to the All-Ireland club final in the summer of '73, where they had come up short against Nemo Rangers. Heff was bursting to have a second good run at it. He explained himself to Gray, and let it be known that Dublin would only get in his way.

A week passed.

Every second day Gray was being asked by Seán Óg Ó'Ceallacháin, who was busy as a bee filling his column in the *Evening Press* newspaper with Dublin happenings and opinions, who was going to be in charge of Dublin for the new football season. Ó'Ceallacháin was irrepressible. Finally, Gray mentioned Kevin Heffernan, and trotted out a slim-line version of his big idea.

Ó'Ceallacháin was a neighbour of Heff's on the Howth Road, a former teammate and opponent, and never one bit afraid to hop a ball in Kevin Heffernan's direction. The following Wednesday evening he announced Heff as the new Dublin manager.

Heff was furious.

The first wave of fury was directed at Jimmy Gray.

Seán Óg Ó'Ceallacháin was served up the dregs, which were still sufficient to fill both of his ears.

Heff told both men he had no choice.

He'd now have to do the job.

Whatever else, he'd get them fit.

Fitter and stronger than every other football team. And harder at the back. Tough as nails back there. Then he'd see what he could make of them.

He'd want them to play the Vincents way.

Teak-tough at the back, big and strong in the middle, and sort of crazy and bamboozling up front. He'd need an Ollie Freaney on the '40'. He'd need one Des Ferguson, at least, who would forage on the half-forward line. In the full-forward line, he'd need two of himself. Two men who would stay or take off down the field as though they had no intention of ever coming back, and always have the other full-back line thinking, and worrying, about what was happening.

But, to begin with, he needed them fit.

Of Heff's dozen or so needs, that was number one.

And in getting that done right he needed Mickey Whelan.

In 1969 Mickey Whelan had emigrated to America, but now he was back. Whelan knew stuff that no football managers and trainers in Ireland knew. Heff was fairly sure of that.

Whelan had taken off to America at 30 years of age. He had a wife and two small kids, and restarted his life over there as a student. The Whelans cleaned apartments and worked odd jobs to get by. Later he would get a scholarship, but at first he had to give up almost everything. He'd studied biology and sociology in Westchester, and then majored in PE and biology in Davis & Elkins College in West Virginia, before returning to Westchester to complete his masters.

Whelan was a Clanna Gael man, but Heff liked him. And Whelan liked nearly everything about Kevin Heffernan's ways and means of getting things done. He was on the Dublin team at 19 when Heff was one of the old boys.

It only took a short conversation before Whelan agreed to help Heff's Dublin become fit enough to win something decent. But Heff wasn't finished there, and he talked Whelan into first playing for Vincents' intermediate football team, then Vincents' senior football team, and when Heff would lead Vincents to the All-Ireland club title in 1976, Mickey Whelan was centrepoint to what was happening on the field.

In the winter of '74, Heff had his new Dublin squad of footballers up to the new tricks that Mickey Whelan now had up his sleeve. They took them out to Finglas, to a new hall in Coláiste Eoin secondary school and, there, Dublin footballers tiptoed their way in and out of two lines of tyres. They'd be told to get up on a beam of wood best suited to young slips of lassies and fellas, and try to be gymnasts. They dropped medicine balls on each other's stomachs. They did sit-ups and press-ups until nearly everyone moaned. They stood opposite one another, chest to chest, and pummelled one another's stomachs with crisp, fast moving fists, until one man might be half bent over and another man might have his arms falling off him.

In the early spring, in Parnell Park, there were bundles and bundles of 800-metre runs in every training session. As the evenings lengthened in mid-spring there were more and more faster laps, and there were evenings in St Anne's Park in Raheny, running the hills. They got fitter, and fitter.

Fit enough to be able to run 'the circle' as Mickey Whelan and Kevin Heffernan knew it could only be run by a team in which every last man Jack was, pretty much, fitter than he had ever been in his life.

The circle would be 50 or 60 yards in diameter. Flags marked its circumference, four or five yards apart. One footballer stood at each flag. On the whistle every man chased the man in front of him. Full out. Chasing hard, shouting loudly. A footballer who grabbed the jersey of the footballer in front of him was allowed out of the circle. And the chase continued, and continued, footballers grabbed, footballers released from the circle, until only half a dozen remained, and were now sprinting, heads down, sprinting but half banjaxed, with no hope of ever catching the jersey of the man in front of them.

The whistle would blow, finally.

Everyone would get back in the circle, including the half-banjaxed.

The whistle would blow again, to start everyone off all over again. Tuesdays, Thursdays, and Saturdays. And before and after every training session the team would have a 'warm-up' and a 'cool-down', new-fangled thinking that Mickey Whelan had also found out all about in America.

That thinking included making use of Saturdays.

Mickey Whelan had informed Heff that long, restful weekends with only a game of football to stretch everyone's legs were no good to anybody. There was last-minute work that could be done on Saturdays. And with the players having to turn out on a Saturday morning there was less chance of anyone deciding to have an extra pint or two on a Friday night.

Saturday became the most important day's work of the whole week.

On Saturday mornings, nobody was racing from work to training. And nobody was racing home after training.

Heff had time to mooch around a little bit more himself, and that included wandering into the small bookie's shop on Collins Avenue, just down the road from Parnell Park. Heff liked his little bets. Horses or dogs, didn't matter, as long as he thought the price looked good.

One Saturday morning in April, Heff was in the bookie's, studying the odds, knowing his players wouldn't be turning up at the ground across the road for another ten or fifteen minutes. With his bets laid, Heff was on his way out of the shop when he noticed a board with the prices for the Leinster football championship hurriedly put together in someone's handwriting.

Dublin were 8/1.

They were behind the Leinster champions, Offaly. Kildare had just beaten Dublin in the league, so they were behind them as well. Meath were also at tighter odds. Heff didn't ever think of putting his money on football matches.

He stuck to the horses and dogs.

They didn't answer back. Most of them ran as though there was no tomorrow. They didn't drop their heads or give up, as footballers easily did.

A week later Heff was back to put on some money.

Dublin to win Leinster, at 8/1.

Heff didn't put anything on Dublin to win the All-Ireland. If he'd asked, the same bookie would have offered him odds of 33/1.

18

'The young fella in the back of the car said he went to all the Vincents games with his dad and told me Jimmy Keaveney never missed a free.'

KH

Sunday, 26 May 1974

Kevin Heffernan was not in the best of form.

He was driving away from Croke Park. It was nearly tea-time, and traffic wasn't too bad. Dublin had beaten Wexford in the first round of the championship. The game was due to warm up the crowd for the National League final replay between Kerry and Roscommon. That was the main event of the afternoon.

A win for Kerry, with not many Kerry folk there to see it. There wasn't a whole lot of support from Roscommon or Wexford either.

Hill 16 was quiet as a large mouse.

The whole place was only a quarter full.

Heff was halfway home before he knew it. And he'd been grumbling for the previous five minutes. About how bad Dublin looked, and about how good Kerry and Roscommon were, for sure. Listening was his wife, Mary, in the seat next to him. In the back seats were Mary's friend Lily Jennings and her seven-year-old son, Terry.

Heff had formally announced to himself and his companions that Dublin had been poor, and that there's not much hope for a poor team unless it has a free-taker who can nail every single free the team gets.

'Why don't you get Jimmy Keaveney?' asked little Terry Jennings from over Heff's left shoulder.

*

Bernard Brogan had played on the edge of the square against Wexford. He'd twisted his left knee just after Christmas but worked around the clock to get himself right for the first round of the championship.

Brogan was glad that he had listened to Heff.

It was good being part of the Dublin squad, and even though there was nothing to show for it in the Monday morning news-papers for the first eight and half months of Heff's reign, he loved the sense of professionalism about the weekly training regime. He had done all right against Wexford.

But, in the second round of the Leinster championship against Louth, he was told that the team didn't need him in the full-forward line. Bernard Brogan was named amongst the big list of substitutes.

Jimmy Keaveney was No.14 instead.

It was a big change of mind. Bernard Brogan was tall, slim as a reed, and a complete athlete. Jimmy Keaveney was three or four inches shorter, and perhaps two or three stone heavier.

It simply didn't make sense to Brogan, or to most of the Dublin players. Eyes were shot up to heaven when Keaveney, and his Vincents buddy Leslie Deegan, showed up for training on the Tuesday after the first-round win over Wexford. Hauling Jimmy Keaveney out of retirement was the last thing anybody who'd had a long winter, and an even longer spring, of brutally hard work in the gym and out on the training field wished to see.

Nobody was amused, not even the Vincents boys who palled around with Keaveney, and loved knocking him, and loved even more being on the receiving end of Keaveney's cutting wit.

Against Louth, Keaveney slapped over four frees.

He got six points in total in his comeback game. When Dublin badly needed a point or two against Offaly, in the Leinster quarter-final, Keaveney slotted them over with hardly a care in the world. He scored four more frees, five points in total on the day. But it was Deegan who had made the world of difference against Offaly.

Again, Croker was a quarter full, at best. But Dublin burst into life from the very beginning, and grabbed Offaly by the throat. It was an Offaly team that had beaten Galway and Kerry in All-Ireland finals in 1971 and '72, and had just won three exquisite Leinster titles in a row. They'd played their part in the last five. Dublin hadn't even been anywhere near a Leinster final for eight years.

But David Hickey cracked a shot off the crossbar early on. Hickey too had returned late. He'd been a minor for Dublin in 1968 and '69, and got to wear a Dublin senior jersey for the first time in '69. Heff was back as a selector in 1970 and picked Hickey for his first championship game. Heff liked his grittiness. Hickey was fast, like Des Ferguson. He could also forage like Ferguson, though unlike Ferguson he wasn't a natural fighter. But neither was Hickey one bit afraid. All told, he was just enough like Snitchie.

But in 1973, Hickey was playing more rugby than football. He had taken up the game during his medical studies in UCD, and had only played one game the entire year for Dublin. Dublin lost in a Leinster championship replay to Louth. That meant that David Hickey had completed three short summers as a Dublin footballer, and had three losses in the first round to show for it. Laois, Westmeath and Louth.

The evening that UCD were knocked out of the senior cup in Leinster by Bective Rangers, Heff phoned him. It did not need to be a very long conversation.

Twice more Dublin hit the woodwork.

In the first half, Offaly didn't look like a team that had come for a fight. Shortly before half-time, Paddy Reilly thundered a big kick towards the Offaly posts, but as he came to collect the high ball Offaly goalkeeper Martin Furlong didn't sense too much danger. He didn't even see Leslie Deegan. Before he knew it, Deegan had darted in and knocked the ball with his hand into the corner of the net.

Dublin were one point up at half-time.

When the teams re-emerged, Dublin's tails were still up. Offaly now had their sleeves rolled up, and they were not playing well, but they were seriously getting stuck into their opponents. Every possible way, but Dublin handled the physical stuff and, at the same time, it pleased Heff that they were also able to keep playing good football. The teams were level with sixty seconds remaining.

Offaly had possession.

Their centre-back, Sean Lowry, was about to unleash a long drive from defence, when midfielder Stephen Rooney dived in and blocked the ball. Rooney collected the ball also, and passed it off to Brian Mullins.

He found Deegan, mainly because Deegan was the only man free, and Leslie Deegan's soaring kick took an age in defying gravity. Deegan had kicked the ball up as high as he could because four Offaly defenders were about to devour him and ball at any second.

It went up and up.

The game was also pretty much up. The ball then started to descend. It was coming right down in the Offaly goalmouth. Nobody expected it to land on the far side of Martin Furlong's crossbar.

It did.

Dublin 1–11, Offaly 0–13.

Heff now realized that Dublin had every chance of winning the Leinster final. But Bernard Brogan wouldn't play again in 1974. Late in the game against Offaly he had twisted his right knee, and messed up his cartilage completely. He faced a fortnight in hospital. Two months in plaster, and a full nine months of painful rehabilitation.

Gay O'Driscoll, like every second man who came through Scoil Mhuire in Marino, and Joey's, and was Vincents through and through, was more of a hurler than a footballer.

O'Driscoll was also steel.

Full-back line steel, which meant that O'Driscoll was steel of a vastly superior quality to anyone else who played in front of him on Vincents and Dublin hurling and football teams. He didn't look fast. But any opponent he ever met never looked that fast either after the first ten or fifteen minutes of a match. Gay O'Driscoll played the game tight.

Sometimes too tight when the ball was at the other end of the field. In the county finals in 1970 and '72, he was sent to the Vincents line, though he had the consolation on each occasion of being accompanied by his opponent.

At 19, O'Driscoll had played hurling and football for Dublin. For Vincents too, of course, where he got to team up with an ageing Heff. He'd played on the Dublin Under-21 hurling team that lost an All-Ireland final to Tipperary by a single point, and for five years he gave hurling and football everything he had. In 1972 O'Driscoll got married. In '73 he decided on one game.

At 25 years of age, Gay O'Driscoll became a footballer, first, foremost, and last.

Gay O'Driscoll was definitely his own man. As a footballer, and as a businessman who would soon be selling his own office furniture and would have his own successful manufacturing company employing twenty people.

Heff liked that about him.

What Heff didn't so much like about O'Driscoll was that, unlike almost every other man in the Dublin squad, O'Driscoll paid little heed to his manager's warning to neither befriend, nor pass the time of day with, newspapermen.

Equally, the mind games, and the temptations and veiled threats that Heff liked to trot out in the dressing-room concerned O'Driscoll less than most of those around him. Heff had left O'Driscoll off his team for the Leinster quarter-final against Offaly.

O'Driscoll wasn't impressed.

When the team had finished listening to Heff in the dressing-room, and as they fussed over last-minute necessities, Gay O'Driscoll took to the floor.

He told everyone who was starting the game that if they were feeling any pressure or experiencing any doubts that they should stay put in the room. He then told them all that there were substitutes like himself who were only too ready to do the job, if the job wasn't being done properly on the field.

O'Driscoll wanted back into the team. Most lunchtimes, unknown to the rest of the lads, he made it out to Seapoint and there, ever so quietly, got in three or four miles on his own. He had started the Division Two play-off game against Kildare. But he'd been dropped for the match with Wexford, and was still on the bench when Dublin played Louth in the second round. He came on that day. But he was still not named on the starting team against Offaly.

Dave Billings started in the corner for Dublin. But Billings found Seamus Darby more than a handful and at half-time O'Driscoll got his chance. He was back on for the second half against Offaly.

Problem was, Dublin hadn't won two championship games in a row in years. In May, nobody had talked about June. In June, nobody had talked about July. Nobody was thinking about anything other than the next game, and in July some Dublin footballers had their holidays booked. That included Gay O'Driscoll.

He was going away for a week. Heff did not ask him to cancel the holiday. He knew that everyone, himself included, would have to learn from the lessons in 1974 and talk and plan full summers in future. O'Driscoll was home on the morning of the Leinster semi-final. Heff still wanted him to play against Kildare. As soon as O'Driscoll arrived into his house he got a call from Heff. He was wanted down in Vincents, where Heff wanted to have a look at him. There was a game starting at 11 a.m. and Heff wanted O'Driscoll to play the first half.

O'Driscoll did.

And Gay O'Driscoll started the semi-final against Kildare, and also the Leinster final against Meath. He would stay on the team until 1979, when he was again dropped by Heff, though Heff would bring O'Driscoll on for the second half of the All-Ireland final that year. The next day, at 32 years of age, Gay O'Driscoll called it quits with Dublin.

Dublin 1–14, Meath 1–9.
Jimmy Keaveney 1–8.
Jimmy Keaveney 0–7 from frees.
Dublin were 1974 Leinster champions.
Kevin Heffernan made a pretty penny when he dropped into the bookie's at the tail end of Collins Avenue the following Saturday. And he had one and a half men to thank for that, Jimmy Keaveney, and seven-year-old Terry Jennings.

Would he have ever thought of Keaveney, he wondered privately, and sometimes aloud, at the end of 1974? He had been watching Jimmy Keaveney playing for Vincents, same as the child was watching Keaveney in every game he was brought to by his father.

'Why don't you get Jimmy Keaveney,' the boy had suggested from the back seat of Heff's car two months before.

'My dad brings me to all his games . . . and Jimmy Keaveney never misses a free, Mr Heffernan.'

'After 1974, we always expected that we should beat Cork.'

KH

Monday, 5 August 1974

Jimmy Keaveney had spent the night with some of his Cork friends. He was leaving Frank Cogan's house the following morning when someone came to the door, and gave him a shout.

'JIMMY . . . wait there!'

Keaveney turned, just in time to see Cogan and Billy Morgan holding the Sam Maguire Cup over their heads.

'Take a look at it, Jimmy boy!' said Cogan.

'It's the nearest you'll ever get to it!' chimed Morgan.

Even when surprised, Jimmy Keaveney was never short of a few fast words. He had a couple of things to say to his Cork buddies, but as Keaveney drove back up to Dublin he also thought about exactly what he would tell Kevin Heffernan.

Heff would like the story.

Keaveney knew that, and knew Heff would use it at just the right moment later in the week, probably when all the players squeezed into the old Nissen hut at the far end of the ground after Thursday night's training session. On Sunday, Dublin were meeting Cork in the All-Ireland semi-final.

Cork were everybody's favourites.

Dublin had had their year. It was early August, but Dublin's year certainly appeared ready to have the envelope licked closed on it within a matter of days.

Cork had talent to burn all over the field.

Everybody knew that.

They'd seen it in the All-Ireland final the previous September when Cork beat Galway by seven points. They'd seen it in the Munster final of '73, to begin with, when Jimmy Barry-Murphy was picked at corner-forward and Ray Cummins at full-forward, but swapped under instruction from team trainer, Donie O'Donovan just as the ball was thrown in. Ray was followed into the corner by Paud O'Donoghue. Jimmy Deenihan found himself in at full-back on the tall, rangy kid with the crew cut and attitude.

Cork 5–12, Kerry 1–15.

To Heff, any team beating Kerry by nine points in a championship match was a team to be one hundred per cent feared.

The important thing was not to be scared stiff.

Cork got over Kerry again in the 1974 Munster final, and beat them by double scores, in fact, 1–11 to 0–7.

Heff had a busy Sunday ahead of him.

The timesheet for the Lord Mayor's Cup at Clontarf Golf Club had him down for an 8.32 a.m. start. There was a big entry for the Cup that was limited to handicappers of between five and nine. It was going to be a day's serious golfing, before the final sixty-four would be decided by Sunday evening. The next day and for the following week, the Cup would continue as a matchplay competition.

Heff was due to be first off.

Having friends in the highest places in the golf club was a good thing for the Dublin football manager. He'd eventually be in high places himself in Clontarf Golf Club, accepting the job of president in 2001. Years later, he didn't worry about the club's airs and graces too much.

His old black Toyota Camry was usually parked facing the first tee, and most usually in the space reserved for the club professional. If the car was filled with smoke, Heff was still inside. If not, the pro knew he could be found in the clubhouse lounge, a cup of tea in front of him, a copy of the *Racing Post* receiving his fullest attention.

But all through the summer of 1974 Heff was playing the best golf of his life. In June, on the morning of Dublin's victory over Offaly in the Leinster quarter-final, he'd also been helped to the earliest possible tee-time.

That morning was the Captain's Prize day.

Heff got his first shot off at the ungodly hour of 6.30 a.m. He had a good score under his belt three hours later, and he birdied the last two holes to finish up with 42 Stableford points. He was told that he was in with a right good chance of winning Dr P. J. Smyth's prize.

Heff finished up at 10 a.m., and then got home to prepare himself for the more important sporting event of the day. Dublin ousted Offaly from the championship, and Heff was back home when he got a phone call from the club. He had to head back for the prizegiving. Dr Smyth was waiting for him.

He'd won.

Two months later, on the morning of the All-Ireland semi-final, Heff carded an excellent 77, and his playing colleagues didn't know if he had golf or football on his mind when he came to the club's notoriously difficult 12th hole.

Clontarf's tightness and its narrow fairways always called for decently high levels of concentration. To make up for its shortness, the club liked to keep its 'rough' more on the rough side than most city clubs. Then, of course, Clontarf had its trademark 12th, 'the Quarry Hole', carved out of a plot of land once owned by Donnycarney Quarries.

Heff drove his ball expertly on to the raised plateau on the 12th. To his right was 'out of bounds', and to his left and front there was water. Heff knew the hole by heart. But that didn't mean the hole ever offered itself up to him or others.

Not for a second.

His second shot was down into the valley, to the green. Two ponds and two greenside bunkers vied for his attention as always. He hit the heart of the green, and was safe, and on his way down the last few holes with his score almost secured. As fine a 77 as he had ever carded.

*

Billy Morgan grabbed Jimmy Keaveney with both hands in the 68th minute of the All-Ireland semi-final. It was an eighty-minute game. And it was a penalty.

The second penalty of the second half.

Twelve minutes earlier Jimmy Barry-Murphy had rifled the ball to the net from the penalty spot, and did so amid raging argument. Cork substitute Martin Doherty had been pulled down in the square by Seán Doherty all right, but at the time Ned Kirby, the man Martin Doherty had run on to replace, was still on the field.

Cork had that piece of luck.

Barry-Murphy's goal got Cork on the road to a victory that everyone in the attendance of 50,000 still half-expected of them. One big final quarter was all Cork needed, and now with the penalty that big finish was set up for them.

But Cork still stalled.

Then Keaveney grabbed the ball, which was dropped by his marker, Humphrey Kelleher. Keaveney next wrong-footed Billy Morgan who had no option but to grab him and pull him to the ground as he strode through.

Keaveney landed on the ground, one foot from the Cork goal-line. This time, referee Patsy Devlin heard nobody shout at him when he gave the penalty. Brian Mullins struck the ball poorly. Morgan almost got a hand to it, but the ball made its way, low and ugly, to the corner of the net.

Fifteen minutes into the game, Cork had missed the first big opportunity for one team to land a blow on the other team's chin. Jimmy Barry-Murphy found himself in possession and with an open goal in front of him, but he smashed the ball over the bar. A goal would have put Cork two points up.

Instead, the teams were level, and for the next thirty-five minutes Cork flustered and flapped, and did not get one more score. In fact, forty-five minutes went by with Cork failing to get a score from play. Over the full eighty minutes, with Seán Doherty pinning down Ray Cummins and taking him out of the game as a target man, Cork would only manage five points from play.

Heff was delighted that his lads had been mean and tough in defence and had shown Cork damn all respect as All-Ireland champions, and he was just as happy that they also had belief in themselves and their great fitness by powering home in the final ten minutes of the game.

Dublin 2–11, Cork 1–8.

Before the game, and at half-time, Heff had promised his players that good Cork teams never defeated good Dublin teams. It wasn't true, of course.

Cork had beaten Dublin before when they both strode on to the big stage in Croke Park. They'd beaten them in a National final in front of 50,000 people.

That was back in 1952.

Heff knew that, he could never forget it. But he also knew that his players would have no memory of, or interest in, how the '52 National League final had ended. There was the League title at stake that year and an awful lot more, a brilliant trip to New York for the winners. It would be the first time the vast majority of the Dublin football team would have set foot in America. Everyone wanted it.

In the final seconds of the game Dublin had a final, last attack into the Canal End when they were awarded a free 40 yards out.

Cork were leading by one point.

The angle was tough enough, but Heff was at the height of his power as Dublin's free-taker. The pressure was doubled on Heff when the referee, Dan Ryan from Kerry, told him that his kick would be the last kick of the match.

Cork's trainer in 1973 and '74, Donie O'Donovan, played on the half-forward line that victorious day in '52. Heff had lost to O'Donovan that afternoon. Heff had lost the League final, and he had lost the brilliant trip to America for everyone in the Dublin dressing-room.

Heff's kick had the length all right, but it had struck off the right upright. Ollie Freaney grabbed the ball, but, as he had warned, the referee blew the final whistle without further delay.

Heff had lost to Cork.

All because he could not nail one last free-kick that someone like Jimmy Keaveney would certainly have relished, and really fancied.

Heff was back in Clontarf for the first round of the Lord Mayor's Cup on the Wednesday after the All-Ireland semi-final. It fitted nicely between the Tuesday and Thursday training sessions in Parnell Park.

He was playing Limerick's Rory Fitzgerald, an 18-year-old, and Heff was two down after four holes. But Heff was square at the turn. It was nip and tuck between the pair of them on the back nine, and when they arrived at the par five 18th they were still all square. Heff hit his drive immaculately. Locals told him afterwards it must have been all of 300 yards. Heff doubted them. But his tee shot had left him with a two iron to the final green. Heff pulled his shot into heavy country on his left.

He scrambled for a five, and a half on the hole. Heff kept his nerve on the tie hole. He safely took his par four, while his opponent saw his second shot trickle over the back of the green, and then lost his nerve with a weak chip.

In the second round, Heff was drawn against his brother-in-law, Jimmy O'Neill. Heff had no mercy. But the best golfing summer of his life was ended on the Friday after the All-Ireland semi-final at the hands of a Clontarf man and a Corkman, Dermot Condon, who turned into the back nine three up, withheld Heff's fightback over the next four holes, and then finished him off 'two and one'.

Another loss to Cork for Heff.

But his Dublin team were in the 1974 All-Ireland football final.

'They were experienced footballers. Once they got their confidence and the team game came together, the jump to top-class football was not as difficult as it would have been for some young team with no experience.'

KH

Sunday, 22 September 1974

An early mass on the morning of the All-Ireland final fitted itself into the plans of most of Heff's footballers. His captain was amongst that number.

Seán Doherty was on his knees.

On the altar in his local church were his boots, and his Dublin football socks and shorts. His jersey too. Sixty seconds earlier the parish priest, Fr Lucey, had blessed them. Seán Doherty was 28 years old. He had been a Wicklow boy, born and bred. But he'd played all his adult football with Kilmacud Crokes and Ballyboden Wanderers, and before his career with the two clubs concluded he would have an extremely light haul of one junior football championship medal, one junior hurling championship medal, one intermediate football championship medal and one intermediate hurling championship medal to show for all of his years' service to both of Dublin's south-side clubs.

In other words, sweet feck all.

The decision of the Doherty family to move from the Devil's Glen, in Ashford, up to Ballsbridge in the mid-fifties had not made any great difference to Seán Doherty's GAA career.

Seán was 13 years old when they moved to the city.

Seán, however, still went 'home' to be a Wicklow footballer. His home county chose him at full-forward for the first round of the Leinster Under-21 championship in 1967. Within a year he played with the Wicklow senior team.

Dublin had never shown any interest in him, so Wicklow's invitation could not be turned down. Doherty's career as a Wicklow footballer included picking up four other players twice a week for training and heading down to Aughrim, and his career as a Wicklow footballer ended after a short enough enquiry from him about food and petrol money.

He had just started his own plumbing business. Money was tight. And all the lads in his car were hungry by the time they were dropped off after training by Doherty at the top of their individual roads. Sometimes it would be close to midnight.

The Wicklow county board had replied to Seán Doherty's enquiry with a question of their own. He was asked, did he not play football for the love of the game?

Twelve months earlier, as Cork and Galway ran out on to the field in Croke Park for the 1973 All-Ireland final, Seán Doherty's love for the game had him standing on Hill 16, where he was working for the day as a GAA steward.

Now, on the morning of the 1974 All-Ireland final, he was the captain of the Dublin team. Heff had chosen him to be captain.

Heff had never explained why.

Doherty had been Dublin full-back since 1968. He was a big man on a team of losers, but he didn't suffer fools. That's what Heff liked about him. Heff didn't make a drama out of it when he told Doherty he was Dublin captain. Two years later, when he came up to Doherty and informed him he was no longer Dublin captain, Heff made the conversation even shorter and seem even less important.

Seán Doherty's socks, shorts and jersey were folded neatly and sitting on his boots, on the altar. His wife hadn't told him that Fr Lucey had asked for them the previous evening. Teresa Doherty had given them to the priest without Seán's consent or knowledge.

Seán Doherty was at the end of the most nerve-racking, the most amazing week of his life as a footballer. But he could not show it, to anyone. Everyone on the team called him 'the Doc'.

He had no medical kit in his hand. But one of his jobs, on and off the field, was to look after everyone else. Make sure everyone was ready. Leave no man in any doubt about that man's own health and ability. The Doc had a fearsome strength. He was made hard.

His teammates knew that.

Opponents quickly discovered it.

In the years to come, every Kerry footballer would know it. And the toughest Kerry footballer of them all, Páidí Ó Sé, would repeatedly warn everybody not to forget it. Once, Páidí had over-heard a dressing-room plot to give Dublin goalkeeper Paddy Cullen a thump early on in the 1976 All-Ireland final.

The plotters thought the immaculately presented Cullen, socks pulled up, shorts tight, jersey even tighter, might be unnerved if he found himself sitting on his arse or, better still, sitting there and see-ing some stars. Páidí interrupted the conversation of the Kerry full-forward line, and told the boys the problem would not be getting in and hitting Paddy Cullen.

The problem would be getting out after hitting him.

The plot was dropped.

Nobody messed with the Doc.

Nobody messed with his goalkeeper, nobody did any messing of any kind for very long in his full-back line.

That's what Heff also liked about his captain.

Heff was all business.

An All-Ireland final was a precious place to be. He'd found out himself as a young man that an All-Ireland final, and the weeks and days leading up to it, was as exciting and brilliant as the last days in school before the summer holidays.

September 1974 was just so.

It was carnival time, and wild.

Everyone was happy. Everything seemed right with the world. Nobody thought, for one second, about what could go wrong. But

Heff knew that everything could go wrong in slightly over eighty minutes.

He'd been that kid on the last day in school.

He'd been that young man who'd been a fool, who'd feared nothing. He had woken up the morning after the 1955 All-Ireland final, he'd woken up early, woken suddenly in a cold sweat. The realization that it was all over, and that nothing could be done about it, grabbed him by his shoulders. There was a knot tightening in his stomach, and the longest day of his life had not even started.

Heff felt he might never forgive himself for what happened in the All-Ireland final that was already a day old. A whole year went into darkness. A flick of a switch.

And it had all happened so fast.

Kerry were 1955 All-Ireland champions.

Dublin were nothing.

Already, the worst had happened.

One week after beating Cork in the semi-final, Brian Mullins had lined out for Dublin against Mayo in the All-Ireland Under-21 semi-final. Dublin lost, and Heff's giant, blond and long-haired midfielder, 19 years old but with the naturally grumpy disposition of a man three times that age, had landed awkwardly on his left ankle in the second half.

On the Monday morning he'd taken a phone call from Mullins telling him the bone was chipped. His whole lower leg was in plaster. Heff knew that Mullins had played on and finished the game. That same evening, he'd also turned up in Parnell Park to watch Dublin play against Offaly in the Player Wills Cup tournament.

While the thought of playing in the All-Ireland final without Mullins was shuddering, Heff also saw an immediate upside. He was actually quietly pleased that Brian Mullins had everyone sick with worry. The fellas had been lively, and noisier than they had been the whole year, when they came back into training on the Tuesday and Thursday after beating Cork. Heff had stood back looking at them, and they looked like lads who felt that they had reached the finishing line.

They sounded like lads ready to celebrate.

They weren't euphoric, but they weren't too far away from it. Heff had been worried about them all that week, but the news of Brian Mullins' injury had shut everybody up straight away.

They weren't talking rubbish any more.

There was no more shouting about the T-shirts people were wearing on the streets. Stores in the city centre were selling T-shirts by the hundreds every day, with just two words emblazoned on the front.

HEFFO'S ARMY.

And there were flags and banners. One on Westmoreland Street was already bursting to immortalize Anton O'Toole.

ANTON O'TOOLE,

THE BLUE PANTHER.

It was all unbelievable and fantastic. It was brilliant, and it had happened so fast. But the 1974 All-Ireland final had still not been played.

Mullins coming into training on a pair of crutches, with his left leg wrapped in plaster and swinging heavily in the air, had done the trick. That night Heff looked at the fellas good and close. To a man, they were heads down. Nobody laughed, not once, all evening long.

It was a cold, sober training session.

There were things Heff had to do, and things he didn't have to do any more, thankfully. He didn't have to keep an eye on Jimmy Keaveney.

Neither did he have to ask other people to keep an eye on Keaveney, in Vincents' clubhouse to begin with, and later in some quiet pubs closer to the city centre. Jimmy liked to retire for a pint or two, and one or two more, some evenings. When he brought him back into his squad at the beginning of the summer, Heff needed two things from Jimmy Keaveney.

He needed him to nail every crucial free-kick.

And he needed him to stop sitting on a bar stool and behaving like just another Dublin football fan.

Through August and into September, there were no reports

of Jimmy Keaveney having a quiet pint anywhere. Only Heff knew Jimmy's weight. He had been 14 stones and 11 pounds when he appeared back in Parnell Park. That was in June. By September, Jimmy was down to 13 stones and 8 pounds. Also, for all his old guff, and daily bravado, Jimmy Keaveney knew that, as a footballer, he was sitting high on a stool in a whole different and important place, in the last chance saloon.

Heff knew that too. Jimmy Keaveney had retired as a Dublin footballer at 27 years of age. That was two and a half years earlier. He'd broken an ankle, and broken a wrist and a collar-bone playing for Vincents and Dublin down through the years.

Heff and Jimmy both knew that they might never get into an All-Ireland final again. They might never get near one.

The game began slowly.

And fearfully.

The 1974 All-Ireland final was a game of football that was played by two teams that were absolutely terrified of losing. The referee, Tyrone's Patsy Devlin could not do very much to let the game flow. From the very start Galway played like a team that was determined not to lose a second All-Ireland final on the trot. But neither did Galway look like a team that was determined to win one.

Galway wanted to stop Dublin.

Dublin, too often for long passages, were struggling with a similar intent. Over the eighty minutes there were fifty-six stoppages and the referee could have doubled that number if he really wished.

Heff made sure his fellas were on the field early. He wanted them out there, and to have a good look around them. See all the colours, and take in the noise. Heff wanted them out there as long as possible.

Dublin were out on the field almost twenty minutes before Galway appeared out of their tunnel under the Cusack Stand. Seán Doherty was only too happy to get out of the dressing-room. He'd never been in a Dublin dressing-room like it.

The place was so quiet.

It was completely different to the semi-final, when everyone wanted to size themselves up against the All-Ireland champions. And then get stuck into Cork. Then, the place had been full of energy. It was an exciting place. But, the early afternoon of the All-Ireland final, the minute all of the Dublin players sat down and began to take off their clothes, and slowly change, Seán Doherty felt that something was wrong.

He could breathe it.

A simmering fear.

Everyone around him looked worried.

Heff looked uptight. He'd never looked more serious. When the time came to lead the lads out of the dressing-room, Heff had told his captain that he would feel like he was entering a whole different world. Some place he'd never been before in his long football life. A place that looked and sounded nothing like the Croke Park, where Seán Doherty had played dozens and dozens of times.

The Doc could not feel his legs as he took off down the tunnel. He was not sure if he was running fast or slow.

He remembered that Heff had told him it would be so.

The Doc would never feel quite himself at the start of the 1974 All-Ireland final, and at the end of the eighty minutes he was certain that he had not played all that well.

He had played deep.

And behind his man.

He didn't want to lose his man, Liam Sammon. If he went shoulder-to-shoulder with the Galway full-forward, or tried to get out in front of him and beat him to the ball, the Doc knew that there was a chance, a big chance, a small chance, that disaster could befall him. Who knew?

He feared losing Sammon.

Or letting Sammon inside him, so the Doc stayed put, stayed behind his man. He had defended his own square. Therefore, it confused him all the more when he discovered that evening and late into the night that a great many people thought of the Dublin full-back line as a line of real heroes.

The full-forward line of McDonagh–Sammon–Tobin had been

a greater source of worry for Heff and his army of supporters than any other combination on the Galway team. Sammon was a genius, and John Tobin was a tricky devil who some imagined might simply be too fast, too slippery, for Gay O'Driscoll.

All through the week, in the team meetings after training, in the Nissen hut in Parnell Park, O'Driscoll had promised his teammates that Tobin would be handled. And that's what he did. He kept a tight handle on Tobin for the eighty minutes, and by the end Tobin had scored just a single point from a free. Sammon got no score on Doherty. And in the other corner, Robbie Kelleher also gave his man nothing.

Galway got a one-point return from their prized full-forward line.

Kelleher's man, Colin McDonagh, had taken an inch-perfect pass from Jimmy Duggan early on and, with the Dublin goals wide open in front of him, had failed to give Galway the perfect start, blazing wide. Galway would fail to score another goal in the 12th minute of the second half when Liam Sammon had his penalty kick expertly saved by Paddy Cullen. A goal would have put Galway four points in front. And four minutes after that Pat Sands would race through only to drive a shot across the face of the goal and wide.

Dublin too were edgy when it most mattered.

They too missed goal chances, most unbelievably when John McCarthy got possession six yards out and had only the Galway captain, Gay Mitchell, to beat. McCarthy dropped the ball, and Galway scrambled it far away.

The teams were level after 13 minutes, 0–1 apiece, but Galway had the big wind at their backs, and in the middle of the field Billy Joyce was dominant. Brian Mullins had made a miraculous recovery, and Heff boldly insisted on starting him, but it was a day in which Mullins looked more uncertain about himself than any day before or after in his mighty career.

Galway were doing enough, just, to take advantage of that wind. In the 31st minute Sammon got away from Doherty on the end-line underneath Hill 16 and lobbed the ball into the square. Michael

Rooney got a hand to it. It was in the net, and Galway led 1–1 to 0–3.

It was 1–4 to 0–5 at half-time.

Dublin now had the wind.

They also had to pick up their game. Nobody had played well in the first half, and the game was passing Brian Mullins by faster than anybody else. Heff had run on to the field late in that first half and grabbed Mullins' head with both hands.

He shook Mullins' head.

And shouted at the young man who, for the first time all summer, looked lost on the field.

'Keep going . . . KEEP GOING!' Heff had roared twice.

Mullins said nothing.

'Keep going,' Heff shouted once more. 'You'll get into this!'

Mullins and Stephen Rooney finally got into the game in the opening ten minutes of the second half, and started winning the ball. And in the 55th minute, Dublin were back level. Keaveney stood over the ball near the sideline underneath the Hogan Stand, he looked up, kept his head down, and struck the ball delightfully and straight from the free-kick.

Dublin were level.

Then Dublin began to power into the game. There was half an hour left, but Heff knew that Dublin had all the power in the world still stored up. There was nine months of hard work still to be fully unleashed.

Mullins and Rooney got to grips with the game for that final half an hour. Paddy Reilly and David Hickey worked harder than anybody else on the field looking for the ball and chasing down opponents. From the corner pockets, O'Toole and McCarthy came far and deep, and worked wonders.

Dublin played some football, at last.

In total Jimmy Keaveny scored eight points.

Five of them frees.

And Dublin won by five points.

Dublin 0–14, Galway 1–6.

*

A BRILLIANT MIND

Seán Doherty strode up the steps of the Hogan Stand, towards the awaiting Sam Maguire Cup. The rest of the Dublin players tried to follow him as fast as they could through the hustle and craziness.

Heff, on the other hand, decided to disappear.

In the next few minutes the thousands of supporters would shout, 'WE WANT HEFFO . . . WE WANT HEFFO,' but Heff could not hear them.

When the final whistle sounded, Heff had stood in front of the Dublin dug-out beneath the Cusack Stand for several seconds. He said nothing. He looked at Donal Colfer and Lorcan Redmond.

His pair of lieutenants said not a word either.

All three were in a state of shock.

It had happened.

They told each other in the weeks leading up to the All-Ireland final that it could happen, that it would happen. But all three refused to believe, one hundred per cent, that it would be done.

That a team that had been falling over itself only a few months earlier were now All-Ireland champions.

That the team that could not win a game for almost a decade, and could lose a game as easily as win a game in the first four and a half months of 1974, had actually managed it.

Dublin 3–9, Wexford 0–6.

Dublin 2–11, Louth 1–9.

Dublin 1–11, Offaly 0–13.

Dublin 1–13, Kildare 0–10.

Dublin 1–14, Meath 1–9.

Dublin 2–11, Cork 1–8.

Dublin 0–14, Galway 1–6.

Paddy Cullen could not stop crying.

Days later, he would be told that he had cried for forty-five minutes in the Dublin dressing-room.

Cullen did not argue.

Paddy Cullen had pointed to the sky so often through the summer of 1974. Every second time he saw a jet high in the sky over Parnell Park he would turn to the man next to him and tell that man

149

that Dublin would soon be on a jet like that. The whole friggin'
Dublin team.

'That'll be us!' promised Paddy Cullen, pointing skywards.

He'd been an Allstar replacement in '73, and Cullen had looked
at the Cork boys getting to travel to America together and he
thought it was the greatest thing in the world any team could ever
get to experience. To be All-Ireland champions. To be looking down
at the world from 30,000 feet.

Cullen liked to keep promising his teammates that they would
be up there, at that great height. He knew they always laughed at
him, and he liked them to laugh. But they never told him he was
mad.

Like so many of the others, Cullen had eight years of losing
under his belt.

But, unlike the others, Paddy Cullen was a dreamer.

He'd been an electrician as a younger man.

One of ten children, his mother wanted him to have a trade.
Cullen would swap different places of work through his Dublin
football career, fixing cranes over the Liffey for one small period,
and when it was all well and truly over he would celebrate his football career with sports stars from all over Ireland in his own famous
pub in Ballsbridge, in the heart of Dublin.

In 1974, he won the first of three All-Ireland medals, thanks
principally to Heff. Two of those medals would be stolen in a theft
at his home. The third medal, that had been left in an old jug, would
remain his for ever.

When Seán Doherty finally got back into the dressing-room with
Sam Maguire, Paddy Cullen was still in the floods. The place was a
mass of people, old faces, and some new. Heff asked everyone to
leave for a few minutes.

Heff wanted to be alone with his team.

He wanted to thank them.

Congratulate them.

And warn them that their lives had changed for ever, and that
from that very day they were all living their lives at 30,000 feet.

21

'Beating Kerry in an All-Ireland final ... it's as good as two All-Irelands!'

KH

Sunday, 27 July 1975

Jimmy Keaveney couldn't kick straight.

It was amazing.

As weird and confusing as watching the Golden Bear himself, Jack Nicklaus, fail to land a ball in the heart of the green, or anywhere on an immaculately curved green for that matter, for well over an hour.

Jimmy Keaveney didn't miss free-kicks.

In the 1975 Leinster final, however, Jimmy missed them. Five of them. And he also was wide with four or five shots from general play. People never counted Jimmy Keaveney's wides. They usually only counted his scores.

It was simpler, shorter maths-work that way.

But Brian Mullins had the most outstanding game in his short Dublin career, and he stormed down the centre twice in the first half, in the 18th and 33rd minutes, and cracked home two goals. Two points from Pat Gogarty, and one each from David Hickey, Bobby Doyle, Tony Hanahoe and, yes, one from Jimmy Keaveney, left Dublin out of sight of Kildare by half-time.

It was 2–6 to 0–2, and the game finished 3–13 to 0–8. Heff told reporters afterwards that he had nothing much to say. But he did hint that he was fairly delighted with what he saw in the middle of the field.

Bernard Brogan started the game alongside Brian Mullins and, together, Brogan and Mullins had been nothing short of colossal. Brogan won everything in the air. He also barrelled forward on several occasions with a great, big, ambling stride that left him virtually uncatchable. However, it was Mullins who ended up with even more ball in his hands than his midfield partner.

Mullins was an extra man in defence, and any time the ball popped up in attack that unruly blond head of his was nearly always to be seen close by. Mullins, by some distance, was the Man of the Match.

Dublin were in outstanding shape.

At the beginning of May, they had toured America as All-Ireland champions and Paddy Cullen had lived his dream.

Not that he or too many of his teammates could remember very much about the earliest days of the dream trip. Dublin had flown to New York initially. They had a three-hour stopover in JFK airport, before taking off again for San Francisco. There, the team was welcomed by local GAA families, who were putting the All-Ireland champions up in their homes.

There were no four- or five-star hotels.

Heff was just as glad. Any class of hotel would have had a bar, and after watching his finely primed group of athletes guzzling alcohol for almost twenty-four hours non-stop, in the air and on the ground, Heff just wanted everybody in their beds.

A teetotaller himself, Heff guessed the drinking had probably come to a halt. For a few days at least.

They could hardly go again the next day?

Heff was wrong.

The next day the Dublin team was invited to the Irish Cultural Centre in the city. A group of local businessmen were launching a new brand of whiskey. It was, unfortunately, called Dubliner Whiskey.

The Dublin football team found that it loved Dubliner Whiskey. And the new whiskey sent the All-Ireland champions off into the San Francisco night with a wholly renewed pep in their stride. Heff

was in his bed early. The next morning he had planned a light training session in the nearby Balboa Park on the southside of the city.

The session started at half-past ten.

It ended less than half an hour later. There was no point looking
at such a sad lot any longer.

Heff was furious.

He called a team meeting, but quickly found out that there was
no talking sense to them. Half of them were ready to go back to their
beds. The other half had designs on a quick shower and a couple of
early afternoon pints to set themselves up nicely for whatever the
evening might hold.

With Heff fighting a losing battle for two weeks, and with all his
players living Paddy Cullen's dream, Dublin hadn't any chance of
playing good football. They turned out of their beds and turned up
for the games against the Allstars selection, but everybody, Heff
included, thought it best to take absolutely no notice of the results.

At home, Dublin's performances were politely excused. 'Dublin did
not perform with their usual brilliance during the American tour,'
explained the always respectful Paddy Downey in the *Irish Times*,
'but small pitches may have been the cause of that.'

One week after returning home from America, Dublin had a
National League final against Meath top of their agenda. It was top
of Heff's list too. He wanted to do the 'double' of championship
and league and, besides, Dublin had not won a League title since
1958, when he was in the full-forward line and captaining the
team.

Meath had not won a League title since '51.

And with Mick Ryan and Joe Cassells in outstanding form in the
middle of the field, and the flying figure of Ken Rennicks walking all
over centre-backs from every other county, Meath had come out of
Division Two and totally outplayed Kerry in the quarter-finals, and
then taken Mayo apart in the semi-finals.

Meath also beat Dublin in the National League final.

Meath 0–16, Dublin 1–9.

*

Meath also looked Dublin's biggest threat in Leinster in the early summer of 1975 but, like Dublin living the dream at 30,000 feet, the Meath football team decided to celebrate their National League victory with maximum gusto at ground level.

Two weeks after beating Dublin in the League final, Meath fell at the first fence in the Leinster championship, losing to Louth in the first round.

Sobered up and back in Heff's strong hands in Parnell Park, Dublin walked through what was left in their own province. Winning a second Leinster title in '75 was twice as easy as the first.

Kevin Heffernan was on his feet at the top of the room.

He knew most of the men sitting down in front of him. A great many of them he had played against. Now they were all coaches and managers, and they had paid for a weekend in Gormanston College in County Meath to learn more.

Amongst those sitting down in one of the classrooms in the secondary school, sitting next to the young, bushy-headed Kerry footballer Mickey Ned O'Sullivan, was Mick O'Dwyer.

Heff didn't know O'Dwyer all that well. They'd crossed paths on the field but O'Dwyer was seven years younger, and his career as a Kerry footballer was only getting up to full steam when Heff was preparing himself to finish up with Dublin.

In Gormanston College, Heff paid no particular attention to Mick O'Dwyer all day long.

He'd agreed to turn up in Gormanston and help give the course on Gaelic football against his better judgement. He knew the courses were good. Des Ferguson had been one of the men who had started the ball rolling with the whole idea of new-fangled coaching courses in the 1960s, and every year a goodly number, sometimes as high as one hundred men from clubs and counties all over the country, turned up.

Heff was happy to help.

But a few months after winning the All-Ireland, Heff would have much preferred not to be standing up on his feet and telling people how to play the game. Some people might come to the conclusion that he had developed serious notions about himself.

That worried Heff.

Mick O'Dwyer's big worry was to get the hell out of the place before the examination began at the end of the course.

He didn't believe he'd learn a thing.

He'd only driven the whole way up from Kerry because people down home were pestering him. That included the county chairman, Ger McKenna. It also included Mickey Ned, who was sitting beside him. Mickey Ned was training the Kerry football team all through the spring of 1975 because there was nobody else to do it after Johnny Culloty decided, after the Munster final the previous summer, that he was finishing up.

Mickey Ned just wanted to play football. As a Kenmare man, it also looked like he would be named Kerry captain for the championship, so Mickey Ned definitely didn't need to be doubling up on jobs.

Mickey Ned wanted O'Dwyer to take over as manager and trainer. So too did Ger McKenna. And Mickey Ned knew that talking O'Dwyer into doing the job would be that much easier if he could have O'Dwyer's ear all to himself in a car for ten hours. Even if O'Dwyer drove as fast as he always did, Mickey Ned would be sure of nine hours.

He knew it would be long enough.

He also knew that O'Dwyer was curious about the two men who were giving the course in Gormanston.

Only the course.

'I'm not doing any exam!' he'd warned Mickey Ned.

'No . . . no exam, then,' agreed Mickey Ned. 'We'll see what it's all about. Then we'll get away.'

'I'm telling you, I'm not doing any exam!' O'Dwyer repeated, for a double measure of absolute certainty that he was not being quietly railroaded into taking up a pen and paper, and having Joe Lennon, of all people, give him a mark on what he knew, and did not know, about Gaelic football. The course in Gormanston was being presented and marked by Joe Lennon.

Kevin Heffernan was the main speaker. Hearing what Kevin

Heffernan might have to say for himself half-interested O'Dwyer.

The other half of Mick O'Dwyer wanted to sit back in the classroom and listen to the man who had announced some years earlier that Kerry football was twenty years out of date. That was Joe Lennon. Lennon had published his own book on Gaelic football in 1964. It was called *Coaching Gaelic Football for Champions*. Mick O'Dwyer never purchased a copy of that book.

Joe Lennon also had a commanding role on the Down team that had defeated Kerry twice in the first half of the 1960s, by eight points in an All-Ireland final, and six points in an All-Ireland semi-final. In '68 Down beat Kerry by two points in another All-Ireland final, and it was then than Joe Lennon broke the bad news to the people of Kerry.

Not in a thousand years would O'Dwyer pick up that book.

However, O'Dwyer had it in his head, though he was not admitting to it, that he'd take on the Kerry team for the rest of 1975.

He'd taken the team for half a year in '71 while he was still playing himself, and won a League with them. He'd coached the county Under-21s in '74 and liked the cut of that group of young lads, even though they didn't get out of Munster. O'Dwyer had decided that he would not give Mickey Ned even half a clue as to what he was thinking, not until they said their goodbyes back home. And that would be well after midnight.

Mick O'Dwyer had trained under Dr Eamonn O'Sullivan, and sat in the back seat of the great man's car often enough, with Mick O'Connell and Johnny Culloty, as Dr Eamonn said the rosary on the way to games. Dr Eamonn liked his prayers, but O'Dwyer also knew Dr Eamonn was way ahead of his times. O'Dwyer trained under Jackie Lyne, and then under Johnny Culloty. They knew as much, probably more, than anybody.

However, he had listened to Heff in the morning, and then in the afternoon Heff had taken everyone outside and across the road. Opposite the grounds of the college were four massive GAA fields covering one huge open expanse. There Heff put on a real live training session, with some young lads that were borrowed for the day, which opened everyone's eyes.

O'Dwyer's included.

The session was brilliant and brutally hard.

Mick O'Dwyer slipped out of the building with Mickey Ned, before any exam papers were handed out. They got into the car, and O'Dwyer immediately asked the younger man what he thought of it all. Mickey Ned explained in some detail why he thought it was all fairly interesting.

O'Dwyer agreed.

It hadn't been a total waste of a weekend.

'The first team that beats Dublin . . . they'll have to be fitter than them, to start with!' stated O'Dwyer.

22

'Who's going to be the Judas . . . in this game?'

KH

Thursday, 21 August 1975

The door to the Nissen hut was shut.

Inside it was warm, and stuffy. And Heff lighting up his second cigarette didn't help very much.

They were already in there twenty-five minutes, nearly half an hour. And that meant they might be at an end any minute. Or, it might mean that they were only halfway through.

Quickly enough, Heff could decide either way.

But only when nearly every man in the room had spoken, and only when Heff felt that everyone had received exactly the right message. Not necessarily from him as team manager. But, from somebody? Anybody?

Surprise me.

That was always the wish on Heff's straightened face when he called out a man's name and asked him what he thought.

Heff loved his hut.

It was not a place where the Dublin team manager wanted to hear any old guff or worn-down platitudes. Any of that and Heff would light up a third time, and even a fourth Sweet Afton. In the hut, he had all night long.

Once, outside the Nissen hut, Jimmy Gray had approached him all happy and chairman-like. Gray was one of Heff's few close friends, and thought he was being helpful as he suggested knocking down the hut and building a proper meeting room in its place.

The response almost bit Jimmy Gray's nose off.

'Don't . . . TOUCH IT!'

The chairman sought to explain himself.

'But—'

'No . . . !' replied Heff.

Nissen huts had been around the place since the Great War, and the even greater war that followed, and were named after a Major Peter Nissen in the British army who thought them up, and thought that housing fighting men under rounded corrugated steel was close to the height of luxury. The Nissen hut in Parnell Park was placed at the far end of the ground, far from prying eyes, and nosy parkers.

It was Heff's private place for his own fighting men, though Heff didn't normally dominate team conversations in the hut.

All the same, he conducted his team meetings with a military-like intent. Team meetings were designed to find out who was strong and, far more importantly, who might be weak. And team meetings on the Thursday night before a big game were meetings that did not take any prisoners.

Prisoners were shot.

Weaklings were shot.

Everybody else? At the end of a Thursday-night training session, after grabbing a glass of milk, and perhaps being lucky enough to get a couple of biscuits, Jacob's Goldgrain rather than Marietta if they were fast enough, everybody sitting on the wooden benches in the hut, waited.

Until their name was called out by Heff.

The hut was different to the other meeting room where Heff would also hole up for hours on end. In the other meeting room Heff had two television sets side by side at the front of the room showing the game that had been played the previous Sunday. One television covered one half of the field. The second television covered the other half of the field. The whole field was in view thanks to two video recorders that Heff requested for every game.

Every man was in view, for every minute, every last second of the game. And even though there were endless arguments as players often struggled to identify some of the small blue figures on the screens in front of them, every man could privately go home with sound knowledge of what he had done, or what he had failed to do.

In the more formal meeting room Heff wanted to know what was happening on the field, but in the hut Heff wanted to know what was happening in men's heads.

That was the difference.

The hut sorted men out from boys.

And it searched down other men.

'Who's going to be the Judas . . . in this game?' Heff would ask.

'In this game . . .

'. . . who's going to be our Judas?'

In the All-Ireland semi-final in '75, Jimmy Keaveney was no Judas. Not two games running. He quickly put his faltering kicks in the Leinster final far out of his mind. Against Derry, Jimmy Keaveney kicked six points from dead balls. One of them was from a '50', but four of the other five points were also from anywhere between 45 yards and 55 yards.

Jimmy also kicked three points from play.

However, at the other end of the field, while several Dublin defenders were not exactly taking turns to act like Judas at different stages, neither were they being very helpful. It was 1–9 to 2–2 at half-time. That meant that Dublin had conceded nine goals in three and a half games in the defence of their All-Ireland title. By the end of the semi-final, that number would be ten goals in four championship games. Three Wexford goals. Four Louth goals.

And three Derry goals.

Worse still, Dublin were letting an old man score a goal.

Though Sean O'Connell was not simply an oldie. He was an outstanding veteran of the game who had been on the field in 1958 when Kevin Heffernan had captained Dublin to his only All-Ireland title. He was right half-forward that afternoon. In the All-Ireland semi-final in '75 he was a burly, stronger full-forward who was way past worrying about the hits or the different levels of intimidation that the Dublin full-back line might have up its sleeve.

Sean O'Connell was 38 years of age.

He scored the first of the Derry goals, cleverly smashing the ball past Paddy Cullen on the volley from ten yards out after receiving a punched pass from his midfielder, Tom McGuinness. That gave Derry a one-point lead.

John O'Leary got their second when he got enough force behind his angled shot, and Cullen could not hold it. Derry led 2–2 to 0–6.

Dublin needed Jimmy Keaveney every time they got the ball. He kept the team alive and kicking. First he kicked another point from a free, and then he flicked a high ball into the path of the speeding Anton O'Toole and the corner-forward scored the first of his two goals for the day. O'Toole's goals came in the 33rd and 63rd minutes, and Tony Hanahoe worked himself into position for a third Dublin goal in between those scores.

Dublin made hard work of it.

It was 3–13 to 3–8 when referee John Moloney from Tipperary called an end to a game that had too much raw action on the field for Heff's liking. But, they were back in the All-Ireland final.

And there, they would have Kerry. A young Kerry team that nobody knew much about, and a team that did not even have a manager at the beginning of the summer.

Mick O'Dwyer was less than four months into the job.

He would quickly become known all over the country as 'Micko', but in Kerry all they ever called him in the past, and in the future, was 'Dwyer'.

In the previous eighteen months, Mick O'Dwyer and Kevin Heffernan had crossed paths a handful of times without taking too much notice of one another.

Dwyer was sitting at a desk in Gormanston College earlier in the spring of '75 as Heff calmly explained to his classroom of coaches and managers how Gaelic football should be played. And, in the early summer of '74, Dwyer was sitting in Croke Park, a Kerry substitute, and a Kerry player for the very last time, the day Heff sent Dublin into a championship match for the very first time as manager.

Kerry were playing Roscommon in the replayed final of the National League that Sunday. Dublin played Wexford in the first game of the day.

Dwyer hadn't bothered to sit down in the Cusack Stand and watch any of the Dublin game. He'd gone straight to the dressing-room, though there was no good reason why he should be in a hurry. That afternoon, he wasn't needed on the field at any stage.

At 39 years of age he was finished with Kerry as a footballer. At 40 years of age he started with Kerry as their manager.

Like Heff, Mick O'Dwyer was not born and reared in a football house. Like Heff's father, Dwyer's father loved the outdoors, but fishing and shooting were his passions. He made his money by running a taxi service. The money for the cars had come from Canada and America where John O'Dwyer had spent some years before marrying and settling back in Kerry.

Micko was a footballer, but he also liked his cars. And his first job earned him £2 a week as an apprentice mechanic in Austin Lucey's garage, just down the road from the family home, in Waterville. At 20 years of age, in 1956, he would buy the business for £1,350. Soon, he'd have his own Opel dealership. Micko would also start up a self-drive business that was good for turning money. He built a house on to his garage for £2,500. Then he bought another house in Waterville from a friend for £2,000.

Micko and his wife, Mary Carmel, built on to their home and made it into their own hotel, Villa Maria, that had its own bar licence. They joined with some neighbours and also bought the Sea Lodge Hotel. They would rename it the Strand Hotel. Some years later Micko and Mary Carmel bought out their business partners.

Mick O'Dwyer owned a garage, two hotels, and an undertaking business, and, incredibly, he also found the time to become one of the most famous Kerry footballers of his generation.

In September 1953 Dwyer had stood in Croke Park for the first time. He was 17 years old. He stood on Hill 16, and took the deepest breath he had ever taken in his life. Himself and his best friend, Eric Murphy, had taken the 'Ghost Train' up to Dublin. It was a ten-mile cycle to Cahirciveen to get the train that took its name from its long, dark journey through the thick of the night.

It was seven o'clock in the morning when they arrived in Kingsbridge, after a night of sandwiches and tea, and listening to and watching the theatrics of several hundred Kerry football supporters who had plenty of the dark stuff and the hard stuff in flasks and bottles.

Dwyer was not tempted.

Like Heff, Dwyer found himself sufficiently twisted and inebriated by Gaelic football and, like Heff, he would remain a tee-totaller all of his life.

Dwyer and Eric took off down the quays, stopping regularly to stare over the wall into the Liffey. Out of Kerry for the first time, the pair of them had so many things to see that the morning raced by. The Liffey and, finally, O'Connell Street, where they found a café on a side street that served them up a good fry-up.

It was the start of an amazingly good day. By the end of it, Kerry would be 1953 All-Ireland champions.

Dwyer and Eric would be among an official attendance of 86,155 on the day, though it was estimated the next day that another 8,000, at least, had also gotten into the ground after the gates at the Hill 16 end had been broken down.

Six years later, Dwyer would be out on the field in his first All-Ireland final. By then, Dwyer was on his way to becoming a right good Kerry footballer.

One of the greats.

But not immediately.

The first time he pulled a Kerry jersey over his head, in 1957, he had no idea that he was also taking his place in history as part of the Kerry team that would lose to Waterford in the first round of the Munster championship. It was, and remained, one of the greatest upsets in Gaelic football history. Waterford had not beaten Kerry in the championship in over half a century. Dwyer was a half-back.

That's where he still was in 1958 when Kerry took Munster and were raging-hot favourites to defeat Derry in the All-Ireland semi-final. Victory that day would also have brought Kerry into the final against Dublin.

In '58 it might have been Dublin v Kerry.

In '58 it also might have been Heff v Dwyer, for the first time. But Derry, led by Jim McKeever, ruined the prospect of that meeting with a one-point win, which came courtesy of a late goal from a young Sean O'Connell.

Heff v Dwyer was delayed a year. They finally came together on the field in the All-Ireland semi-final in 1959, when All-Ireland champions Dublin were beaten 1–10 to 2–5. And one month later Dwyer won his first All-Ireland medal when Kerry made light work of Galway in the final. Dwyer won his first All-Ireland medal in the half-back line. He would win a second in '62.

Still in the backs.

His second pair of All-Ireland medals would be won in the forwards.

In 1969 Dwyer was Texaco Footballer of the Year. He was the country's top scorer, with a tally of eight goals and 96 points in twenty-two games. Kerry took Offaly's scalp in an unmemorable All-Ireland final. Mick O'Dwyer was 33 years old.

In 1970 he was still the country's top scorer.

Kerry were again All-Ireland champs.

In '74 Mick O'Dwyer retired.

For the second time.

For good. And he did so just in time to become manager of Kerry and start the job of building the greatest Kerry team of all time.

Heff knew that Kerry were waiting for him in the 1975 All-Ireland final. Dwyer's team had beaten Sligo in the semi-finals, two weeks before Dublin had beaten Derry.

Heff had Kerry to think about again.

His oldest and most personal of enemies.

Though Kevin Heffernan really had no idea what exactly was lurking around the corner in green and gold.

23

'I always felt that whenever I was in Kerry, the only All-Ireland that was ever played was in 1955, and I wanted to change that.'

KH

Saturday, 27 September 1975

Heuston station.

Kerry had landed in Dublin.

The Kerry senior and minor teams took the same train. The young lads were playing Tyrone the next day.

Páidí Ó Sé got his kit bag and his clothes bag down from the rack above his head. He wanted off the train fast. Wanted to stretch his legs. Take off. Páidí was rarin' to go, and there were still twenty-four hours to wait for the All-Ireland final. But, as he hopped out the door, someone grabbed him by the arm.

Tugged him, urgently.

Bringing him to a standstill.

'Hey . . . do you know which carriage the senior team are in?'

A photographer, sweating heavily underneath a ruffled anorak, was asking Páidí if he knew where the senior footballers were.

'The Kerry senior team?' Páidí was asked again.

Páidí had no interest in stopping to talk.

'Back there . . . somewhere!' he replied.

'There'll be time for photographs tomorrow,' Páidí thought to himself, as he marched away '. . . with Sam Maguire.'

'Then they'll feckin' know . . .

'They'll know the Kerry senior team when they see them!'

Páidí Ó Sé would sleep Saturday night in the Grand Hotel in

165

Malahide. Before hitting the pillow, and just after a good steak for dinner, Dwyer would take them all across the road from the hotel, and down on to the beach.

The whole lot of them.

Dwyer wanted to walk off the big feed.

Help the lads clear their heads.

Get them to relax, after being cooped up in the hotel for a few hours. More than anybody, Páidí wasn't happy when cooped.

Páidí Ó Sé was one of ten Under-21s that Dwyer had brought into the Kerry dressing-room right away upon his appointment. Páidí was born in 1955, four months before Kerry had met Dublin in the All-Ireland final that year. The last time Kerry had met Dublin with the whole country watching.

He'd been on the Kerry team in '74 when Cork came to Killarney as All-Ireland champs, and went home, still champions of Munster and the whole damned country. Páirc Uí Chaoimh was being built in '74 and was still slowly taking the place of the old Athletic Grounds in the summer of '75.

Cork were back in the second dressing-room in Fitzgerald Stadium in the high summer of '75, ready to give Kerry another slap. Páidí was into year two as a Kerry footballer, but he was still learning.

Learning from the very best.

Tralee's Joe Keohane had a grip of Páidí's shoulder in the minutes before the '75 Munster final. Keohane had five All-Ireland medals, ten Munster medals, and for some reason he had taken to calling Páidí Ó Sé by the name 'Patrick'.

'Patrick . . . you're a defender!' started Keohane.

'And the bigger the game Patrick, the closer you must be to your man,' continued Keohane, still pressing his giant of a right hand down on Páidí's shoulder.

Keohane wasn't finished.

'Patrick, if I ask you at any stage of the game, "Where's Your Man?", you tell me . . . "HERE!"'

Joe Keohane pressed down on the shoulder one last time.

' "HERE" . . . Patrick.'

Páidí was supposed to be marking Ned Kirby that afternoon in Killarney. But Cork switched Dinny Allen on to him pronto on the first whistle. Páidí was up for it, up for anyone.

Allen scored a point.

'They'll be taking you off now, boy,' Allen then told him.

'If I'm going, you're fucking coming with me!' roared Páidí. He gave his man a thump. Allen elbowed him back.

The noise in the stadium switched directions, and zeroed in on the pair of them. Páidí Ó Sé settled after that. Pat Spillane calmed the entire Kerry team when he bagged a dodgy enough goal.

The rest?

There was no rest of the game.

Kerry 1–14, Cork 0–7.

Cork had lost their All-Ireland title in '74. They lost their Munster title in '75, and they would win only one Munster title over the next dozen years. In the All-Ireland semi-final, Kerry met Sligo, who had just won their first Connacht title in forty-seven years.

Kerry 3–13, Sligo 0–5.

Kerry were in the All-Ireland final.

The average age of the team was just over 22.

Dwyer told them that Dublin were not all that brilliant. The Dublin media were saying Dublin were brilliant, Dwyer told them all. Dwyer said '74 was a bad football year. It didn't take a brilliant team at all to win the All-Ireland last year, proclaimed a defiant Dwyer.

As for Heffo's Army?

Dwyer left all of the young men in his company in absolutely no doubt what he thought of that malarkey.

Heff was in a funny mood, and it wasn't a good thing. Nobody much liked the mood of the man. He wasn't himself.

Years later, decades later, some of the footballers who watched Heff and listened to Heff in the second-last week, and then the last week, before the 1975 All-Ireland final would admit to believing that the amazing man was actually, sort of, rattled. Something had gotten into his head.

It definitely was not a good thing.

He was edgy.

Angry.

Heff would never admit that it was Kerry.

As he fussed and second-guessed himself, Heff refused to let anybody think for one minute that an All-Ireland final against Kerry had him slightly unnerved. But Kevin Heffernan was unnerved.

Kerry had taken almost everything from him as a footballer. Minor and senior, and now Kerry were threatening to take away Dublin's All-Ireland title. Only one county had ever left him in a maddening tizzy in his 46 years on this earth. More than that, it was more than that!

He had buckled as a man against Kerry.

Heff felt he had failed himself and everyone who knew him in 1955, in that All-Ireland final that he would never let himself forget. His failure was deep, and personal. He only blamed himself.

In days before the 1975 All-Ireland final, Heff was not Heff.

Dublin had played Kerry three times in the previous nine months. Twice in challenge games, and once in the league. The reigning All-Ireland champions had lost both challenge games. They had drawn the league game.

Three times they had 'failed' against a Kerry team that, on each occasion, looked raggedy, looked young and giddy.

Heff believed he had the fittest team in the country.

Dwyer believed that Dublin were now the second-fittest team in the country. There were weeks when he absolutely creased his lads in training. And they'd come back the next night for more.

It was crazy stuff.

Mick O'Dwyer knew it was mad, but after losing to Meath in the quarter-finals of the League, he had made up his mind to make every last man in his dressing-room completely believe that there was no man who could run longer or further in any other county in Ireland.

Crazy.

Before the Munster final, for twenty-seven evenings in a row, he had taken them out on to the field. Twenty-seven. It hadn't been planned quite like that. That was not a number he had written down on any sheet of paper.

It happened.

Crazy.

Crazy, crazy business.

Dwyer had five physical education teachers in his dressing-room, including Mickey Ned O'Sullivan, who'd all studied the best and most scientific training methods in either Thomond College in Limerick or Strawberry Hill College in London. Dwyer didn't give a damn what they taught lads in Limerick or London, or what they had taught Mickey Whelan over in wherever the hell he was in America.

Dwyer would allow them their warm-ups.

But warm-downs?

That would only use up precious time on the field as far as Dwyer was concerned. He was always happier to have laps as warm-ups. And one good, hard, full pedal-to-the-metal lap as a final warm-down.

Laps were gifts from the gods.

Sacred.

Laps to get everyone in the mood started an evening's work. And then some real laps, with the final length of the field a full-out sprint. After that some more laps. Laps that were jogging and sprinting, a handful of them some evenings.

Then Dwyer got down to the serious work.

Wire-to-wire.

Dwyer loved his wire-to-wires. The width of the field. Three men in each group. Every man holding the wire on one side of the field. Every man to touch the wire at the opposite side. Full sprint.

Ten of them most evenings.

There'd be football too. But no mind-numbing talking about it. Dwyer believed he had picked the very best young footballers in Kerry, and letting them loose was the most important thing. Confusing them was not necessarily a good thing. Making them think too much about what they were doing could be a fierce, bad thing.

And one last lap.

A mighty lap to honour the gods and the Kerry dead, and all of the outstanding footballers who had been on the field before them.

One lap.

One big sprint of a lap.

And straight into the dressing-room.

Straight into the showers.

Straight to the table for steaks and pints of milk.

Twenty-seven evenings.

One after another.

The second-last week before the All-Ireland final, Heff called the lads into training every evening. He wanted to make sure.

He worked them hard.

Six evenings in a row.

Even the evening when the reporters from the national newspapers were invited into Parnell Park to have a look over the Dublin team, and talk to Heff and his players afterwards, there was no let-up.

That evening came at the end of a particularly wet day. It had been coming down all afternoon, and out on the field everyone was drenched inside five minutes. The reporters didn't venture out of the pavilion. They all huddled inside the door.

It was a deluge by then.

But Heff kept them out on the field.

He made sure it was a long night. There were things he wanted to hammer home, especially amongst the forwards. Also, the longer the players were on the field the less time they'd have to talk to the newspapermen afterwards.

By the end of the week most of the Dublin players agreed that they had finished up the longest week of the whole summer. Some of them had no idea why Heff wanted it so.

It had been gruelling.

Too many of them felt whacked. They all looked forward to the last week before the All-Ireland final so that they could get some kind of rest.

They presumed Heff would now calm down.

Heff was far from calm.

Lads had opened their big mouths.

They had ignored everything he had ever told them, he thought. It wasn't that Heff disliked newspaper reporters.

Most of them were decent.

There were some who could always be trusted. But newspaper reporters were dangerous. They could cause problems, and even when they were not looking to cause problems, they could still cause problems.

'We respect Kerry.'

That was the line Heff used to every reporter who questioned him about the All-Ireland final.

'We respect Kerry,' he told them individually, and also told them collectively. 'We respect them . . . but no more so than we would respect any other opponent.'

That was it.

Heff repeated that long sentence two dozen times the night all of the reporters were getting in the way in Parnell Park. But, other people had opened their mouths far too wide.

Worse!

The reporters had turned up in Parnell Park ten days before the All-Ireland final, but their reports did not appear in the morning newspapers until the Wednesday and Thursday and Friday before the game itself. Dangerous.

Bloody dangerous.

Heff had been asked about 1955.

And he'd said too much himself. When he read his own

comments in the morning newspapers, three days before the game, he felt like kicking himself.

'That match took place twenty years ago, and we are not concerned with history,' Heff had replied. 'Most of this team was still in rompers when we played Kerry in 1955. This is the 1975 All-Ireland final, and they're going out to win it.'

He wished he hadn't said that.

He thought Seán Doherty would have known better as well.

'We are very keen to win this one,' said the Doc, 'the second leg of the treble, and I believe we're capable of doing it, but perhaps only by a point or two.'

'Good reading,' thought Heff, '. . . if you're a Kerryman.'

Robbie Kelleher also had a juicy morsel for Mick O'Dwyer and his young team. Kelleher reminded everyone that this was the first time in an All-Ireland final for most of the Kerry lads. Then Robbie Kelleher announced that Dublin were the fitter team.

'I know that Kerry have been training very hard,' he emphasized, 'but I think that we are the fittest team in the country and will prove it in the final.'

'Brilliant,' thought Heff, his heart sinking.

And he crunched the sides of the newspaper more tightly.

They'd all opened their mouths.

Even Donal Colfer, his smart, alert lieutenant.

'No matter when or where the crisis comes,' declared Colfer, boldly, '. . . we have more match winners than Kerry.'

'*Jesus Christ.*'

24

'I never took Kerry for granted in my life . . . nobody's that crazy.'

KH

Sunday, 28 September 1975

The day was sodden.

There was nothing more that could be done, and Kevin Heffernan had done enough, perhaps too much. He'd made some mistakes. He'd trained the lads too hard. In the hut, he had been on the very edge of merciless for too long.

But it was Sunday morning.

All-Ireland final morning.

Heff had to live with his decisions.

It was good football weather for a poor football team, but for everyone else it was potentially disastrous. A day when a game of football could be far too fickle. Dublin would have to live with it, and cope.

Same as Heff would have to live with his week of decisions, and his team selection. It was a tough team to select. He'd always warned everyone who knew him that he'd drop his own mother if he thought it was the right thing to do. The Sunday before, Heff had done just that.

He'd dropped his own mother.

Her name was Doyler.

It might have been a grave error of judgement. And that became apparent to him almost immediately, but as players came to him to question him, and question his thinking, Heff had been defensive. He'd told them it was his job to pick the team.

173

He had decided not to pick Bobby Doyle.

It was their job to play in the team.

He didn't give them an inch. Pat Gogarty was in the corner instead, and Heff didn't explain why. But Heff realized that his selection had created a circus.

A 'big top'.

And having a 'big top' in Parnell Park coming into the week of an All-Ireland football final was the last thing that Heff would have wished for. He wanted clear heads, full concentration on the job ahead. No unnecessary discussion, or distraction, or fellas worried about who was playing where on the team.

Bobby Doyle was the one true Dub.

Unlike everyone else, Doyle's parents were born and reared, all of their lives, in the city. Bobby Doyle had unmixed Coolock blood. Pure blood. Everyone else came from country stock. Heff too.

Bobby looked every inch the team's blue mascot, with his locks long, and his socks down. His jersey lapped over his shorts. Bobby Doyle began every game looking like a man who had already long completed his day's work. But Bobby would work all right.

All day long. In games he would usually wear the No.13, but Bobby would visit every nook and cranny on the field, mischievously turning up with the ball anywhere and at any time. In Parnell Park, when the team trained hard, and ran and ran, it was always Bernard Brogan at the very front, John McCarthy immediately behind him, and then Bobby.

The difference was that Brogan and McCarthy were born to run, whereas Bobby had shorter legs and bigger thighs, and he had to make it a firm decision in every training session that he was not going to lull in the middle of the long, strung-out group of footballers completing lap after lap.

Bobby Doyle was dropped once before in his career. He was 15 years old, and Vincents were in a championship final. Nobody saw him again in the club for four years. He turned to soccer, and didn't show up in Vincents again until he was 20. Three years later, in '73, he was Dublin captain.

By '75 Bobby Doyle was one of the true blues, and trusted. He was a Vincents man, one of Heff's own men in the club. In addition he was with the Electricity Supply Board, which was also Heff's place of employment. By 1975, Heff was personnel manager in the ESB. He was there to help and guide employees like Bobby.

However, Heff was not about to be weakened in his decision making, and Bobby might be a true blue, and he might be a Vincents man and an ESB man, but in Kevin Heffernan's head he was out.

Pat Gogarty was the kind of man who always thought he was good enough. He always thought he was in the running. He was a better man at getting the one or two points that could make the difference in very tight games. Bobby Doyle might gather up all the possession in the world out the field, but Gogarty had more of a forward's greedy instinct.

Macker was more surprised than Gogarty.

Macker was John McCarthy.

He'd been out of the picture the whole summer. In the opening round of the championship he had his jaw slightly fractured in Wexford Park. Three weeks later Heff informed him he was fine. Dublin were playing Louth in round two. He was a substitute, and in the dressing-room he was looking the other way when Heff walked up to him and gave him a slap on the jaw. It was more than a slap.

McCarthy jumped.

'You're fine,' announced Heff.

Midway through the first half, Heff threw McCarthy into the action. He was still jumpy and, as he ran on to the field, McCarthy decided upon a policy for the next hour of accepting absolutely no stick from this man. He did not last an hour.

His man had him by the jersey, and McCarthy turned . . . and . . .

BANG!

He got a three-month suspension.

He was still suspended the day of the All-Ireland semi-final. But in training between the semi-final and final, Heff kept putting John

McCarthy into his 'A' team. Everyone knew what was going on. McCarthy was the only one who was mostly unsure. Everyone was happy for John McCarthy, and nearly everyone was sad for Bobby Doyle.

Bobby was home less than an hour on the Sunday evening before the All-Ireland final, when other Dublin players began arriving at his front door to offer their condolences.

Nearly all the Vincents lads came.

One of their own had been taken out and shot, by Heff.

Shot by one of their own in the club!

The Vincents lads had trouble thinking straight as the days disappeared before the All-Ireland final. The general mood on the whole field was dour, if not ever so slightly troubled.

Heff knew he had been responsible for the circus. But he was damned if he was going to do anything about it. He had to do his job, and that meant getting the right team on the field for Kerry. Nothing could get in the way of that.

It wasn't a week for being soft.

Neither was it a week when he should be explaining himself, and his exact thinking about Gogarty and Bobby, to every single man who crossed his path during training in Parnell Park.

Lads' feelings could wait until the middle of the winter and, by then, they'd probably understand that some things are roughly one hundred times bigger than one man's feelings.

Like the size of an All-Ireland final.

Mickey Ned O'Sullivan had needed a quick word with Dwyer in the team hotel on the evening that Kerry tore Sligo apart in their semi-final.

He picked his moment.

'I'm going to be away for a month,' stated Mickey Ned.

Dwyer said nothing.

The All-Ireland final was six weeks off, far away in the distance. Dwyer was delirious with excitement. Nothing could have upset him.

He had no idea what Mickey Ned was doing for the month. In

fact, he was not even sure that Mickey Ned had said that he was away for a month.

'Away . . .?' asked Dwyer.

'I'm going around Europe . . . for a month,' Mickey Ned confirmed.

'He's telling me he's going on his holidays?' thought Dwyer.

He had no idea what to say.

Mickey Ned kept doing the talking.

And Mickey Ned O'Sullivan was gone the next morning with one of his best friends, Donncha Lucey. They travelled everywhere. And everywhere they went, Mickey Ned found himself somewhere to run and kick a ball, and run after that ball.

The All-Ireland final was 17 minutes old.

Mickey Ned O'Sullivan lay on the wet and muddied ground like a man who was stone dead. Seán Doherty looked down at him, and knew that the Kerry captain was done and dusted with, for the rest of the game.

Rest of the day, probably.

The Doc had spoken to as many defenders as he could grab four minutes earlier, when the referee, John Moloney, had stopped play for another injury up the field. The Doc had run out to his half-back line. Alan Larkin in the No.6 jersey was his number-one destination. But he wanted to talk to everyone in a blue jersey.

He wanted to know what they were up to.

Mickey Ned O'Sullivan had been tearing down the middle of the Dublin defence since the very start of the game, and the Doc wanted no more of it. He wanted answers from Larkin, and the men either side of him, Paddy Reilly and Georgie Wilson.

But Mickey Ned had the ball again.

He ducked inside one challenge from Reilly, and scampered to his right. Mickey Ned was not going in a straight line. He was zig-zagging, and when he arrived in front of Alan Larkin he dummied left, but darted right.

Larkin hit him high.

Mickey Ned slowed only momentarily, and then got in a solo, and he was off again. In Kerry, nobody soloed the ball longer or further than Mickey Ned O'Sullivan, and it drove some men mad. He wouldn't pass. He didn't see anybody. How could he with his head down all the time?

Mickey Ned was bearing down on the Dublin goal. He had no intention of passing. The Doc decided that he had to leave his own full-back line.

He had to abandon his own man inside.

He'd have to meet Mickey Ned himself.

The Doc went.

Alan Larkin was about to catch up on Mickey Ned. He did, finally, as the Doc arrived in front of Mickey Ned. Larkin got his hands on his man, but only managed to push him forward.

Mickey Ned met the Doc like a blind man meets a tonne of bricks.

'Stand back . . .

'Leave him breathe!

'Back . . . BACK!'

Mickey Ned could hear the voices above him.

He could not see anything. Nothing. He couldn't breathe. He felt as though his body was crumpling up into a ball without any air whatsoever inside.

Mickey Ned thought he was dying.

It was the beginning of the end of Mickey Ned O'Sullivan's football career all right. He'd live. He'd fully wake up at nine o'clock that night in the Richmond Hospital in Dublin city centre, and realize he was alive and that the All-Ireland final was long over. But as a footballer, he'd struggle.

He'd start the 1976 All-Ireland final against Dublin, but thereafter Mickey Ned O'Sullivan was a Kerry substitute in the summertime and early autumn.

Brian Mullins had opened the scoring when he was planted with a shoulder but bounced back up off the ground, and surged forward to lash the ball over the bar from nearly 40 yards out.

But Kerry's first score of the game was weightier.

They won a free 40 yards out from the Canal End, and Mikey Sheehy stood over it. There were only three minutes gone but already the ground was giving away, and Sheehy did not quite hold his balance as he struck the ball.

The ball rose, and quickly darted in low just in front of the Dublin goal. Paddy Cullen was behind it, but Gay O'Driscoll claimed the ball. The ball spun up off the ground and into O'Driscoll's hands, and it kept spinning.

It fell to John Egan who was six yards out.

Cullen, Doherty, and especially O'Driscoll, panicked. O'Driscoll threw himself in Egan's direction, but the fastest thinker of all amongst the Kerry forwards simply side-stepped O'Driscoll's lunge.

Egan belted the ball to the back of the net. Afterwards, when it was all over, Heff would tell the reporters milling around outside the Dublin dressing-room that it had been a toe-poke from Egan.

Heff also would say it was the turning point in the game.

He was wrong on the first point, and he was probably also incorrect in his belief that Egan's goal had slammed some sort of door in Dublin's face.

Egan's shot had been clinically struck.

And the game was still less than a handful of minutes old by then, and Dublin had all day to come back. Games of football did not turn after three minutes. Dublin had time to assert their authority over the young boys in the green and gold jerseys who, admittedly, did throw themselves into every minute of the game that followed with a complete and copper-fastened belief that becoming All-Ireland champions in 1975 was their natural destiny.

Kerry became cocky too.

Sheehy, who had been a fattened-up teenager when Dwyer first got a good look at him twelve months earlier, was now slim and majestic on the ball, and he was in the mood to put on a show in his first All-Ireland final.

His fourth point came midway through the second half.

On a day when a great many men found it fairly impossible to control the ball, and other men clutched the ball tight against their chests when they did get a hold of it in the dodgy conditions, Sheehy was completely unfussed.

He had chipped the ball up and into his arms for that fourth point. One fluid movement, which was completed with him steering the ball over the bar without as much as a solo, and without a second look at Paddy Cullen's posts.

Pat Spillane was still some months from his 19th birthday. He was in his element going on long spiral solo runs, and threatening to run every Dublin defender off their legs. He would finish the afternoon with three elegant points. Brendan Lynch popped over the same number.

Egan kept bobbing and weaving, and should have scored a second goal but hit the crossbar with a casual fisted effort. Egan would conclude his summer with five goals in four games. Ger O'Driscoll, who had replaced Mickey Ned, had scored Kerry's second goal when Ogie Moran broke through the centre, and sent a long hand pass into Egan, who found O'Driscoll unmarked.

In the middle of the field, Kerry had dominated the first half. Heff decided to take Bernard Brogan out of it at half-time, though twelve months later the table would be turned in the All-Ireland final when Brogan would have the satisfaction of watching his man, Pat McCarthy, being hauled to the line long before the finish.

Bobby Doyle came on for Brogan at half-time.

He did OK. He got involved, as everyone knew he would, and he won loose ball. And Pat O'Neill came on for John McCarthy.

McCarthy had been unable to get into the game from the very start.

He felt it.

Straight away, he knew that he did not have enough games under his belt, and whenever he did get a ball into his hands he was well bottled up by Jimmy Deenihan.

Heff had not helped either man.

Left: A young Kevin Heffernan in action at the beginning of his Dublin career in the 1950s.

Above: Kevin Heffernan poses formally at the start of his 'long war', carried out over four decades with Kerry.

The Dublin team before the 1955 All-Ireland final against Kerry.

Above: The 1955 All-Ireland final ended with an agonizing defeat by Kerry that trailed Heff throughout his Dublin career until the brilliant victory over The Kingdom in 1976. Heff looks on in the middle of the photo, with his greatest ally Dessie Ferguson the first Dublin player to his right.

Above: Dessie 'Snitchie' Ferguson (*far right of the back row*) with the Dublin team that won the 1961 Leinster hurling championship. Des Foley is second from left (*back row*) and his brother Lar is fifth from the left. The Dublin captain, Noel Drumgoole (*third from left in the front row*), was another St Vincents legend.

Below: The Dublin team that lined out against Kerry in the 1965 National League semi-final: Lar and Des Foley are fourth and fifth from left (*back row*) and Jimmy Keaveney is third from the right; Mickey Whelan is second from left in the front row.

Above: The Dublin team before their breakthrough All-Ireland final victory over Galway in 1974.

Right: Heff keeps a close eye on proceedings deep into the second half of Dublin's 1974 All-Ireland victory over Galway.

Below: Mickey Ned O'Sullivan leads the Kerry team on the pre-match parade before the 1975 All-Ireland final against Dublin.

Left: Heff and his Dublin captain, Tony Hanahoe.

Above: Seán Doherty climbs highest during Dublin's brilliant 1977 All-Ireland semi-final victory over Kerry. Kevin Moran and Jack O'Shea look on.

Eoin 'the Bomber' Liston beats Mick Holden in the air during the 1979 All-Ireland final between Kerry and Dublin.

Above: Jimmy Keaveney, who came out of retirement to help kick Dublin to their historic All-Ireland victory in 1974, lands another majestic kick over the bar against Kerry in 1981.

Right: Legendary RTE commentator Mícheál O'Hehir chats with Heff in Croke Park in the summer of 1981.

Below: Heff and David Hickey walk off the field at half-time during Dublin's famous 1983 All-Ireland semi-final victory over Cork in Páirc Uí Chaoimh.

Above: Referee John Gough sends Brian Mullins to the line during the first half of the infamous All-Ireland final in 1983, when just twelve of Heff's Dublin footballers finished the game against Galway.

Below left: Brian Mullins leads the Dublin team in the pre-match parade before the All-Ireland final against Kerry in 1985 – a game he didn't finish on the field after being substituted by Heff in his last great defiant act to try and stop Kerry at all costs.

Right: Kevin Heffernan was forced to watch Kerry footballers, over four decades, lift the Sam Maguire Cup high into the heavens. The last of them was Páidi Ó Sé, who captained Kerry to victory over Dublin in the 1985 All-Ireland final.

Above left: A jubiliant Mick O'Dwyer celebrates his eighth All-Ireland final victory with Kerry in 1986.

Above right: The day after the 1985 All-Ireland final, after Heff's last great battle with Kerry, he offers an affectionate congratulations to Jack O'Shea, who would captain Heff's Ireland team on their victorious tour of Australia a year later.

Above: A proud Kevin Heffernan sits amongst his Irish squad (*centre, second row*) for an official portrait shot before departing for the International Rules series against Australia in 1986. Directly behind Heff stands Dublin's Joe McNally, with John O'Leary and Meath's Mick Lyons behind McNally.

Above: Team of the Millennium: Heff stands between Kerry legends Pat Spillane and Mick O'Connell in Croke Park with the portraits used for commemorative postage stamps in 1999.

Below: The surviving members of the Dublin team that captured the National League title in 1953 regrouped in 2012 after Dublin's All-Ireland victory over Kerry. Photographed (*from left, back*) are Mick Moylan, Jim Crowley, Jim Lavin, Cathal O'Leary and Paddy O'Flaherty, and (*from left, front*) are Dessie Ferguson, Norman Allen, Kevin Heffernan and Cyril Freaney.

*

Kerry 2–12, Dublin 0–11.

'We have absolutely no complaints,' Heff told the reporters, some of whom had now come into the dressing-room.

'We were well beaten . . . the team as a whole didn't do itself justice at all. It was just one of those days.'

Heff had not helped his own team either.

Not as much as he should have. He'd worked them too hard, for far too long, as the All-Ireland final approached.

He should have let up.

But, it was Kerry, and how could he stand back and just wait for Kerry, just wait for them as though they were any other team.

Kevin Heffernan didn't say it.

But, he knew.

All-Ireland finals.

They could sucker-punch any team, any time.

All of the glory, and the fun, and the intense satisfaction which 1974 had brought Heff and his footballers was gone.

Suddenly, it all seemed very old.

Aged, and half-worthless. And a sucker-punch was always more sickening than painful. Its effects would remain for days. Weeks.

For Heff, when Kerry performed the awful deed, it seemed like a lifetime of nauseating regret and anger within himself. Not with them, and not solely with the footballers in his own dressing-room.

How could he completely lay the blame with his lads?

They were all wet, and cold. The showers were not working when they trooped back into their dressing-room after the 1975 All-Ireland final.

One of the stewards on duty apologized, before very quickly explaining that he had set up a hose in the showers instead.

'You can hose each other down with that,' he suggested, '. . . if you like?'

25

'The weight of champions can affect different teams in different ways. We carried that weight in 1975. Now the positions are reversed. A trip to America and its effects on players is another imponderable. We made the tour in 1975. Kerry were out there this year.'

KH

Sunday, 21 March 1976

There were 7,000 people in Navan to watch the final of a competition that was two years old. Dublin came to town in '76 to play Meath in the final of the 1974 O'Byrne Cup and by the end of it the home supporters felt confident that their team was on track to become Leinster champions.

Heff, by the end of the game, also had some thinking to do.

Dublin had lost their All-Ireland crown the previous September. If they lost the Leinster title as well, he guessed it might all be over.

Too many of the Dublin fellas had waited for too long to win one All-Ireland, and if a second did not appear to be right around the corner then there was no doubt but that some of them would pack it in. And quickly enough.

The grave disappointment of losing to Kerry was still dragging its feet across the dressing-room floor.

Heff knew everything had to go exactly right in '76. But, with two minutes left in the 1974 O'Byrne Cup final, a young 18-year-old kid, all left foot, but with one hell of a left foot, who was playing in the middle of the field for Meath, had kicked the winning point.

Meath 1–9, Dublin 2–5.

Colm O'Rourke sent a high arcing ball over the bar from all of

55 yards out. The crowd erupted and the buckled old tin roof rose a couple of inches off the stand in Páirc Tailteann.

Heff didn't want to lose to Meath.

They had beaten Dublin in the National League final twelve months earlier, and now Meath had a second win, which they thought was sweet enough at their backs, even though Heff had only half his first-choice team on the field. He knew that Meath would now make even greater trouble in the summer.

It was not an entirely worthless day, however, from Heff's perspective. After losing the All-Ireland final he had sat down for several weeks and, in addition to blaming himself, he decided that his half-back line would have to be taken out, and shot. They'd have to go.

Paddy Reilly was a bustling ball of energy. Alan Larkin was a huge, intimidating figure in the centre of the line, and Georgie Wilson was a good fella whom Heff had all the time in the world for.

All three had to be shot.

But first he'd have to get others who could do a better job. It wouldn't be easy. Though Pat O'Neill was one option. A good option. Heff had seen so much of him playing for UCD over the previous three years, and he'd also got value out of O'Neill in a blue jersey from time to time.

O'Neill was a classy footballer.

Also, there was cold-bloodedness in him as a footballer.

Pat O'Neill played centre-back against Meath.

He was playing on Ken Rennicks, who was a flyer, and built like a brick-house. But O'Neill had held him, held him scoreless, and delivered some good, old-fashioned tackles that further livened up the Meath folk roaring abuse at the Dublin centre-back. Reilly was on O'Neill's right. Vincents' Brendan Pocock on his left.

Heff was happy enough with his half-back line. Though he didn't want to lose the game, and he'd sent Jimmy Keaveney and Bobby Doyle in as second-half substitutes to try to pull the game out of Meath's arms.

However, as he drove home, Heff found himself thinking more

and more about one player. He'd always liked Kevin Moran, from the first day he saw him on the field for Good Counsel. He played in the middle of the field in Navan. The first time he spoke to the young, tousled-headed fella he liked him even more. He was his own man.

Young Moran was good with the 'Yes, Sirs!' and 'No, Sirs!' but he was also someone who talked and managed himself as though he was far, far older than his years. Sometimes Moran would look at Heff, and he'd leave Kevin Heffernan with the definite impression that young Moran thought he was Kevin Heffernan's equal in understanding the old game.

Kevin Moran had lapped up the hostile goings-on in Navan.

But Heff wanted to see more of him in his defence.

Heff also needed the older fellas to start again. He needed them to be as strong, and eager and hungry. Some of them who had quit the fags in 1974 had been back smoking again a year later.

Small thing.

But the only packet of cigarettes Heff cared to see on the floor of the dressing-room were his own. And Heff never threw an empty packet on to the ground. He always found good use for his packets, breaking them open at the side and giving himself a perfectly sized scribbling pad.

Bobby Doyle was back.

Doyler was on the edge, no doubt about that, and while Heff's broken relationship with his corner-forward would require some mending in the future, there was no doubt in Heff's mind that Bobby Doyle was not going to wait on ceremony any time in 1976.

Doyle had gone missing when the National League resumed the previous October, one month after the All-Ireland final defeat to Kerry.

Dublin played Cork.

They'd travelled down south and won, and it had been a long day, but a good way nonetheless to start back on the long road to another All-Ireland final. Bobby Doyle had simply not turned up.

He'd taken the whole business of being dropped from the team badly. And he hated being the centre of attention for entirely the wrong reason. When the rest of the team headed down to the Listowel races, as they had planned the week after the All-Ireland final, Doyle stayed at home.

He worked all week while the others took a week's holiday.

Then Doyle got out of the country for a week on his own, on his own holiday. All week long either Donal Colfer or Lorcan Redmond rang the Doyle house to check that Bobby was OK for the trip to Cork. Nobody in the house had the heart to deliver the message that Bobby was out of the country, and would not be home until the Sunday morning.

On the Sunday morning, Bobby told everyone in his own house that he was not travelling down to Cork.

He'd had enough.

More than enough of Heff, to begin with.

Late on the same Sunday night, the front door bell rang in the Doyle house. It was Jimmy Keaveney and David Hickey.

They'd come to tell Bobby that he was being a fool, and that if he quit because Heff had dropped him from the team then he was only proving that Kevin Heffernan was probably dead right in his decision making.

They told him to prove Heff completely wrong.

The Kerry team were guests of honour at Tralee races.

It was a Thursday.

The craic was good, and the drink was free.

And that left a problem. Nobody was going to be fit for training that evening, and by the third race on the card nobody wished to go training. It was decided to call Dwyer, and explain the problem.

Mickey Ned O'Sullivan was hand-picked as the man best equipped to handle the situation, and present the problem delicately to Dwyer on a plate.

Dwyer wasn't too happy.

There was no training that evening.

The bigger problem, all winter and well into the spring, was that nearly everyone in the county wanted to get to know the new bunch of heroes on the Kerry team. And that meant barrels of drink. Every single month.

The Allstars trip to America passed off fine. No drinking records were broken, in the air or at ground level, though Dwyer watched, like Heff had watched a year earlier, as his fellas did their best to maintain the high and worthy tradition of an All-Ireland winning team going half mad each night. Kerry hit San Francisco, Los Angeles and New York.

It was the places they had hit in their own neck of the woods all winter long that did the real damage.

The drinking had finally stopped in the early spring, apart from the odd day at the races.

And physically, the Kerry team was in more than decent shape when Dwyer summoned them in for the serious stuff in March and April. Most of the lads were ready for Dwyer.

Páidí Ó Sé, as the years passed, would officially call his own preparation in the spring as 'getting yourself arranged for Dwyer'. They were all at it, all arranging themselves, because they knew what lay in wait. John O'Keeffe had a gymnasium in Tralee. Pat Spillane had a hill behind his house that must have been nearly 100 yards from bottom to top. Mickey Ned had a handy weights room in his school in Ballyvourney. Páidí preferred small mountains. Two- and three-hour runs on average, with stones in his pockets in the second half of his career in case he was not punishing himself sufficiently, over the mountains.

Behind the Ó Sé home was a steep road called the Clasach. It rises to a peak on Mount Eagle. And it then drops down into Dún Chaoin. Páidí took that road in a decent stride two and three times a week in the spring. From Dún Chaoin he'd then stretch it out around Slea Head, and back into Ventry.

Fourteen miles.

If he got bored, Páidí would sometimes slip off the road and tear up different inclines, like a demented goat.

Nearly all of them got 'arranged' for Dwyer in their own way.

But, as Heff knew, and as Dwyer was half-guessing, Kerry might be in the best of shape by the middle of the summer, but what sort of shape would their heads be in?

The championship was on the horizon.

Kerry had Waterford in their semi-final, in the middle of June, which meant a spin over to Dungarvan. There was no danger.

Brendan Lynch, Mikey Sheehy and Pat Spillane scored the goals that would have been enough to win the game on their own. Waterford scored six points in total. Kerry finished with 3–17.

Four weeks later, in the Munster final, there was another spin east. The Cork county board had finally completed the build on Páirc Uí Chaoimh. The stadium was a magnificent bowl ready to be coloured in by supporters. But too many supporters got into the ground. Camped on the perimeter of the field, by the time the game got under way, were about one thousand supporters. Most of them wearing red.

The atmosphere was red and white hot.

And the forwards found it hardest. Mikey Sheehy remained calmer than the others and slotted over five points, and Pat Spillane got two. But no other starting forward was able to bag a score.

Pat McCarthy burst through from midfield and kicked two more vital points, but the most important score of the entire afternoon came from the boot of Sean Walsh, a young lad who'd been minor the year before. Walsh and another promising kid, Jack O'Shea, had been on the Kerry minor team that had beaten Tyrone by nine points the previous September. The goalkeeper on the team was a block of a young lad called Charlie Nelligan.

Walsh was the first of this promising bunch to get the nod from Dwyer. He came on in the second half, in the brand new Páirc, and booted a point that helped Kerry to a draw, 0–10 each. Dwyer knew they were all blessed. They should have lost their Munster and All-Ireland titles, the lot.

But Kerry were alive.

Daylight robbery, no question about it.

Dwyer was livid with himself during the game, and for the rest of the week. He knew he'd been too easy on them. He'd let them play puck. Drinking, and carousing, and not enough laps.

But Cork had come to Killarney two years running while their ground was being built, so Kerry owed their neighbours. The replay was back in Páirc Uí Chaoimh a fortnight later.

On 25 July Kerry met Cork again and the pair went toe-to-toe for one hundred minutes. It was 3–20 to 2–19 at the end of extra-time. Once again, Sean Walsh had come in and this time he had scored a goal and three points. Mickey Ned and Spillane scored the other two goals for Kerry. Sheehy scored 11 points.

It was still too close for Dwyer. They were seven points down at one stage. Six down with twelve minutes left. Five down with ten minutes left. With five minutes to go, Cork were still four points clear.

They were lucky.

Sheehy had an easy free, but he didn't pop it over the bar. He chipped it to Sean Walsh. He duly beat Billy Morgan all ends up, but Cork's tough corner-back Brian Murphy got in the way of Sean Walsh's blistering shot. He held the ball, but the umpire reached for his green flag. Murphy was ruled to have crossed his goal-line. A little later, at the other end of the field, Sean Murphy floated the ball deep into the Kerry goalmouth. Declan Barron got up highest and punched the ball into the Kerry net. The referee, John Moloney, ruled for a 'square ball'.

No goal.

That was a six-point turnaround.

Pat Spillane grabbed the equalizer.

Sheehy seemed to have won the game for Kerry, but Moloney blew his whistle as the ball was about to dissect the posts. Kerry could have won the game against the run of play. It wasn't until extra-time that Kerry looked any way in control. They won the game in additional time by 0–7 to 0–3.

'Thank God for the wire-to-wires,' thought Dwyer.

Kerry had escaped Munster, and escaped more than captured their own province, and were heading back to Croke Park.

Dublin had no more trouble than Kerry did in reaching their provincial final, but there the hard work was certain to start.

Meath also made it through to the Leinster final in double-quick time, and they had no slip-ups like that against Louth in the first round in '75. Meath had beaten Dublin in two finals in the previous twelve months. They feared nothing about Dublin.

Heff?

Heffo's Army?

The 1974 All-Ireland winning Dublin team?

In Meath, it was believed throughout the whole county that their team was good enough to win the All-Ireland. Leinster might only be the stepping stone.

26

'You never knew with Meath. You never knew until you had beaten them, and when you had them beaten you still worried until the final whistle went.'

KH

Sunday, 25 July 1976

Cormac Rowe was a mountain of a man.

He was from the north Meath village of Syddan.

But he was not full-back or centre-back on the Meath team. The Meath coach, Mick O'Brien, didn't have him in the middle of the field either.

The Meath team was bigger than most teams, and far stronger on almost every position on the field. And in the right corner-forward position there was a human mountain.

The Mountain ran into his corner.

There, Robbie Kelleher shook hands with him. The Leinster final was about to start. Croke Park was only three-quarters full, but every man, woman and child in county Meath appeared to be present.

In training sessions, in Navan, Cormac Rowe would mark Brendan Murray every evening in the practice game that Mick O'Brien liked to have for thirty minutes, to get everyone up to a proper level of intensity, and round off things for the night.

Every evening, one of the highlights of the game was Rowe and Murray taking lumps out of one another. Brendan Murray was a concrete block of a man. The Mountain v the Concrete Block got everyone's attention on the field.

When Cormac Rowe got the ball it was usually best that he did not try to solo it. The ball could go anywhere. It could go up in the air, or it could roll down the back of the Mountain. That's why Mick O'Brien liked to have Cormac Rowe very close to the other team's goals.

Meath were not just big, and ferociously strong. There were good footballers on every line. Kevin McConnell had succeeded the majestic Jack Quinn at full-back, and would be the county's Footballer of the Year in '77. Joe Cassells was always able for Brian Mullins and was undoubtedly the most outstanding midfielder in all of Leinster, and in '77 he would be joined in the middle by Gerry McEntee, giving Meath the most naturally talented midfield partnership in the whole country. In the forwards, things really hotted up for Meath's opponents.

Mick Ryan was the best all-round footballer in the county, bar none, and he was on the '40'. Martin Coyne was one side, Gerry Farrelly on the other. Young Colm O'Rourke was full-forward. The Mountain was on his left. On his right was the smartest, the most unbelievably skilful forward that Meath had produced in over a generation, Mattie Kerrigan, who had been the brains on the 1967 Meath All-Ireland winning team.

Heff had good reason to be very worried. Like Meath folk, he knew that the Meath team was good enough to win an All-Ireland.

Heff had other things on his mind as well in '76.

St Vincents had their sights set on an All-Ireland club title. Vincents having been named Dublin champions in 1975 without having to play the final against UCD, after the students had been slapped over the head by the Dublin county board for not doing what they were told.

Vincents chose to be Dublin's 'representatives' rather than Dublin champions in the Leinster championship, which they won in due course, and then came up against the brilliant Nemo Rangers in the All-Ireland semi-final in the early spring of 1976.

Heff had the Vincents lads in strict training for ten weeks before the semi-final. It was all hands on deck. Vincents went down to the

Mardyke in Cork and demolished the Cork champs. Vincents won 0–10 to 0–3.

Heff and Vincents would be All-Ireland club champions a short time later. But, in between the All-Ireland club semi-final and final, Kevin Heffernan was named as Leinster manager for the Railway Cup.

Heff was manager of Vincents, Dublin and Leinster in 1976.

On 15 February, Leinster beat Connacht by two points in the Railway Cup semi-final. The next week Vincents beat Nemo Rangers.

On 17 March, Leinster lost to Munster by seven points in the Railway Cup final. Three days before that, Vincents had beaten Roscommon Gaels by 17 points in the All-Ireland club final.

Heff had Mick O'Brien to out-think.

Out-manoeuvre, and, hopefully, leave clueless on the sideline.

And that was not going to be easy.

Mick O'Brien was the first fully accredited genius to manage the Meath football team, and O'Brien did not just build large, powerful football teams. His football teams were brilliant machines.

Mick O'Brien's football teams liked to play ducks and drakes with other teams. His own parish, Walterstown, would become one of the most accomplished, and completely mesmerizing, club teams in the entire country. Walterstown had been a small junior club. They were dressed in black from head to toe. They were dressed for funerals. Usually their own.

But, at the end of the seventies and early eighties, as he managed Meath at regular intervals, Mick O'Brien was as busy as Heff, and he would instruct the small clutch of footballers at his disposal in Walterstown how to win five Meath championships in seven years, and how to become Leinster champions twice.

Twice O'Brien would also bring his parish to the All-Ireland club final, but each time they would be beaten by Cork's Nemo Rangers and St Finbarrs.

Heff had two great opponents in 1976.

Mick O'Dwyer would come later.

Mick O'Brien was first up in Croke Park in July.

Meath were on the rampage, and the Leinster final was only midway through the first half. From the very start, they had torn into Dublin.

Brian Mullins and Fran Ryder, two of Heff's Vincents men, were being completely overpowered in the middle of the field. Cassells was lording it over Mullins. But little Dermie Rennicks, who could leap as high as any man, and stay afloat longer than any man in Meath, was, incredibly, winning just as much ball as Cassells.

Dublin were in early trouble.

Clearly, Heff could see that the game was going to remain some sort of wild-west shootout right to the very end. Coming up to half-time Dublin had finally begun to play some football of their own. They had pushed Meath back. They began to make Meath think about where they were.

Who they were playing against.

The second half would be an edge-of-the-seat experience for everyone sitting in the old ground. Even for those standing. For those mostly standing on the sideline, it was a game that refused to slow down.

It was hard to think.

Even harder to see what was happening out there on the field.

Heff would make two moves in the second half to try to help the game fall his way. He'd bring on Bernard Brogan, and also Jim Brogan. He'd bring off two of his defenders, Paddy Reilly and Robbie Kelleher.

Mick O'Brien would also make two moves.

The second of those was forced upon him, when he substituted Cormac Rowe with Ken Rennicks.

The first was a mistake. A huge mistake that was made with ten minutes left in the game.

Mick O'Brien brought his own brother, Ollie, in for Gerry Farrelly. Ollie O'Brien was a good, clever footballer and an excellent playmaker, and there was a good chance that he would help create more chances for Meath in the final clattering minutes of the game.

But Gerry Farrelly was Meath's number-one free-taker. And he was also the team's number-one penalty taker, and nobody in Meath could remember the last penalty that Gerry Farrelly had missed. Farrelly, always, seemed to blast the ball straight into the top right-hand corner as though the white object had been dispatched by a small cannon.

Dublin got a grip on things at the start of the second half. But, ten minutes in Rowe got the ball and created enough consternation in the Dublin large square, and attracted sufficient enough defenders towards him, that Colm O'Rourke was left in room to his right.

Rowe quickly punched the ball to O'Rourke, and he scrambled his shot past Paddy Cullen. The teams were level.

Cormac Rowe was bulldozing through Robbie Kelleher every time he got the ball. In the other corner, Mattie Kerrigan was fifty-fifty with Gay O'Driscoll. In the middle of the full-back line, even though he'd end the afternoon with a goal and two points, Colm O'Rourke was slowly but surely being wrapped up by Seán Doherty.

Rowe was the mammoth problem.

Kelleher was unable to deal with the problem, and in the middle of the second half the problem would be dealt with on his behalf.

After that, Jim Brogan replaced Kelleher, who had to peer out of the Dublin dug-out for the last hectic ten minutes.

As well, by then, Cormac Rowe was gone.

Kelleher was probably the most cultured defender on the Dublin team, and that was not always a good thing.

A Glasnevin boy and a Scoil Uí Chonaill footballer, he would admit that Heff was the only coach he ever knew in his entire career. Heff had first taken Robbie Kelleher under his wing when he was a selector in 1971. It was he who taught Kelleher how to defend. But there were other things Heff could not pour into any man.

Like badness, for instance.

Heff liked some badness in a defender. A little bit of evil intent, but the problem with Robbie Kelleher was that he was a total footballer to begin with. He could really play, and sometimes he liked to play with the ball too far away from his corner of the defence. That instinct would rear its ugly head more and more, closer to the finish of Kelleher's Dublin career.

Robbie Kelleher's life off the field was economics.

There was a lot going on in his head, and more things being weighed up all the time in that head than the heads of all the other Dublin defenders put together. The rest of them would as soon knock the head off their man and get on with the game.

That was not Kelleher's style.

Kelleher was a success story on and off the field, and when he handed in the blue jersey for the last time he had won four Allstar awards in the left corner of the Dublin defence. He was also one of the brightest economists in the country, but that was absolutely no help in Croke Park when he found himself dealing with a man who was a good two inches taller and easily three stones heavier. Plus, Cormac Rowe had the strength of two medium-sized bulls.

Rowe had the ball.

Again.

The noise level in the ground soared every time he took the ball into his giant hands, and made one of his big, defiant turns, shoulders first, in the direction of Paddy Cullen.

Kelleher had pawed at him.

Rowe was moving towards the Dublin goal with some speed, when . . .

BANNNGGGGG!

Gay O'Driscoll had charged straight at Rowe. He came in from an angle, and struck Rowe just underneath his left shoulder. Except O'Driscoll didn't bounce off Rowe. O'Driscoll's right shoulder connected just under Cormac Rowe's chin. Rowe had gone down.

That was hard to believe.

Harder still was the sight of Rowe crumpled up on the ground.

He wasn't getting up.

There wasn't a stir out of him.

Referee Seamus Aldridge from Kildare had not stopped play.

Seán Doherty had gathered up the ball that had fallen out of Rowe's hands, and lashed it up the field. Gay O'Driscoll reported back to his own corner to check on Mattie Kerrigan.

Half of the population of Meath was stunned.

Those who sat in the Cusack Stand stopped watching the game. Two Meath selectors were bringing Cormac Rowe off the field. He was being dragged off.

There was no stretcher in Croke Park in the summer of 1976.

With his feet dragging along the ground, and with his head slumped over his own right shoulder, Cormac Rowe was brought over to the Meath dug-out. His jersey was covered in sweat, mixed with a good amount of blood.

Cormac Rowe was laid out on the Meath sideline, directly in front of all of the Meath substitutes sitting and standing in the dug-out.

Rowe was gone.

Kelleher was not far behind him, as Heff has seen enough from his tidiest of corner-backs for one afternoon.

The game was still finely balanced.

O'Rourke had the ball, and had a half-chance inside the large Dublin square when he was clattered by Doherty. Aldridge blew for a penalty.

Gerry Farrelly, the man who never missed a penalty in his life, was sitting in the Meath dug-out with a tracksuit top on.

Farrelly had been taken off two minutes before Rowe.

Nobody stood over the ball that Seamus Aldridge had placed on the penalty spot. There was confusion amongst the Meath forwards. Amongst the Meath selectors there was a big conversation under way. Finally, word was sent out of the large circle.

'Colm . . . tell Colm to take it!

'Colm . . . *Colm O'Rourke* . . . YOU . . . !'

The previous summer in Croke Park, O'Rourke had taken two penalties for the Meath minor team and scored both.

He heard them.

O'Rourke strolled up to the ball, and replaced it.

*

Paddy Cullen lay against the inside of the net.

As O'Rourke placed the ball a second time, and then reversed back and looked up at the Dublin goal, there was no sign of Cullen.

Paddy Cullen stayed where he was, holding the left-hand side of his net. Five, six, seven seconds passed.

Seamus Aldridge did not blow his whistle.

The referee and Colm O'Rourke were waiting for Paddy Cullen.

Then, Cullen walked over to the centre of his line. Aldridge blew. O'Rourke had been waiting an eternity. He was just 19 years old and he was not going to wait a moment longer.

O'Rourke struck the ball perfectly.

And hard towards the left-hand side, to Cullen's right. High to Cullen's right. The Dublin goalkeeper did not move.

The Meath supporters waited for the ball to stop and wrap itself up in the back of the net. To them the penalty had looked absolute perfection. Meath were going to be back in the lead. They were on their feet.

The ball kept travelling.

It did not stop.

The ball struck the iron railings behind Paddy Cullen's goal.

Dublin held on to Leinster!

Dublin 2–8, Meath 1–9.

A year later, back in Croke Park, Meath and Dublin would again go toe-to-toe in a Leinster final.

Again Meath expected to win.

They had lost by two points in '76. They had missed a penalty. And they had started the game without the hugely industrious presence of Ken Rennicks, who was injured, on the '40'. Meath folk were certain that justice would be served in '77. Though Colm O'Rourke had sustained a savage knee breakage four months before the Leinster final that looked certain to end his career.

In 1977 Dublin held Leinster again!

Dublin 1–9, Meath 0–8.

Meath had lost three Leinster finals in four years to Dublin, in

1974, '76 and '77, and Meath's faith died by the end of that summer in 1977.

The Meath team threw in the towel.

Heff had beaten Mick O'Brien.

The grave danger of Dublin losing their Leinster title, losing everything, had passed. The distinct probability of winning everything back, from Kerry, now lay in front of Kevin Heffernan.

It had been touch and go, and there had been some luck involved, but three victories in three Leinster finals left him happy, and absolutely certain in his own head, that the better team had won each time.

Mick O'Brien's attention would turn full-time to Walterstown.

And a heart-broken, defeated Meath team would pass into the hands of others, beginning with Heff's best of friends, his best of Vincents buddies, Des Ferguson.

27

'I've waited twenty-one years for this.'

KH

Sunday, 26 September 1976

'Do you want to play . . . OR NOT?'

Bobby Doyle noticed that Heff had thrown his jaw to one side, as he completed the question.

Heff's jaw to one side meant one thing.

He was not amused.

Shit . . . or get off the pot.

Bobby had carried a hamstring injury for the previous month, since Dublin had slipped by Galway in the dour, dirty All-Ireland semi-final. He knew that Heff had less interest in amateur dramatics than he had one day managing the Dublin cricket team.

Bobby had seriously pulled his hamstring.

But Bobby Doyle had decided, upon re-entering the Kingdom of Kevin Heffernan and sitting down in that little hut, to be examined and cross-examined, that he would never, ever again be dropped from the team.

It was more than a decision.

It was a vow. But in the kickabout before the All-Ireland final, with Kerry at the other end of the field and all systems go, he had felt a definite twinge. He trotted over to Heff.

'I think I felt something wrong,' he told Heff, as he rubbed the offending hamstring with his right hand.

If looks could kill.

Bobby Doyle would have been six feet under within half a

199

second of uttering the word 'wrong'. Heff had watched Bobby jogging around the field in Parnell Park for the previous seven days, all by himself. Heff was no nurse. Neither was he at all fast in dispensing any sympathy.

It wasn't Heff's job.

He didn't do it.

Watching Bobby trot and worry had only annoyed Heff intensely. Twenty-four hours before the game, on Saturday morning, Bobby was still not able to report to Heff that the hamstring was one hundred per cent.

Heff held it in.

On the morning of the game, he turned up at the front door of the Doyle home unannounced. He said he wanted Bobby out on the road. He didn't give a damn if neighbours were watching or not. Heff had two footballs with him.

'Let's get out here!' he told Bobby.

Bobby Doyle was dressed for mass, not a full physical examination, but Heff got him out on to the road, and started kicking footballs at him, high. Then lots of them low on either side.

'That's enough,' declared Heff, at last.

'How do you feel?'

Bobby said he felt good.

'Good,' said Heff, and off he went.

And now, at the last minute, with Kerry ready to defend their All-Ireland title as though their lives depended upon winning this one game, Heff had Bobby Doyle telling him that he was not sure.

He kept rubbing his right thigh that was heavily bandaged, as he looked at Heff for confirmation that he would be able to play or, better still, a miracle cure.

Kevin Heffernan didn't do sympathy or miracles.

'Do you want to play or not?' he had been asked by Heff.

Bobby took one more look at Heff's jaw.

'I'm OK,' replied Bobby.

'I'm OK . . . never mind . . . I'm good.'

Heff watched Bobby Doyle run off twice as fast as he had arrived.

*

Three days earlier, on the Thursday evening, Heff had surprised them all in the hut after training by saying he had said and heard enough.

Heff got up and walked out of the hut.

He told them to talk amongst themselves.

The intensity of the meeting had reached boiling point before Heff said he was going. Heff had been ratcheting it up, minute by minute, calling out names. Pushing lads, prodding lads. The hut was ready to spill over. That was when Heff left.

And closed the door behind him.

Nobody else would leave the hut for another hour and a half. Though nobody jumped in to restart the conversation. For a few seconds there was a nervous silence, and then Anton O'Toole had something to say for himself.

O'Toole's paws were all over the team's performances in the summer of 1976. 'Tooler' they called him on the field. Others in Dublin football circles knew him as 'Anto'. The match programmes in Croke Park had also shortened his name to Anto O'Toole. His younger brother, Peter, would also be called in briefly at the beginning of one summer by Heff. On the training field they called him 'Pedro'.

Anton O'Toole took to the investigations and machinations in the hut with as much fervour as anyone else. But O'Toole also liked to cut to the chase.

The summer of '76 belonged to Anton O'Toole more than anybody on the Dublin team, and he was winning games on the field, and telling it like he saw it in the hut. In the Leinster final it was O'Toole more than any other person in the Dublin forward division who was able to find vital chinks in the steel unit of the Meath defence.

O'Toole's probing, and his natural and confounding instincts, his special elasticity, made the greatest difference against Meath. He would score a vital goal against them in the '76 Leinster final.

And in the Leinster final in '77 he would again confound the entire Meath defence by winning the ball with his back to goal and, with his back still to the Meath goal, whip a handpass into the top-right corner of the Meath net. It was O'Toole, more than anybody, who undid Meath in two Leinster finals.

O'Toole was a Synge Street footballer. The same club as Heff's selector, Donal Colfer. He had broken through and made his debut for Dublin in 1972. Heff didn't frighten him. O'Toole was quiet when he wanted to be quiet. When Heff called out his name in the hut he was just as happy to let everyone know exactly what he thought of the situation.

O'Toole understood the hut.

So too did one of the new boys. Kevin Moran was a natural in the hut from day one. When Heff called his name out, he always delivered from the hip. Moran did not wait on ceremony for any of the older crew, or for the Vincents gang, who were led by Keaveney and Hanahoe in the hut.

Moran did not always tell Kevin Heffernan what he wanted to hear either. But, in the hut, when Heff walked out everyone instinctively knew that it was Hanahoe who was left in charge.

He was team captain.

Tony Hanahoe had been the fast and easy choice once Heff decided that he wished to take the job away from Seán Doherty in the full-back line.

Kerry had pulverized Derry in their All-Ireland semi-final. They'd scored 3–13 against Sligo in the '75 semi-final, and in '76 they scored 5–14 against Derry. In their own semi-final, on an afternoon that was unmemorable, apart from the bad-tempered attitude of both teams, Dublin had beaten Galway 1–8 to 0–8.

Heff had known that it would come to this.

Winning the All-Ireland back from Kerry would have to begin with stopping them from running through his defence.

That meant stopping them early.

And further out the field.

In August, the week of the semi-final, Heff had finally completed the job he set out to do. He shot Paddy Reilly four days before the game against Galway.

It was a shock to most people.

O'Reilly, Larkin and Wilson, the half-back line that had been so sturdy all through 1974 was now gone. All shot. Wilson was the first to go. He'd played little or no part for Heff in almost two years. Larkin had played only once in '76, and his biggest appearance in '77 would not be in the middle of the defence but in the middle of the field, when he partnered Brian Mullins in the Leinster final in Bernard Brogan's absence. But Reilly had stuck to his job.

Reilly was also one of the easiest and wittiest lads in the dressing-room. Everyone liked Paddy Reilly. He kept everyone in good form, and together with Georgie Wilson he had helped to lighten the load that weighed down on the dressing-room, and grew heavier as every summer drew to a close.

No prisoners.

No weaklings.

No defenders who couldn't defend against marauding Kerry for-wards. No kindness, no loyalty, no sympathy.

None.

Kevin Heffernan was in no mood for anything other than throttling Kerry, and after it he'd see what damage had been done to friendships.

Or not.

Heff's whole life as a football man was now in microcosm.

Dublin had not beaten Kerry since 1934.

Forty-two years, in which time Dublin had lost two All-Ireland finals and four All-Ireland semi-finals to Kerry. Heff's own misery on the field with Kerry came in the middle of that time-span. A great need was gnawing at Heff more fiercely than he could ever remember.

He felt consumed. It had been a brutally busy year. He had managed three teams through the first half of 1976, and now he was down to just one last game. St Vincents were All-Ireland champions. Dublin had retained their Leinster title, and they had also won the National League title, shipping 15 points in the final, far too much, but beating Derry 2–10 to 0–15.

He felt his whole football life had come down to just one more game.

Seventy minutes.

Win or lose, Heff thought his job was just about done.

He did not believe there was anything more he could do with the team. In the weeks and days before the 1976 All-Ireland final he had accepted his fate.

Win or lose.

It was probably time for him to leave.

'Every now and then, coaches should change,' he had admitted to one reporter. 'Dublin should win the All-Ireland fairly frequently in the future. It doesn't mean that it will follow in a mathematically precise way.

'But it will happen.'

Kevin Heffernan felt that Sunday was his own Judgement Day. And not so much a do-or-die day for the Dublin football team. Dublin would survive. The team he had built might not live on, but the county would get by, win or lose against Kerry. What more could he do?

'I've been three years as a trainer,' he continued, never before thinking aloud in the presence of a newspaperman. 'There should be a progression in that length of time. As the team improves, then gradually the manager's impact should be less and less. It should come down to the team.'

Con O'Leary, Croke Park's groundsman, cut the grass for the last time on the Friday before. Reporters wanted to know, was he happy?

It was two days before, possibly, the greatest game in the GAA's fantastic history, and everybody hoped that the sloppiness and stickiness of the weather and the field, which had conspired against both teams in '75, would not be back at work twelve months later.

Con O'Leary reassured people.

He broke ranks with the normal level of guardedness he displayed when questioned about his pitch. He told reporters that he had to use an iron bar to create holes for the sideline flags. It was that hard.

'It's like it has never rained at all,' stated O'Leary. 'And it doesn't matter how much rain falls now, the pitch will absorb it.'

There was a depression over Ireland on the Friday, but the analysis division of the Meteorological Service promised that the torrential rain witnessed in so many places in the country on Friday would have moved on by Sunday morning and afternoon.

They expected lengthy showers on Saturday. Intermittent showers on Sunday, and, as it turned out, they were right.

Though Heff was not taking any chances.

Parnell Park had been hard as a rock for several weeks, and with the weather breaking Heff was worried. He didn't want lads panicking. He didn't want them slipping and sliding, and he didn't want any of them complaining rather than playing football.

Six days before the All-Ireland final Heff had a word with the greenkeeper in Clontarf Golf Club. The 16th green in Heff's club wasn't a million miles from Parnell Park. From the green, Heff was able to organize a water hose that ran on to the field in Parnell Park.

On Tuesday and Thursday evening, Dublin trained with a wet ball.

Twenty seconds into the game, Kevin Moran charged upfield.

Brian Mullins slipped the ball to him.

Moran had nobody following him. The Kerry forwards were as open-mouthed as everybody watching in Croke Park. Moran played the ball to Bernard Brogan and raced on for the return pass. He was too far out, but Moran had run so far that he thought he was much closer to the Kerry goal.

The Kerry goal looked huge.

Kevin Moran drop-kicked the ball, meeting it flush with his right boot, perfectly, and the ball roared a couple of yards wide.

Suddenly, everyone was awake.

Moran was the gatekeeper of the Dublin defence.

On his right was Tommy Drumm. On his left Pat O'Neill.

Two gentlemen and a doctor.

Two of Dublin's three half-backs were hard and fair, and had hardly a mean bone in their bodies. Two out of three was not good in Heff's book.

But he liked his new half-back line.

It meant that Pat O'Neill would have to lay down the law on his own more than ever before, and it also meant that Gay O'Driscoll and Seán Doherty would also have to breathe fire more often than at any time in the recent past.

Pat O'Neill, at a young age, had reached a definite conclusion about himself as a footballer. He felt that he never played well when he was afraid of his opponent, but that he played well when his opponent was afraid of him. It was as simple as that. And he played every game as though it was the last game that Heff, or anybody else for that matter, might deliver judgement on him as a footballer and as a man.

O'Neill was a lucky man indeed to be playing at all in 1976. He had missed out on '74 after a serious illness that began with a kidney problem, which left him on a life-support machine for two days.

If Heff liked his half-back line, he loved Pat O'Neill.

Heff liked men who saw life on a football field without colours, just black and white. That was Pat O'Neill. Tommy Drumm, on the other hand, was not handmade as Heff's type of footballer. Drumm played soccer in school with future Irish captain Liam Brady. Like Heff, Drumm was still a Trinity student, but there he played the other game as well and was coached by Liam Tuohy. Tommy Drumm was good enough to get selected for the Combined Universities first eleven.

Heff never said hello to Drumm.

First time they spoke, Heff told him, 'You go in left half-back!'

Drumm was young, far too good-looking to be a Dublin foot-baller, and just 21 years old. Kevin Moran, on the other hand, looked like he had just exited a tumble dryer.

Moran's Dublin career was nine months old when he walked on to the field for the 1976 All-Ireland final.

Tommy Drumm, Kevin Moran and Pat O'Neill had the biggest task of all on the Dublin team. They faced Denis 'Ogie' Moran, Mikey Sheehy and Mickey Ned O'Sullivan. The two men on the wings were flyers. The man in the middle, on Kevin Moran, was a magician and a footballer.

The three Dublin defenders had only played together once before, in the semi-final win over Galway.

The previous January, Kevin Moran had arrived at Parnell Park on a Honda 125 motorbike. When he got off the bike Heff liked the walk of him. He was the same age as Tommy Drumm. Same as Drumm, he was just as interested in soccer. He had already spent a year with Bohs.

He would spend from January 1976 to February 1978 with Dublin, and then Dublin supporters would get only rare glimpses of him in a blue jersey, and then he would be gone for good, playing the other game 231 times for Manchester United, 33 times for Sporting Gijón, and 147 times for Blackburn Rovers. He'd also play the other game for Ireland in European Championships and World Cups, 71 times in total he'd play the other game in green.

Heff had taken a good look at how Kerry were ripping up defences. The five goals they had put past Derry was a good starting point, and Heff had devoured that video tape, hour after hour.

He got it.

It wasn't really rocket science. Kerry had their corner-forwards, Brendan Lynch and Pat Spillane, coming out of their pockets all of the time. Mick O'Dwyer wanted space inside, space that the likes of Ogie Moran and Mickey Ned could race into. Heff saw one good way to put a stop to that.

He told Moran that he wanted him to play deep, and cover right back inside the Dublin full-back line for long periods.

Two weeks earlier, Heff gave Moran his instructions, and explained the thinking behind it. But Kevin Moran wasn't satisfied. He asked Heff to let him see the Kerry videos for himself.

A special sitting with Kevin Moran was arranged, and lasted over two hours. It continued until Moran knew exactly what was going on, and exactly why Heff was telling him not to be the gate-keeper on this one occasion.

Jimmy Keaveney took a quick pass from David Hickey.

He was 45 yards out, 50 yards.

Keaveney didn't like pot shots.

When he kicked the ball for a point he only ever wished to think about accuracy, not length. He also knew Heff had not brought him out of retirement to be a big-time gambler. Jimmy Keaveney was there to make certain.

And the team had to know that they were in good hands every time Jimmy Keaveney had the ball, or stood over a ball on the ground before striking another free-kick dead centre. 'Get up off the ground . . . and go get me another free,' Jimmy had once ordered a horizontal Anton O'Toole, who had just won Jimmy a free that had almost cost him his life.

Jimmy was the team's shot of high-octane morale.

This time, instinctively, Keaveney looked up and drop-kicked a sweet, floating ball towards the Kerry large square, where he himself should have been, alongside Kerry full-back John O'Keeffe. Tony Hanahoe had roamed into the space left vacant by his full-forward.

Hanahoe said thank you very much.

He slotted the ball over the bar.

Dublin were on the scoreboard.

If Dwyer had his ideas about the Dublin defence, then Heff had his private thoughts about how the Kerry defence could be prised open. One of these thoughts was taking O'Keeffe away from the square. O'Keeffe knew he had to stick to Jimmy Keaveney. Though even when he did, and stuck like glue, it was still hard to stop Keaveney from getting possession.

For starters, there was the size of Keaveney. He was a big man to try to get around. And, for a big man, he was able to cover ten yards as fast as any man O'Keeffe played against in Kerry's training games. Keaveney could do ten yards as fast as Egan or Spillane.

It was freaky, but true, and John O'Keeffe had found that out more than once in the recent past. And John O'Keeffe, a modern day prince amongst full-backs, an athlete and footballer sculpted from stone, born a midfielder, and built into a full-back by Dwyer at the start of 1975, was not going to be a big-time gambler in an All-Ireland final any more than Jimmy Keaveney was.

What Heff didn't know was that Dwyer had picked two defenders who were injured. Ger O'Keeffe and Jimmy Deenihan were not right, and they had not been right in training for weeks.

Their manager defiantly ignored their aches and pains.

Dwyer had gone for a big gamble of his own.

The gamble was actually huge.

His goalkeeper was also in bad shape.

Paudie O'Mahoney had damaged his Achilles tendon playing in the East Kerry championship semi-final in July, but, like the others, he was told by Dwyer to run it off. Dwyer did not tolerate having a dressing-room doubling as some class of hospital ward.

Neither did he see any point in having men standing on the sideline in their street clothes, hands in their pockets, watching their teammates being half-flogged to death like mules. Paudie O'Mahoney was told to tog out the first night he turned up and complained to Dwyer about his Achilles. Same the next night.

John McCarthy had scored Dublin's first goal.

Dublin were on the attack again.

Paudie O'Mahoney jumped to field a high centre. Then, disaster. His Achilles snapped. It felt like someone had sliced through the back of his ankle with a jungle knife.

O'Mahoney could not move.

Before he knew it, O'Mahoney was having his jersey stripped from his back by Dwyer. Kerry, for no good reason, had no sub goalkeeper's jersey. O'Mahoney's jersey was handed to 19-year-old Charlie Nelligan.

The dominoes kept collapsing.

Kerry's goalkeeping problems would soon be Jimmy Keaveney's

problem. At the start of the second half, John McCarthy was fouled in the large square. Paddy Collins from Westmeath blew for a penalty.

Jimmy Keaveney faced Charlie Nelligan.

Keaveney liked to hit his penalties low to the goalkeeper's left. That was his trademark spot kick. Hard and to the left.

But between the semi-final and final, Jimmy Keaveney had taken a phone call from Billy Morgan. And his Cork pal explained that he had taken a run over to Killarney the previous evening. He'd noticed something small.

But could be important, Billy told Jimmy.

Dwyer was happy to keep nearly all his training sessions 'open' to the people of Kerry, and any other visitors who came down to Fitzgerald Stadium in Killarney to view the wonder of the Kerry football team. It was the opposite to Heff's policy. Heff, nearly all the time, liked the gates to Parnell Park to be shut tight. Entertaining people midweek was not in his job description.

Billy Morgan was no tourist.

Neither was he a Kerry fan. He was Cork's All-Ireland winning captain, and he was just curious.

Morgan stood there, and he watched the Kerry forwards practising penalty kicks on Paudie O'Mahoney, and every single time they had shot to O'Mahoney's left. Without fail. In fact, O'Mahoney had dived to his left more than twenty times in a row that one evening, and saved most of the kicks too.

Billy Morgan thought that Jimmy Keaveney might like to know that Paudie O'Mahoney was waiting for him.

Except Paudie O'Mahoney was now gone.

Keaveney placed the ball.

'Who's this young lad?'

Keaveney stepped back, and stood still.

'Does he know to dive to his left?'

Right or left? Jimmy Keaveney had to choose. Keaveney had to gamble with a penalty kick. And Jimmy Keaveney was not on the team to gamble.

Jimmy Keaveney planted the ball to Charlie Nelligan's left.
Dublin's second goal.

Kerry never led Dublin, not once in the seventy minutes.

The third goal would come from Brian Mullins. Tommy
Drumm booted a great ball up the field. Anton O'Toole deftly
flicked it down. Mullins took the ball and was lucky to squeeze his
shot between Charlie Nelligan's legs.

Mullins had been monstrously good from the very start. He was
all arms and legs and shoulders under the ball. By the end of the
1976 All-Ireland final, Dwyer knew that he needed to build himself
a new midfield partnership.

Mullins was getting better and better.

Bernard Brogan and Mullins were young, and they were pure
athletes. Dwyer needed to do something about them fast.

It was a day of redemption.

For Heff.

And for Gay O'Driscoll, Bernard Brogan and Bobby Doyle more
than any other trio in blue.

Bobby Doyle did not score. He was the only Dublin forward not
to get a score, but he ran himself silly and wiped out the sickening
sense of loss he had lived with for a full twelve months, before Heff
took him off two minutes from the end.

Bernard Brogan also met his day of complete redemption. In '75
he had been substituted by Heff, after struggling against Pat
McCarthy for too long. Twelve months later, he had thrived in the
middle and run McCarthy all over the field. Until McCarthy was
substituted.

Every Kerry forward scored.

But the Kerry full-forward line only got four points between the
three of them, Brendan Lynch, John Egan and Pat Spillane.

Ogie Moran scored two on Pat O'Neill.

And on the other wing, Mickey Ned got one on Tommy
Drumm.

211

In the middle, Mikey Sheehy scored three points. And only one from play against Kevin Moran, who had shepherded Sheehy, and also dropped back and picked up so many passes that had been kicked into open space in front of and behind his full-back line.

There were no Kerry goals.

It had taken Heff nearly the full twelve months to build the defence he wanted, and finalize his half-back line especially, but Dublin had conceded one goal in five championship games. In the same number of championship games in '75 they had suffered twelve goals.

Dublin 3–8, Kerry 0–10.

At the end, Heff wandered on to the field.

It was not his style.

Nor his place, in his own view, but this time he walked across the field. And he grabbed Kevin Moran.

'I've waited twenty-one years for this!' Heff shouted.

'TWENTY-ONE YEARS . . .' he shouted into Moran's right ear.

The next evening, the story on the streets of Dublin was that Kevin Heffernan was quitting as Dublin manager.

'It's simply not true!' Heff replied.

Newspapermen had nothing else on their minds, and Heff ruled out his imminent retirement a dozen times, more.

Two weeks later, the management committee of the Dublin board asked Heff, and his two men, Donal Colfer and Lorcan Redmond, to stay in their jobs. The board asked for an answer in one week.

Eight days later, Heff told them he was finished.

28

'I know the difference between a boisterous, joyous dressing-room and the almost wake-like scene when you lose. You're only as good as your last match anyway.'

KH

Tuesday, 19 October 1976

Heff wanted to talk to his fellas first.

They were told that there was going to be a meeting with Heff after training. They left Parnell Park, and headed for O'Connell Street.

They were told to report to the Gresham Hotel. Heff hadn't been at training. The players were suspicious. They had heard the talk same as everyone else. None believed it.

Heff had never said a word to them all year long.

But Heff was there, at the top of the meeting-room on the first floor of the grand hotel. There was ribbing and laughter about the rich formality. They also had football on their brains. The National League was back up and running, and Dublin had a journey down to Tralee five days later.

It was to be Dublin's third meeting with Kerry in less than a month, as the two teams had lined out in the Wembley tournament in London two weeks after the All-Ireland final. Bosom buddies indeed.

The only man who knew what was in Kevin Heffernan's head was Jimmy Gray. Heff and Gray were closer than anybody else. The respect between the two men ran full steam ahead each way. Gray had been in London for a week's holidays. He'd asked Heff to hold off on any final decision until he came home.

Heff respected the wish.

But, now, he was not going to wait a moment longer. There was no big farewell speech, no grandiose beginning to what he had come to say. The rules of the hut still prevailed, even in the fancy surroundings of a famous hotel, founded by a man who'd been abandoned as a baby in London. Thomas Gresham's old lodging house. Now the most famous hotel in Ireland. But the Dublin football team may as well have been back in their hut.

Heff spilled it out.

He was going.

Actually he was gone! He was resigning with immediate effect. No reason was given. And no explanation sought.

That's because everybody in the room, apart from Jimmy Gray, was in a state of shock, and couldn't think straight. Or get words out.

'No . . .!'

'No . . . Kevin . . .!'

Those were the only words heard initially.

Later there would be some tears. Paddy Cullen was emotional. So too Jimmy Keaveney. Others were white in the face.

The only other words uttered belonged to David Hickey, who was standing at the back of the room, his hands in his pockets. Given the damned historic importance of the moment, several Dublin players would remember that Hickey's trousers were white.

'Is that it?' asked David Hickey.

It wasn't a question at all.

Hickey was not impressed at being brought to the Gresham Hotel. Neither was he one bit impressed by Heff.

The management committee of the Dublin county board were not happy either. They had awaited a response from Heff and his two selectors the day before, when they sat down for their meeting on the Monday evening.

They got to hear second hand that Heff was gone.

Also, they'd heard from others that Tony Hanahoe was to be Heff's successor. That rankled as well. The management committee decided on who should be proposed as Dublin manager. Not a few lads in a hotel somewhere.

And the man proposed by the management committee then had to be presented to the full meeting of the county committee for acceptance.

The management committee's annoyance lasted three days.

They called a meeting on the Thursday night. The committee proposed Tony Hanahoe as Heff's replacement, and asked Donal Colfer and Lorcan Redmond to continue on, either side of their new 31-year-old captain and manager.

But, during games, it would be Colfer and Redmond side by side on the sideline. Hanahoe would still be on the field.

A great many of Heff players felt he had walked out on them.

It was no resignation or retirement.

Heff had quit on them.

And they wanted to know why. And they refused to accept that Heff had some good or worthy personal reasons behind his sudden decision.

They believed they were more than a football team.

They thought he was more than their football manager.

They had lived their lives together, on the field and in the dressing-room, and in the hut. In the hut, where nothing could ever be hidden from the next man.

Where was the total honesty?

Loyalty? Decency as a friend?

Love?

Kevin Heffernan had never said he loved any of them. Heff would have preferred to swallow his own tongue rather than profess his love for even one of them . . . Keaveney, Mullins, anybody. That was talk for sissies and cowboys in Heff's book. But a great many of them loved him for being a hard, decent, brilliant taskmaster.

Like a father.

And now he had gone and fucked off on them all.

Some were angry.

Some felt deeply betrayed.

A few accepted it was just Heff.

And those few understood that, to Heff, the game was not simply personal. It was as much business. More so business at times.

Even those few, however, had to wonder, had it all been just business?

It wasn't like he hadn't had time to tell them.

The All-Ireland final was followed by days of living in each other's shoes and laughing off the whole, long pressurized year that had preceded the game. For days they had talked. Cried a little. Hugged a lot.

There were days of usual celebrations.

And new, historic days, like the afternoon when a gang of them made their way to the Provost's House in Trinity College. Dr F. S. L. Lyons, a historian known to every young boy and girl in the country for his textbooks, had called for a piece of history to be made in his own very private neck of the woods.

The Provost, Dr Lyons, held a reception for some of the college's old boys. It was the first time the Provost had honoured any group of sportsmen who had not directly represented one of the clubs on campus.

Heff was there, as were Tony Hanahoe, Tommy Drumm and Jim Brogan. All of them had studied somewhere amongst the magnificent buildings. And Robbie Kelleher, a part-time lecturer in economics at Trinity College, was also asked along.

The Sam Maguire was also present, on display in College Park, and after the ceremony Dr Lyons, more of a squash man than a GAA man, to be honest, hosted a dinner for his guests.

Heff, all afternoon long, and into the evening, had not breathed a word to the others about needing to go as Dublin manager.

Heff's needs.

He had put them ahead of everybody. But the worse part was that he did not tell them what was going on in his head.

They all had needs.

And they had all sacrificed their needs.

All it took was one look from Kevin Heffernan and, every time, a man's needs were instantly forgotten, reduced to dust.

In the days and weeks that made up the remainder of 1976, they all had to think, and re-think, of all he had done for them. And some more than others thought about all that they had taken from him.

The punishment on the field, and in the hut. Hounding them. Humiliating them when he needed to do so.

Inciting them.

Pushing, prodding, poking, when he was not brutalizing them with his demands and verdicts.

Hardly ever saying 'well done'.

Rarely a thank you.

At the same time, they knew it wasn't about thank yous.

They hadn't done it for him.

Not him alone.

He had made them the team they were, and whether they liked it or not, he had made them do it for themselves.

He had made them win more, on the biggest stage of all, than he had ever won in his younger life as a Gaelic footballer. He had made them reach their potential, and explore beyond.

That's why he goaded them.

Struck fear into their hearts, and crammed their heads with new demands every single blessed week.

They still wanted to know why.

29

'I wouldn't say that they were afraid of me. There was no fear there. And I don't believe I ever treated any player with disrespect. We were in it together. We all wanted the same thing, and we all did it together.'

KH

Saturday, 20 August 1977

It was the day before the All-Ireland semi-final.

Dublin v Kerry.

It was the end of a week in which Kevin Heffernan informed the Minister for Labour, Gene Fitzgerald, that he would do what was asked of him.

The Jack Lynch government was about to announce an Employment Action Team in early September and Kevin Heffernan, the industrial relations manager at the ESB, was asked to be chairman.

The Action Team was out to help young people.

'Mr Heffernan has accumulated considerable experience of the employment field, including the employment of young people, and their problems. This experience and his continuing and close association with youth in the sports area will be of great value to the Action Team in their work.'

That's how the Department of Labour would announce it on Monday, 5 September. Kevin Heffernan's life, and the good work that consumed his personal time, appeared to be heading in a whole different direction.

*

But it was the day before Dublin met Kerry in the 1977 All-Ireland semi-final, and Heff's head and heart were in the game.

It was still his team.

Almost twelve months had passed since he had walked away from them. Left them as All-Ireland champions, with a rare and cherished victory over Kerry that had taken almost half a century of hard work.

Left them high and dry, at the same time.

He knew how the lads had felt.

The Vincents lads had explained. Heff may have quit on Dublin but he was not going to be allowed to take time off from Vincents. O'Driscoll, Mullins, Hanahoe, Keaveney, Doyle, they were all with him as he guided Vincents to another Dublin football title in 1977.

He didn't tell them much.

They knew better not to ask, though if anyone could find out exactly what had gotten into Heff's head it was Jimmy Keaveney. And Keaveney didn't profess to know very much at all.

In Heff's head, it was simple enough.

Over the course of the next thirty-five years his story never changed. He'd had the longest, toughest year of his life. And that was true, he'd managed Vincents, Dublin, and Leinster in '76.

All three summers in a row, 1974, '75 and '76, had been long, and all extended themselves right into the early autumn, and didn't end until an All-Ireland final left everyone completely exhausted.

Heff worried that the team would go stale.

And that the team might find itself going there fast. Especially if they had to listen to him go on, and on and on. Managing Dublin was the greatest job in the world to Heff, but he was also tired.

And if he was getting tired, pushing them and bullying them, then surely they were bound to be equally tired of him? If not in 1976, then soon enough. They had won two All-Irelands. They had beaten Kerry.

After that, after Kerry, what more was there?

They had achieved everything that he believed they could ever achieve. Two All-Irelands, three successive Leinster titles, and a National League, and all in three storming years.

And his working life was busy.

That was true.

That was the full story in Heff's head. Or the only story he ever told concerning his action in 1976 and '77.

Kerry.

Beating them was a lifetime's target, and an end point.

For Heff, it was that simple.

It had taken almost everything out of him.

Gratitude and general levels of emotional sloppiness were not part of Kevin Heffernan's nature. In three years he had shown his players none of that.

Quite the opposite.

He didn't socialize with them, didn't chitchat with them. Never drank with them. Ate with them at the team table when he had to, but preferred to observe their lives and visit their lives, rather than become a friend in those same lives.

Heff didn't need new friends. His best friends were from a different, earlier generation.

Like Jackie Gilroy.

A former teammate. Vincents chairman, and great friend of Heff.

When both men were in their 60s, in the mid-1990s, Jackie Gilroy spent ten weeks in a hospital bed in St James's.

Jackie had just lost a leg to amputation.

He would lose both legs due to cruel illness. But, every night when visiting time ended, and the staff were hunkered down for the late night ahead, and most patients were dozing off to sleep, Heff would arrive by Jackie's bedside, a coffee in his hand, and no rush on him.

For ten weeks Heff showed up.

Never rushing.

Every single night.

*

Jimmy Keaveney was indeed a friend. But the players Heff managed on Vincents teams and the players he managed on the Dublin team did not necessarily need Heff's close friendship. Nor him theirs. They needed something else from him.

Heff, in his great life, had seen too many teams fail.

Too many under-perform, and waste time, waste football careers. Heff had seen the greatest footballers under-perform, fail to deliver, opt out, make excuses, and he had under-performed himself and he had failed to deliver on occasions.

But he had never opted out.

He had never made blatant excuses.

Heff saw that as his job.

His job was to win an All-Ireland for Dublin, win two All-Irelands, perhaps, and maybe beat Kerry. But the biggest job of all was for Heff to do everything in his power to force every footballer in his dressing-room to live up, one hundred per cent, to his God-given talents on the field.

He didn't fuss over them.

He never allowed them to go soft. That was Heff's number-one most hated characteristic in any footballer. Softness.

Gaelic football and softness did not go well together. And it made him cold-hearted and indifferent to players' needs. Lots of times. Right from the very beginning, in '74, when Georgie Wilson and Stephen Rooney would get out on the road in Balbriggan with their kit bags and thumb lifts to training in Parnell Park. Some evenings, it would take a couple of lifts and the kindness of more than one stranger.

And, after training, after anything up to two hours of working themselves to a standstill, all of Heff's players only ever got a glass of milk or a cup of tea. And biscuits. Packets of Jacob's Goldgrain that didn't last very long, and lots of packets of boring, dry Mariettas.

Other teams, down the country, and down at the foot of the country in Kerry, were sitting at tables after training and being fed steaks. Every night. Tuesdays and Thursdays.

Heff's single-mindedness deprived his footballers of any small indulgence, not until the summer was over, and not until they had won something. His management of his footballers, before and after training, was a style taken from the 1950s. Kevin Heffernan's management style erred on the side of deprivation.

Down in Kerry, Mick O'Dwyer could never be single-minded. Down there Dwyer was always on the go, doing something for himself and getting something more for his footballers.

If Heff lived by rules, Dwyer broke rules. The Kerry manager had his players creating a serious war with the GAA at the end of the seventies by wearing Adidas playing gear, and in the early eighties Dwyer most famously and defiantly lined up alongside a handful of his best-known footballers, and a Bendix washing machine, after a pre-All-Ireland final training session.

Heff would have snarled at the same washing machine.

Gaelic football was not about money.

Or life's little luxuries.

He'd never go soft on a footballer.

In Heff's last great stubborn act as a Dublin football manager, Brian Mullins would find that out.

From the very first summer, from the summer of '74, as Heff shot footballers, or stopped talking to them or turned his back on them, it was always known that the only two games that mattered to Kevin Heffernan was the last game and the next game.

They all knew that.

But, when their time came, they were nearly all surprised at how quickly, ruthlessly, cold-bloodedly, Heff acted. Starting with his full-back, his first captain, Seán Doherty.

It was the run-in to the All-Ireland final in '79.

Seán Doherty had been on the team for six years, permanent, the No.3 shirt his more than any man's, but in the weeks before the All-Ireland final the former captain was told to take up the No.3 shirt on the 'B' team made up of substitutes and panellists. When the Dublin team for the final was announced, 'A. N. Other' was pencilled in at No.3.

After the game, Seán Doherty quickly called it a day.

Paddy Reilly, Alan Larkin and Georgie Wilson were all shot by Heff, at different times after the glorious victory in '74.

In the end, Bobby Doyle met the same fate.

Bobby played in the first round of the championship in 1980. He suffered a stress fracture. He came back to training as fast as he could, and before the Leinster final against Offaly he scored 1–4 for the 'B' team in a final practice game. On the Friday before the game the morning newspaper carried the Dublin team.

Bobby was not on the team.

The newspaper also carried the names of the eleven Dublin substitutes. Bobby was not there either. It was all over. Nobody had phoned him.

No word from Heff.

And then, there was Bernard Brogan.

Bernard Brogan was shot by Heff, and brought back to life.

Then Bernard Brogan was shot again.

He'd been pushed to one side in '79 when Heff felt too many of the lads were finished, but three years later Brogan got a call.

Heff wanted his old midfielder to play full-forward. He told Brogan that he wanted to build the forward unit around him in the No.14 shirt. Bernard Brogan went for it. In his third game back, in the National League, Brogan received a special welcome-back present from Kildare full-back Paddy O'Donoghue.

Bernard Brogan woke up in the Dublin dressing-room.

He was carted off to James Connolly Memorial Hospital in Blanchardstown immediately after the game. There, the nurses could not have been kinder. Leaving the next morning, Brogan gave one of the nurses the Dublin jersey he had been wearing on his arrival.

It was his last game for Dublin.

There was no word from Heff. No mention of the grand plan to have him reborn as a full-forward for the championship. No mention of anything.

All Bernard Brogan heard, one evening when he was at home and the phone rang, was Lorcan Redmond's voice.

He asked Bernard how he was.

'Fine,' replied Brogan.

'Bernard . . .' continued Redmond.

'You don't have that jersey, do you?'

The hut?

The one place where they all made great promises.

Where the Dublin team lived.

Thrived.

Looked one another directly in the face.

Where no man looked down at the floor, no man blinked.

But nothing in the hut ever prepared a Dublin footballer for being taken out and shot by Kevin Heffernan.

30

'You're not enjoying your football? You're not supposed to be enjoying it.'

KH

Sunday, 21 August 1977

A little bit more of human kindness.

That was Tony Hanahoe.

Everything else, mostly, was exactly the same as it had ever been when Kevin Heffernan was on the field, and in the dressing-room.

In the hut.

Tony Hanahoe could hold the attention of men.

He was educated and trained to do so as a successful solicitor. But, before that, in his boyhood, Hanahoe was also reared to be more old school in his posture, and his delivery when he spoke to people.

There was no great football pedigree in the Hanahoe household. His father was a Donegal man who played soccer in UCD, and liked his round of golf. He also owned a pair of boxing gloves that he left in the kitchen for some years for his four boys to try out for size. The Hanahoes had purchased a house in Dublin close enough to Croke Park, on Hollybrook Road, to leave the boys wondering what it was like inside that great, cement palace.

At eight and nine years of age, Tony Hanahoe would make his way down there, usually a couple of hours before the gates opened for the day's games. And down there he always saw another boy waiting, usually alone, too. Though they never spoke. The other boy was called Jimmy, he knew that, and he always wore a gabardine coat.

Jimmy Keaveney's mother always insisted that Jimmy did not go out the front door without his coat.

Hanahoe and Keaveney would make up for that silence.

In Vincents and on Dublin teams in the early sixties they would become firm friends, and understanding friends, and when they up-scuttled one another with a cruel or slap-stick comment in the dressing-room that friendship only tightened.

Jimmy Keaveney was fast with the lip.

Hanahoe was slower, more precise, and as a man who stood up in courtrooms and carefully presented his thoughts to judge and jury, he picked his words carefully. His greatest choice of words, however, was reserved for the hut one evening when all of the Dublin players were relaxed and in jovial mood after a particularly satisfying win the previous Sunday.

Everyone was being up-scuttled.

Then Hanahoe had the floor.

'James, in fairness,' he began, directing his words in the direction of Jimmy Keaveney, 'covered every blade of grass in that small square!'

Hanahoe was well read.

It was he who looked over his shoulder in the Gresham Hotel, after Heff had made his announcement, and looked at David Hickey as he spoke.

Hanahoe reflected that Hickey stood and spoke that famous evening like Gatsby himself, or some notable character who had fallen out of an F. Scott Fitzgerald novel and landed amongst them. Hanahoe read and boxed from a young age. His father encouraged that amongst his boys.

And whenever the hut or the dressing-room required a dash of extra emotion or intrigue, Hanahoe would talk about men laying down their jackets, or rolling up their sleeves. Men arriving at a point in their lives where something honourable and brave was one hundred per cent required of them.

As manager in 1977, Hanahoe was different to Heff in the dressing-room before games. For starters, he liked to talk to every man in the room individually. He didn't try to hold the floor like Heff. But, out on the field, Hanahoe still stuck by Heff's planning.

His role on the field was one that was more sacrificial than heroic. And, naturally, as a man who deeply admired so many tall, strong characters from the boxing ring, Tony Hanahoe would have preferred it if it was the other way around. But Hanahoe was the ultimate team player, even when every member of the team had been nominated for an Allstar award at the end of '74 and he was the only man ignored by the Allstar selectors.

Hanahoe said not a word.

Running out of the picture so often, running away from the ball, and bringing his man with him and leaving a 20- or 30-yard avenue, wide and welcoming right down the middle of the opposing team's defence, was the classic Vincents ploy for many decades. Ollie Freaney had perfected it for the club and county. Hanahoe would further demonstrate the role for Dublin in six successive All-Ireland finals in the seventies.

Everything went smoothly enough for Hanahoe in 1977, until 17 April, when Dublin met Kerry in the final of the National League, and in the defence of that League title. They lost by two points.

Kerry 1–8, Dublin 1–6.

But Meath were beaten back by four points in the Leinster final. Dublin were in the All-Ireland semi-final, and so too were Kerry, who were back and who were tearing up other teams' defences all over again. They completely obliterated Cork in the Munster final.

Kerry 3–15, Cork 0–9.

Kerry were fuelled to the brim at the beginning of August, and there was a lot of talk from both sides. And some big talk. Most of it coming from Kerry.

The talking was interrupted by the giant figure of the *Evening Press's* Con Houlihan, the week before the two teams met in their semi-final on 21 August, in a game that would become the un-disputed greatest football game ever played in Croke Park. One sentence from Houlihan, a proud Kerryman, shut his native football team up for a day or two.

'Never criticize the alligator's mother,' he wrote, in his back-page column in his newspaper, '. . . before you cross the river!'

Dwyer had promised himself a new midfield, and he had it. Páidí Ó Sé and 19-year-old Jack O'Shea. They were facing Brian Mullins, who had missed the League final and who was struggling with his form. Once again, he had been second best in the Leinster final against Joe Cassells and Meath. In that Leinster final, Fran Ryder had come on for Alan Larkin to assist Mullins.

More than anywhere else, the 1977 All-Ireland semi-final would be won and lost in the middle. Six men would be involved in that direct battle.

Pat McCarthy would replace Jack O'Shea in the second half. And Bernard Brogan would come in for Fran Ryder.

Mullins would outshine all five of them.

Jack O'Shea was just 19 years old, and the game engulfed him. But Dwyer refused to budge. He left Jacko in a losing battle almost until the end. With two minutes to go Pat McCarthy came in.

Brogan had been on the move for almost eighteen months. His life as an engineer had him in Cork, in London for six months, in Kilkenny for a time, and in New Ross in the summer of '77. He was working on the building of an oil rig for the Kinsale gas field, but in June and July of '77 the rig was brought to French waters for testing. And that's where Brogan was for the Leinster final, in the French port of Cherbourg. He listened to the game on the radio.

Páidí and Jacko were on top from the very beginning. The challengers immediately kicked the alligator's mother out of their way, and they went for the throat of the alligator itself.

Kerry led 1–5 to 0–3 midway through the first half.

Once more, Jimmy Keaveney's primary job was to take John O'Keeffe as far away from his large square as possible, and it was a job he would accomplish. O'Keeffe was brought left and right and up the field.

Dwyer didn't cop on.

The Kerry boss was far too delighted to see his boys putting away scores at the other end of the field.

But despite his day of wandering, Keaveney had the first brilliant goal chance. Clean through, he stubbed his kick as he looked to tuck the ball to one side of Paudie O'Mahoney.

Sean Walsh, now starting in the No.14 shirt for Dwyer, grabbed the first goal of the game, catching a '50' cleanly, and turning and belting the ball into the net. It was a goal that an Under-14 defence might concede. Kerry were still five points in front with time almost up, but Dublin stole in for two easy scores before half-time.

Kerry 1–6, Dublin 0–6.

Hanahoe remained calm.

Throughout the first half he remained in contact with his side-line. There was no need for Donal Colfer or Lorcan Redmond to come running on to the field to have a word with the manager.

The three of them had an agreed set of signals.

If the worst happened, all three men knew what was to be done, and right up to the 56th minute of the game, until Dublin finally got in front for the first time all afternoon, the worst had not happened.

Dublin led twice in the second half.

Kerry led three times.

The game had become a battle that was intoxicating. The audacity of both teams, their fearlessness, but also the foolishness of the two teams and their extravagance at times, in wasting so much hard-won ball by lashing it out of sight, was all-consuming. It was a battle pitched at a greater height than anyone could remember.

In the final seven minutes John Egan scored his second point of the day to put Kerry two clear.

By the end, Anton O'Toole would surprisingly be Dublin's biggest points scorer. He bagged four of them.

Keaveney had three.

Hanahoe, amazingly, got into some excellent positions and kicked over three points as well.

David Hickey had scored one.

And Bobby Doyle.

One.

But Dublin also scored three goals before the afternoon was finally over. John McCarthy got the first of them after a brilliant drop-kick across the field by Tommy Drumm out-puzzled the Kerry defence.

The other two goals came from Hickey and Brogan. Both came in the last six minutes of the game. Both of them with a final pass dispatched by Hanahoe.

In a flash, really.

Brian Mullins got the ball to Anton O'Toole, and O'Toole's kick was knocked into Hanahoe's path by the outstretched hand of Kerry full-back John O'Keeffe. He fed Hickey.

Hickey crashed the ball past Paudie O'Mahoney.

Four minutes later, Hanahoe received a pass from Hickey. He held the ball, and then floated the ball into the path of Bernard Brogan.

Brogan's great stride shook the whole ground. His shot, like Hickey's, was a bomb. Brogan hadn't had a long, weary summer like the rest of them. And the late summer was more of a gift to him.

He remembered a very short conversation he once had with Kevin Heffernan, when he told Heff that he wasn't enjoying his football much.

'Enjoying your football?' scowled Heff. 'You're not supposed to be enjoying it!' But in the summer of '77 Bernard Brogan got to enjoy every single minute.

Two bombs finished off Kerry.

Dublin 3–12, Kerry 1–13.

There was a big victory at the team's back, but Hanahoe had a bigger job ahead of him. He had to come to terms with what had just happened.

The crowds were gone when he left the dressing-room, though there were still plenty of supporters on the street corners, half-jammed into pubs.

Most of the Dublin lads also had drinking more than eating in mind and were heading for Meaghers public house on Richmond Road, the usual landing spot for the whole team. But Hanahoe got into his car and drove out of the city.

He drove into the country.

In Garristown he found a pub that looked quiet, and the Dublin captain and manager wandered in and sat on a high stool. The place was peaceful.

Hanahoe was left mostly alone.

The All-Ireland final was still not won. That was the recurring thought that jumped up and down in his head. Dublin had beaten Kerry but, for once, unusually, they had won nothing.

It had been quite a summer.

Before leaving the pub and getting back to his teammates, Hanahoe also resolved to work all of them hard, physically and mentally, like Heff would now work them. They'd all believe the summer and the championship was as good as over.

Heff would waken them.

He'd knock that satisfaction, that dangerously false presumption, out of their heads and would enjoy doing so. He'd tear into the whole lot of them.

They'd never know what hit them.

That's what Heff would do.

Tony Hanahoe knew what he had to do. But, it was a job he had been doing expertly for months, as though he had been doing it all of his life. He'd kept everyone serious, focused, scared stiff and fearless at the very same time, in the anxious weeks before the semi-final.

Three weeks earlier Hanahoe had got married.

He told nobody.

None of them in the dressing-room had a clue. Hanahoe didn't want any of them to think that he had anything else on his mind. Only beating Kerry.

On the morning of his wedding Tony Hanahoe had turned up for training, as per normal, his big secret tucked out of sight. No questions. No information offered. There was always so much to be done on a Saturday morning anyway.

31

'What I loved most about the game was getting into the other man's head.'

KH

Sunday, 23 April 1978

Heff wanted to come back.

Hanahoe and himself had discussed the situation. If Heff wanted back in, then Hanahoe was not going to stand in his way.

But, first of all, Dublin were back in another League final. League finals were becoming a habit. This time Dublin won.

Though it wasn't Kerry.

Dublin 2–18, Mayo 2–13.

Heff was coming back to a group of fellas who were All-Ireland champions and National League champions.

The team had not missed a beat in his absence.

Hanahoe had corralled the team and substitutes after the hectic couple of days that followed the most amazing game ever seen in Croker. Nobody was allowed out. Everybody on the field was made to suffer.

In the hut, as usual, skin and hair flew.

On 25 September 1977, Dublin had enacted the All-Ireland final of Tony Hanahoe's dreams. Even if he failed to score himself as the team rattled up a princely total of five goals and 12 points.

Dublin 5–12, Armagh 3–6.

It was a no-contest.

Armagh's great pleasure in becoming the first Ulster team to make it to the final in nine years was tipped on its head. It was 3–6 to 1–3 at half-time.

The second half was more of the same, and mostly a non-event as Dublin increased their lead by 4–8 to 1–3 before everybody called it a day, and Armagh scrambled for some respectability.

But Dublin had won the All-Ireland title for the third time in four appearances, and for the twentieth time in all. And it was Dublin's first time to retain the big one since 1922. The numbers game made the game itself pale into insignificance.

Jimmy Keaveney scored 2–6.

It was an individual record for an All-Ireland final, beating by one point Frank Stockwell's handy tally in Galway's win over Cork in '56. His All-Ireland final tally made sure that his high standards were maintained. Jimmy had helped himself to 101 points in seventeen games in '76. The year before, in twenty games, he had personally accounted for eight goals and 95 points.

There was no red carpet.

As far as most of the players were concerned, if there was a carpet required then Heff could bring his own.

Some felt that Kevin Heffernan had suited himself twelve months earlier, and they thought he should live with his decision and stay away.

Others felt nothing.

They were All-Ireland champions. Twice they had beaten Kerry, the one team that Heff feared more than any other, and as they awaited the summer of '78 most of the lads in the dressing-room felt that they had nothing to fear.

Nobody.

Not even Heff any more.

The majority of the Dublin panel felt that they had outlived the man who had made it all possible in the first place. Outlasted him.

They had moved on.

It was exactly as Heff himself had asserted in a rare newspaper interview, two years before. A good team should outgrow their manager. So, why should they want him back?

They did not understand why he had left in the first place, and they could not understand why he was now coming back.

As it happened, Heff slipped back in.

No big hello.

One evening in Parnell Park, he was there.

Simple as that.

Whose team was it in 1978?

Officially it was still Tony Hanahoe's team.

Unofficially it was Kevin Heffernan's team again. Though Heff liked to keep people on the outside guessing.

The players knew they had Heff to answer to, listen to, and reply to back in the hut. And, on the Dublin team, the rules of the hut ruled.

In '78 and '79, as Dublin went back into battle with Kerry in two more All-Ireland finals, and the country's newspapers juiced up the games on the field with the equally epic confrontation between Heff and Dwyer, as two middle-aged gladiators on the sideline, nobody bothered to correct them.

In the spring of '79, Heff fell ill. He collapsed during a training session and was rushed to the cardiac unit of the Mater Hospital.

That real scare helped with the kidding around.

In July of '79, almost three years after his shock resignation, Heff was still not calling the team his own even though he was back on the field in Parnell Park, after his hospitalization, and was in charge of team training.

Dublin were preparing for the Leinster final against an Offaly team that was looking a serious proposition. The manager of the Offaly team who was in charge of the county's regeneration was Longford and UCD's Eugene McGee. Heff's old foe, and some more.

There was serious business being done on the field in Parnell Park. But Heff denied everything.

'Even if I wished to do so,' he emphasized, 'I couldn't resume where I left off. I'm kept too busy with my job these days. But I'm always pleased to help out, if I have the spare time.'

That same year ended with the Dublin county committee rubber-stamping the decision of the board's activities committee with the appointment of Tony Hanahoe, Donal Colfer and Lorcan Redmond as team selectors for another year.

Oh, and the committee also officially appointed Kevin Heffernan as 'adviser to the team'.

32

'I kept going to 1985. We lost a lot of matches in that time, but I kept going.'

KH

Friday, 28 April 1978

The Dublin football team had been spending a lot of time at 30,000 feet while Kevin Heffernan was away.

Heff had had his fill of the Allstar tour to the United States in 1974, and watching his lads filling up, on everything and anything at all, every single time a bottle was passed in front of them, was not his idea of relaxation.

Excessive drinking only annoyed him.

There was a time and place for it, of course, just not every day for over two weeks, afternoon, evening and night. Dublin went off to America in the spring of '77, a couple of days after losing to Kerry in the National League final. Half of the Kerry team joined them on the trip. They started in Chicago. They got drunk, Jimmy Keaveney had his nose plastered across his face when he was on the receiving end of an accidental punch from John O'Keeffe, and they got drunk again making sure that Kevin Moran's 21st birthday celebration would not be forgotten, and then they flew out to San Francisco.

And it all started all over again.

It was standard for an Allstars tour.

In '78, everybody except Heff was up in the air again.

This time they landed in New York. And this time, the normal enough procedure of the All-Ireland champions playing the Allstars in a game which was half-paced, full of smiles, a few 'excuse me(s)' and the occasional 'sorry about that', was completely forgotten.

It wasn't Dublin versus the Allstars.

Dublin were playing Kerry.

It was a special fundraising game. The next day Dublin were heading off to Los Angeles and San Francisco with the Allstars party. Their holiday was only beginning, but the Kerry players who were not amongst the Allstars were heading home, double quick.

Kerry, therefore, were in a mood.

They'd lost to Dublin two years running, and they had no interest in being 'dancing partners' on another Allstars tour. No thank you.

It bucketed down the day of the game in Gaelic Park.

Hanahoe brought the team to the south Bronx in a handful of yellow cabs, but the drivers were asked to keep their meters running. Nobody thought the game would go ahead, which, for Dublin, was very wishful thinking.

Kerry were already togging out.

They had come to play football.

And get some other things out of their system. And being left in the soaking rain waiting for Dublin to finally come to a decision to leave the slight comfort of their dressing-room meant that the 'systems' of a great number of players needed a lot of clearing out.

Even Eoin Liston needed some of it.

And Liston was new, he'd no history with Dublin of any kind. All of the Kerry lads called him 'the Bomber', which was considered interesting, but tomfoolery, a bit of country foolishness, by those on the Dublin team who had never seen him before.

Eoin 'Bomber' Liston.

Hard to forget that name, whoever he was.

A big man too, and he was in a mood also for no good reason!

He was captain of Kerry in the absence of his club colleague, Ogie Moran, but he was not over-taxed by that responsibility for very long in New York. He was not on the field at the end. Paddy Reilly had been clobbered by Tommy Doyle.

Pat O'Neill had clobbered Doyle.

And the Bomber had clobbered O'Neill.

The whole of the Dublin team suddenly took serious interest in the new boy with the promising nickname, and, in the mêlée that followed, a great many got up close and personal for the first time with Eoin Bomber Liston. Then, the Bomber was sent off by Seamus Aldridge.

At half-time, Kerry ran to the dressing-rooms. Dublin stayed on the field, drenched to the skin, and now slowly freezing as they stood around, waiting.

It had been agreed that both teams would stay 'out'.

The agreement was broken. It turned Dublin into a mood of their own. The mood deepened further when Kerry came back out for the start of the second half in a nice, dry new kit of jerseys.

The game descended further and further into the depths of unruliness.

Then spitefulness.

And, lastly, complete and utter roguery.

It was the dirtiest game of football ever played between Dublin and Kerry.

When they told Heff all about it a couple of weeks later, he didn't really believe them. And when they told him about the big lump of a fella who had started it all, Heff was equally dismissive.

Kerry had won, easily in the end, but two of theirs, Jimmy Deenihan and Pat Spillane, had their noses broken and spent the evening in New York in hospital, in Accident and Emergency. Páidí Ó Sé, Pat O'Neill and Eoin Liston were sent off.

It all sounded like more drunken war stories to Heff.

Soon, however, he would get to see for himself the damage that the Bomber could do on a football field. In the summer of 1978 *The Incredible Hulk* television series was also aired in Ireland for the first time. If Heff watched much television at all he might have caught a glimpse of what awaited his team on the football field by the end of '78.

Heff never caught *The Incredible Hulk*.

*

Heff came back in May of '78.

Over the next seventeen months Dublin would lose twice to Kerry in All-Ireland finals. Whether he was officially labelled manager or not, Kevin Heffernan found himself back in the middle of a war which always appeared stacked against him.

All of his life he had been fighting that war, and losing. Apart from 1976, the only year in his adult life when Dublin were able for Kerry in a game of football that was the last gripping chapter in the whole championship.

In '55 it was John Dowling.

Heff had stayed on the field in his damp blue jersey as the Kerry captain walked up the steps of the Hogan Stand and lifted the Sam Maguire Cup.

In '75 it was Pat Spillane.

Heff stayed put, bravely, defiantly to the bitter end, and watched Spillane take the place of the semi-conscious Mickey Ned O'Sullivan and lift Sam as well.

Both gut-wrenching images were Heff's for life.

In '78 it was Ogie Moran.

Heff would stand his ground in Croke Park as a losing Dublin manager again and see Ogie Moran raise the great prize over his head with both hands.

In '79 it was Tim Kennelly.

Heff would still be out there, still standing, still defeated. Tim Kennelly would walk halfway up the lower tier of the Hogan Stand and collect the cup. Tim and Sam.

The seventeen months would speed by upon Kevin Heffernan's return.

The football decade would be completed faster than anybody could have imagined. The seventies were history.

Heff's Dublin team had awakened the city, and intrigued the entire country. They had come from nowhere. And they would make it to the far end of September six years in a row, playing in six All-Ireland finals in succession.

Three were won.

And three would be lost to Kerry.

Dublin would play Kerry five times in the championship in those six years between 1974 and '79. The score would be 3–2 to Kerry.

It was a war that consumed Kevin Heffernan, that ruled his life. Win or lose. He'd been unable to stay away. At the decade's end, he would find himself totally powerless when it came to walking away.

By the tail end of 1977, it had looked as though Heff and Dwyer were both finished. Heff was out of the Dublin picture and nobody knew that he was thinking of possibly coming back. Dwyer also looked on the way out in Kerry.

His career as Kerry team boss hung by a thread for several weeks, and it was not until his number-one fan, Ger McKenna, somehow managed to keep a grip of his job as county board chairman that Mick O'Dwyer thought he was in any way safe. Too many Kerry folk were sick of Dwyer's style of football, and they were sick to their teeth of losing to Dublin.

Ger McKenna's re-election saved Dwyer's neck from being wrung.

And the revelation of Eoin Liston as a full-forward with super-human powers lifted Dwyer back up on to his pedestal.

In 1978, Kerry were just seventy minutes away from losing to Dublin for the third year on the trot. Another defeat and Dwyer was in big trouble.

Dwyer would be history.

They had lost to Dublin by seven points in the All-Ireland final in '76, and they'd lost again in the semi-final in '77 by five points. Twelve minutes into the final in '78 they were still losing. They were five points down.

There were fifty-eight minutes left to that third defeat on the trot.

Dublin looked powerful.

In the Dublin dug-out Kevin Heffernan sensed that his team were delivering one last, courageous, gigantic performance.

Everything was working out as he had planned. There were no danger signs.

The Bomber Liston?

There was nothing major to worry about there either.

'The drizzling rain seemed irrelevant as Dublin moved the ball with the confidence of a grandmaster playing chess against a novice,' wrote Con Houlihan in the *Evening Press* the next day.

Dublin led by six points to one. Mullins scored one of those points and was having one of his seriously bullish performances. For Dwyer, the game was looking more and more like his last game as Kerry manager. He was now less than fifty minutes away from an appointment with the people of Kerry. He'd be blamed for everything.

No doubt about it, he would be told that he had been fooling around with a precious group of Kerry footballers.

But he'd shaken things up this time against Dublin. He had moved Ger Power up from the half-back line to the half-forward line. Anton O'Toole had run through Power in '77, but let loose up front Power had the legs for any man.

Dwyer had Paudie Lynch back in defence instead. Sean Walsh was no longer full-forward. He was in the middle with Jack O'Shea. John Egan and Mikey Sheehy were in the two corners. The Bomber was between them.

Dublin stayed the same.

Heff went out of his way to keep everything as it had been in '76, and as it had been with Hanahoe in '77. And his only piece of extra work comprised a quick trip to Manchester to hold on to Kevin Moran for one or two more games.

Moran was on the Manchester United books as a full-time professional footballer since February of 1978. His Gaelic football career looked more or less finished at 22 years of age. But Dublin needed him.

Heff wanted him back. Even if it was only for a couple of games, and when Manchester United were in pre-season training Heff and Hanahoe popped over to Old Trafford and got to sit down with their manager Dave Sexton. He was a pleasant, amenable sort of man. A Londoner whose father, Archie, had been a professional boxer, Sexton had an appreciation for all sports.

The Manchester United manager didn't know anything about Gaelic football, but he told Heff he'd like to take a trip over to Dublin sometime and see a game for himself. Sounded like fun to Sexton.

Sure, he was happy for his young Irish boy to play in the little game. It was amateur stuff. His boy wasn't getting paid or anything, was he? No harm could come of it. Heff and Hanahoe came back to Dublin with Kevin Moran's name on the team for the All-Ireland semi-final against Down.

And they got him for the final too.

Dave Sexton gave his boy the full week off.

On the Tuesday before the All-Ireland final, however, as he happily chased around Parnell Park, Kevin Moran pulled his hamstring. He rested it for the remainder of the week. Heff hoped he was right for the final.

But Moran knew he was not even close to being right as he took up his position, shoulder-to-shoulder with Ogie Moran, in the centre of the Dublin defence.

Eoin Liston saved Dwyer.

It was the big, bearded giant of a man who carried Dwyer back home to Kerry on his shoulders, and made sure that every last man, woman and child who had doubted either the cunning, or the absolute genius, of the Kerry manager got a chance to bow down in front of him.

To begin with, Liston had got himself a teaching job in Waterville Vocational School and had to leave north Kerry, and find himself digs just down the road from Dwyer. On quiet evenings, when Liston went over to the football field for a kickabout, Dwyer would turn up and kick the ball back to him.

Dwyer was still playing club football. He was 42 years old, but he had no intention of being some sort of old ball boy. Dwyer and Liston did more than kick the ball about. They began to get testy.

They began to meet up mornings and evenings during the summer, and they didn't stick to football. They'd do anything to beat one another on the golf course. And when it was rainy or gloomy, they'd go one on one in basketball. Or Dwyer would take his badminton rackets out, and string a net across the basketball court. Liston was twice as heavy. But Liston had twice the reach with a racket.

Dwyer hated letting Liston get the better of him.

They played some squash.

Tennis.

Even had a couple of games of handball.

And sometimes they'd squeeze in a game of badminton or squash after their round of golf. It depended on which man had won the golf. But the extra game was normally added when Dwyer was beaten over the eighteen holes.

Coming up to half-time in the 1978 All-Ireland final, however, the Bomber wanted to give up. He was being cleaned out of it by Seán Doherty. The All-Ireland final was too big for him. Too busy, too noisy. Sometimes an All-Ireland final made a man second-guess everything he ever knew about himself.

The '78 All-Ireland final had the Bomber in such a stew.

He felt a pain in his knee. By the time he reached Dwyer on the sideline, he reported a pain in his knee, and another pain up the back of his neck.

The Bomber was ready to turn his huge back on the game.

Dwyer didn't listen to a word.

'Get back out there,' rasped Dwyer.

'Christ . . . it's an All-Ireland, man!'

The first Kerry goal didn't rock Dublin off their feet.

It just stunned.

The whistle was blown on Bobby Doyle for over-carrying the ball. Whether it was fair or harsh, nobody was quite sure, not even Heff, but the full jury agreed that Bobby was messing around with the ball.

The referee, Seamus Aldridge, was the jury foreman.

Heff also saw that Robbie Kelleher had been meddling around close to Bobby Doyle when the play switched direction. A quick free was sent in the Bomber's direction. It was far too high, but he got up for it, and came down with it, and passed it off to Jack O'Shea.

O'Shea found Pat Spillane.

Spillane, for once in his life, according to John Egan, looked up. And he passed the ball inside, miracle of miracles, also according to Egan.

Egan got to the ball just as Paddy Cullen launched himself off his goal-line. The ball was tipped over Cullen's head.

It floated into the net, slowly, like a big round butterfly.

Dublin were stunned only.

Shock followed the second goal.

The second goal?

The most controversial, hilarious goal ever scored in Croke Park. A goal that was mischievous, and instinctive. And wrapped in sheer brilliance.

Paddy Cullen came off his line again.

He was looking to clear the ball when he was on the receiving end of a slightly late tackle from Ger Power. It was nothing much. But Paddy Cullen had taken a disliking to Ger Power on the American trips.

A few minutes later Cullen and Power found themselves involved in another confab, a little contretemps. Mainly it was childish goings-on.

A little bit of nothing.

Cullen again came off his line to retrieve a ball sent in too long from Mikey Sheehy. He got the ball and fisted it off to Robbie Kelleher.

Power was on the scene again.

Cullen and Power said a quick hello and goodbye, once again, with another small jostle. Neither man fouled the other.

The whistle blew.

Free in?

Free out?

Nobody thought it was a free in the first place, but Seamus Aldridge had blown. Robbie Kelleher had the ball in his hands. He was as confused as the next man.

The only person in the ground more wised-up than confused was Mikey Sheehy. And Kelleher handed the ball to Sheehy when he asked for it.

Sheehy saw Cullen off his line.

Sheehy saw the referee wasn't looking.

Sheehy didn't think.

Without waiting for the referee's whistle, or permission, Sheehy placed the ball and deftly kicked it. Sheehy's kick was a light, sublime touch over the retreating figure of the Dublin goalkeeper, over Cullen's flaying arm as he reversed up, and the ball curled into the top corner of the net. Confusion reigned. The referee let the goal stand. 'Cullen had dashed back to his goal like a woman who smells a cake burning,' Con Houlihan declared with lip-smacking drama.

The shock in the Dublin team deepened, if anything, when everyone got back to the dressing-room at half-time.

Heff could not rouse them.

Or clear their heads. They'd been rattled. They thought they had the game half won and, now, suddenly, in the dressing-room they didn't look like a team that had been just stunned or shocked. As they sat there, they did indeed resemble a team that had been rocked off its feet.

The Bomber buried them in the next thirty-five minutes.

BOOM.

BOOM.

BOOM.

The first goal from the Bomber was a gift from above two minutes into the second half. A Jack O'Shea kick for a point came down short, and right into his hands. BOOM. Kerry were five points clear.

The second goal came from a Páidí Lynch free-kick. The Bomber played a one-two with Ger Power. BOOM.

BOOM. The third was fisted into the net by the Bomber after John Egan flighted the ball across the Dublin square.

Kerry 5–11, Dublin 0–9.

The months flew.

The 1978 All-Ireland final merged into the 1979 All-Ireland final.

But, in '79, when they met Kerry in the All-Ireland final again, the entire Dublin full-back line of Gay O'Driscoll, Seán Doherty and Robbie Kelleher was gone. All three of them. Heff and Hanahoe had a new line built in double-quick time in front of Paddy Cullen. It was made up of Mick Kennedy, Mick Holden and David Foran. A full-back line that had to be built from scratch.

Paddy Cullen, however, would also be gone soon enough.

And Kevin Moran would play just one more game for Dublin, in 1980, in a Leinster semi-final against Meath in Navan's Páirc Tailteann, which Dave Sexton did not get to see, thankfully. The Manchester United manager would have watched his centre-back coming off the field, banged up good and proper by the crowd in green jerseys, his head wrapped in white bandages six inches wide at least, and his blue jersey splattered with some of Moran's blood, and some belonging to someone from the team in green.

That completed Kevin Moran's Dublin days.

O'Neill would also call it a day on the half-back line in 1980.

Brogan would be gone in the middle of the field. Up front, Hanahoe and Hickey would be gone. Hickey would be playing rugby in France, in the cities of La Rochelle and Bordeaux, for the next two years. And Doyle would be gone, and on his last day in the Dublin dressing-room, for the Leinster final against Offaly, Bobby Doyle was not counted amongst the eleven substitutes.

In 1980, Keaveney would be a year gone, and his final championship tally in his six-year 'comeback' would be closed off at 12 goals and 142 points in twenty-five games.

On their short journey to the 1979 All-Ireland final, Kerry had scored nine goals against Clare in the Munster semi-final.

Two more followed against Cork in the Munster final.

And they had five goals against Monaghan in their All-Ireland semi-final. Five goals and 14 points, while Dublin scrambled and worked themselves close to the bone to get by Roscommon by one point, one week later in their semi-final.

In the All-Ireland final Dublin were without Jimmy Keaveney, who had been sent off in a tight, two-point Leinster final victory over Offaly. Kerry would be without Páidí Ó Sé by the end when he got his marching orders for pulling Anton O'Toole to the ground when a goal seemed a possibility.

There were three more Kerry goals in the '79 final.

BOOM.

BOOM . . . AND BOOM . . . all over again.

Mick Holden would hold the Bomber to one point, but Sheehy would get two goals on Dave Foran, and in the other corner John Egan would get one on Mick Kennedy.

Two All-Ireland finals.

Eight goals.

Eight goals scored by the Kerry full-forward line.

Kerry 3–13, Dublin 1–8.

The decade had indeed reached a close at high speed.

Heff, mostly, could just sit and watch.

Out on the field, Kerry had an average age that was five years younger than Dublin. Some of the young bucks in Mick O'Dwyer's team were ten years younger than some of Kevin Heffernan's oldest reliables.

In the hut, at times, it was like nobody had ever aged since 1974. Everyone around Heff made the right noises, and said the right things when he probed or charged at them with a fierce demand.

But he could only wonder, was everybody listening?

The young footballers who were sitting in the hut for the first time, they were all ears, naturally. They were all eyes and ears, and, on occasions, and especially up close to the All-Ireland semi-final and final, their eyeballs were springing out of their heads like one of those daft cartoons on the television.

But the rest of them?

The fellas who had been there from the very start in '74, they knew the end was right around the next corner.

They were seeing Heff taking out some of their friends and shooting them. Fellas were being shot, and fellas were talking more and more about finishing up and avoiding a bullet.

There was talk about the end.

For Heff, 1978 and '79 were years he wished to forget.

Both years ended in pain and turmoil, and in 1980, '81 and '82 each summer would come to an even more abrupt halt.

Somehow, and against the natural order of things, Dublin had defeated Eugene McGee's Offaly in the 1979 Leinster final, 1–8 to 0–9, with fourteen men. Keaveney had been sent off before half-time. With thirteen minutes left Dublin were five points behind. Brian Mullins set up Bernard Brogan for the game-winning goal in the final minute.

Dublin's sixth Leinster title in a row was an act of robbery against a younger, stronger team. Eugene McGee had a team that had Dublin on the ropes. Dublin escaped in '79.

They would not escape in 1980.

Heff had a new fight on his hands that was quite personal, though he had nothing whatsoever against Offaly. Heff's father was an Offalyman.

With McGee, it wasn't like it was with O'Dwyer.

Heff could forget about O'Dwyer, half ignore him until it suited him to start thinking about O'Dwyer, and think, 'What the hell was Mick O'Dwyer thinking?'

As Heff watched Dwyer win a third All-Ireland title in 1980, and a fourth in '81, and then get the whole country into a decent-sized frenzy as Kerry prepared to win a splendid and historic five All-Ireland football titles in a row, he could only admire the man.

Besides, Dublin were no longer in Kerry's league.

Part Five

A Long War Lost

'Holden . . . what's your story today?'

KH

Sunday, 31 July 1983

Offaly were one point up.

The first thirty-five minutes of the 1983 Leinster final were almost done. Heff was happy with what he had seen so far. He just wanted his fellas to stay with Offaly, live with them until half-time. And then Heff was going to get it into their heads, good and strong, that they could win the game.

He was fed up losing to Offaly.

More fed up at looking down the sideline at Eugene McGee than ever. In his heart Heff was expecting another defeat.

In his head, however, Heff was busily, crazily, trying to work out how Dublin could beat the All-Ireland champions, and how he could dump McGee's team on its arse. They were serious All-Ireland champions. They'd been lucky stopping Kerry from winning their five in a row the previous September. A little dunt by Séamus Darby into Tommy Doyle's back close to the end of that game had resulted in Offaly's winning goal.

Darby got the ball and smacked it high and diagonally past Charlie Nelligan, who was ever so slightly off his line and out of position.

Heff felt the tiniest amount of sympathy for Mick O'Dwyer. The 'five' would have been historic, and Heff liked watching little pieces of GAA history being made.

But, Heff wasn't going to be fooled by his own likes and dislikes, and he fully accepted that Offaly were damned fine All-Ireland champions, and probably deserving of it as well.

They'd been battling Dublin and Kerry for five years. McGee had built a team that had everything required of All-Ireland champions. Hard as nails at the back. Athletic in the middle of the field. And, amongst his forwards, he had brilliant runners and great ball players, and at least two geniuses. Matt Connor and Johnny Mooney. Once they had proved that they were better than Dublin, Offaly had set their sights on Kerry.

They had done it.

And, in the 1983 Leinster final, McGee had fourteen of his All-Ireland winning team out there on the field.

Beating Offaly seemed unlikely to Heff.

Offaly would fight off everybody in '83 with a real sense of duty. They'd also feel some terror at the very thought of losing the one thing they had spent five years waiting for, working for, four and five days a week. And, as well, defending champions usually had a little bit of extra luck on their side. Heff had always found that out.

Champions made that additional dash of luck for themselves.

A big performance, no dithering in the face of the All-Ireland champions, no fear, nothing stupid, and Dublin might still lose. But they would have learned, and they'd be good and ready for Offaly in 1984.

That was all at the back of Heff's head as he stood in front of the Dublin dug-out and prepared himself for talking to his fellas back in the dressing-room.

One point down was almost perfect.

Barney Rock had the ball.

The red-haired fella was bigger and stronger than people thought. He was also Heff's free-taker. Rock didn't follow through with his kick like Jimmy Keaveney. Rock's kicking action was not poetry in motion. He stabbed at the ball. But Barney had an uncanny accuracy with his kicking, Heff had to give him that.

Barney Rock would kick five points from frees in the 1983 Leinster final. But, with the game into the last two minutes before half-time, he had moved out of the right corner pocket and gathered the ball around the middle. He was moving around the Offaly half of the field.

Liam Currams was unable to get between Rock and the Offaly goal, and Rock threaded a dangerous pass down the middle. The ball broke awkwardly for Anton O'Toole. He failed to gather it cleanly.

But O'Toole fumbled the ball into the path of Joe McNally, the big, overweight former goalkeeper whom Heff thought was interesting. McNally was zippy over the ground and he was hard to tackle. McNally took one quick look up.

Joe McNally then whipped the ball past the Offaly keeper, Martin Furlong. Dublin were two points up.

Offaly hardly blinked.

They immediately worked the ball down to the other end of the field, as composed, cock-sure champions were well able to do, and Brendan Lowry slipped over a point. Heff was now even happier.

He wanted to get into those dressing-rooms.

Ciaran Duff beat his man to a loose ball 40 yards out from the Offaly goal, and slapped in a good centre towards Martin Furlong's small square. O'Toole got one of his long arms up into the air, higher than Offaly full-back Liam O'Connor, and knocked the ball down.

John Caffrey had a golden goal chance. And he drove the ball past Martin Furlong from ten yards out.

Cork, Donegal and Galway were already through to the 1983 All-Ireland semi-finals. All three teams awaited the Leinster final. Cork would be playing the winners. The same as 1974.

In '74, the same three teams got through to the last four of the All-Ireland, and then Dublin joined them. It seemed a lifetime ago to Heff.

He had two men left from that team, however, his first All-Ireland winning team. Brian Mullins and Anton O'Toole. A third, Tommy Drumm, was also part of that seventies extravaganza of Leinster and All-Ireland titles.

*

Tommy Drumm was the man that Kevin Heffernan always thought was too good-looking to be a great Gaelic footballer, though almost everything else about the defender made up for that worry.

He was now Heff's captain.

In the hut, when Heff was finished with his opening, head-turning comments, he was now handing it over to Tommy Drumm to start all of the players talking.

Drumm had just over twelve months left as a Dublin footballer, and at 29 years of age he would tell Heff that he'd had more than enough. Drumm would then set up his new life in Qatar, in the Middle East, where he would happily spend the next four years as a civil engineer and a general manager, stuck a gazillion miles away from a Gaelic football pitch.

There was nothing soft about Drumm, who grew up on Collins Avenue and whose father was a Meathman. And he was extra intelligent. Once those two boxes were ticked by Heff, he didn't have to think very much more about the man.

Heff had named him captain at the start of the year.

When Heff was finished talking in the dressing-room at half-time in the Leinster final, Mullins had a few provocative words to say. Lastly, Tommy Drumm told the team in his sure, clear voice that everyone just needed to keep their heads and play to the final minute.

Surprisingly, the Offaly half-back line remained jittery.

Sean Lowry in the middle would get stronger and stronger as the game entered its final quarter, but Pat Fitzgerald on his right didn't look himself, and the normally implacable Liam Currams didn't seem to be able to get his head into the game at all. Eugene McGee would take his most attack-minded defender off the field nine minutes into the half.

McGee switched three defenders into different position at the same time. Dublin, on the other hand, looked settled and increased their half-time lead to six points within three minutes of the restart. It was 2–7 to 0–7.

Dublin had scored two goals and two points in the six minutes either side of half-time. In the same time frame, Offaly had scored a single point.

Heff realized that Dublin might win.

But, if there was any luck going, McGee would probably get it. He reminded himself of that, cautioned himself about that fact.

P. J. Buckley and O'Toole set up Ciaran Duff for a third great goal chance. Duff wriggled through two defenders, and was about to shoot when he was hauled to the ground. It was a penalty.

Dublin were sure now, perhaps?

Brian Mullins stood five yards behind the ball he had just planted on the ground. He duly struck the ball low and hard to the goalkeeper's left.

Martin Furlong smothered the shot.

Heff steeled himself for the worst.

Offaly would now charge.

Barney Rock shot over two free-kicks from way out, 40 yards, further. But at the other end Johnny Mooney was smothered by three Dublin defenders. It was stupid carry-on, panicky.

It was a penalty to Offaly.

Matt Connor drove his kick badly wide of John O'Leary's left-hand post. A minute later, bizarrely, Connor was also wide with a handy enough free.

At the other end, Rock launched a free from miles out, and over near the sideline, and as usual he had stabbed at the ball, but it floated straight over Martin Furlong's bar.

Then Rock did it again.

Dublin had regained their Leinster title after three years.

Dublin 2–13, Offaly 1–11.

Heff was not a man who cared to spend much time at all in cloud-cuckoo-land. But that's where he was being taken by someone in particular and, the strange thing was, Heff did not seem to mind.

He went to that 'land' with Mick Holden.

Repeatedly.

Heff had decided to be different with his new bunch of footballers.

They were not like the fellas he had almost ten years earlier. They were mostly younger. He knew less about them, and knew less about their capabilities. In the hut, nothing much changed.

However, outside the hut Heff talked to his footballers more.

Holden changed him.

Mick Holden first of all charmed Kevin Heffernan.

To Heff, Holden quickly enough was Jimmy Keaveney and Gay O'Driscoll all rolled up into one funny, gutsy, genuine, tough footballer.

Heff had all the time in the world for the man.

And it showed. Others would see the pair of them and hear them having discussions that entirely belonged in the land of those cuckoos. If one of the fellas in the seventies had ever tried to engage Heff like Mick Holden regularly engaged him, then he would almost certainly have been talking himself into receiving a one-way ticket off the Dublin football team.

But, Holden's guff?

'Holden . . . what's your story today?'

'Why are you late?'

Heff had been on the field in Parnell Park for over twenty minutes on the Saturday morning, when Mick Holden strutted through the gate, and over to Heff.

Holden was nearly always late. He usually told Heff that he had something like twenty-seven or twenty-eight traffic lights to get through on his way to training. And that was true. Of all the players, Holden had the longest journey from Cuala on the southside of the county, the whole way across the city, to reach the gates of Parnell Park just off Collins Avenue.

Sometimes when he arrived he would have a McDonald's bag with him, and he'd dig into his quarter pounder and fries as he togged out in the dressing-room.

'Kevin . . .' Holden began.

He talked loudly in order to attract witnesses. The more people around, the safer a conversation with Heff. That was always Mick Holden's *modus operandi*.

'. . . I was coming across town . . . and I was stopped!

'The guards stopped me, Kevin . . . there was a bank robbery.'

Heff kept listening.

There was no smile on Heff's face.

He was listening, and was more interested in seeing exactly where Mick Holden would go with his ridiculous story.

It amused everyone listening.

Always did.

And it always saved Holden. Everyone got a kick out of having Holden amongst them. The last thing Heff wanted to do was to send Holden home, and tell him to stay there, that he might be in touch with him.

Nobody tested Heff with stories.

Once, one of the new fellas had arrived at training and had given Heff a long story about some injury or other. He then told Heff that he would not be able to get to training the next night. A shorter story this time. But he promised Heff that he would be at the game on the Sunday.

'Why?' asked Heff.

'Sorry, Kevin . . . ?' replied the young footballer.

'Why would you be at the game on Sunday?' asked Heff a second time.

'Because . . . we're playing . . .'

'Why would YOU be there?' said Heff, signing off on the conversation, and walking on.

Mick Holden was near the end of his story.

He had reached the last line.

'And . . . Kevin . . . the guards wanted to have a word with me. They said I looked the spitting image of one of the robbers.'

'Is that right, Mick?'

Heff actually wondered if, on this occasion, there was a half chance that Holden's tale had really happened.

'No . . . it's not true, Kevin . . . But it's better than me telling you I slept it out!'

Mick Holden had been full-back, replacing Seán Doherty, on the Dublin team that caved in to Kerry in the All-Ireland final in 1979. Against Offaly, in '83 in the Leinster final, he was corner-back and keeping a close eye on Heff's new full-back Gerry Hargan.

Holden had been marking Brendan Lowry.

He'd conceded two points to his man.

Hargan, however, had a torrid time of it against Matt Connor. He conceded one goal and seven points, six of the points coming from frees.

It would have been more only for Holden offering protection.

Holden was brave, foolishly brave.

He was a hurler at heart, and on Dublin's GAA fields hurling was a far more dangerous game than football. Holden had first played for the Dublin hurlers. He had first worn the blue jersey as a 14-year-old goalkeeper on the Dublin minor hurling team in 1969. They were beaten by Kilkenny in the Leinster final. Mick's father was a Kilkennyman. And Mick far preferred a game of hurling. It showed when he kicked the ball.

Mick Holden was not Mr Accuracy.

But Mick Holden was in the same category as Heff's mother. Heff told others he would drop the pair of them if he thought it was good for the team.

In 2007, Mick Holden was just 52 years old when he died suddenly.

He was the first of Heff's footballers to go.

The only one of Heff's footballers to go before him, and it broke Kevin Heffernan's heart.

'How could anyone not like Mick Holden?' he had asked.

For Heff loved the man.

34

'Cork's decision to bring us down to Páirc Uí Chaoimh was a good one. Going down there was something that got everyone's full attention.'

KH

Sunday, 28 August 1983

Joe McNally didn't need to lift the ball into his hands.

He let the ball roll ahead.

Glanced up quickly.

Balanced himself, and stroked the ball past the keeper and into the back of the Cork net. It was clinical, and it was perfection.

And, coming at the very end of an All-Ireland semi-final replay, it sealed Dublin's victory with a kiss. McNally's right boot sent Dublin back into the All-Ireland final in some style.

Joe McNally's unorthodox, but excellent late goal sealed a Dublin victory over Cork in the All-Ireland semi-final replay that seemed blessed and delivered to Dublin from start to finish.

Mullins lorded it over every single man who came his way in the middle of the field. He also delicately enough stroked home a penalty to give Dublin a 1–7 to 0–5 lead at half-time.

A Dave Barry penalty eleven minutes later brought Cork back to two points down. Ciaran Duff scored Dublin's second goal.

Barry got through and grabbed his second goal at the other end. Then Barney Rock scored Dublin's third goal. And Joe McNally finished off Cork with a tidy piece of footwork before side-footing Dublin's fourth.

259

Dublin 4–15, Cork 2–10.

Six days earlier in Croke Park, when the two teams met for the first time, Cork had led Dublin by five points with only nine minutes left in the game.

Barney Rock hit over a '50' in the 61st minute.

McNally brought it back to three points when he kicked over a point in the 65th minute.

Thirty seconds from the end a Cork pass went astray in the Dublin defence. Mick Holden picked up the ball and passed it off to Brian Mullins, who seemed astonished to see his Vincents clubmate Ray Hazley a full 80 yards from his full-back line and racing towards the Railway End.

Mullins lobbed the ball through to his left full-back.

Ten minutes earlier, when all looked lost, Rock had drifted out the field and found himself making up numbers in the middle when he came to Heff's attention. Heff let out a roar at him.

Rock ran over to his manager to hear him more clearly. There, he got to hear what Heff was saying all right.

'Will you fucking wake up, Barney . . . we're losing this . . . GET FUCKING BACK IN THERE!'

Ray Hazley tried to find Rock.

Rock slipped inside his marker, Jimmy Kerrigan, as he took Hazley's pass and buried the ball past goalkeeper, Michael Creedon.

Dublin 2–11, Cork 2–11.

Within twenty-four hours Cork had sent a written submission to the GAA's Games Administration Committee seeking to have the replay in Páirc Uí Chaoimh. It was the first time anybody had asked to play an All-Ireland semi-final outside Croke Park in forty-two years.

The Dublin county board asked Heff what he thought.

Heff didn't have to think.

'Let's go down there . . .

'Why not?' he said.

Brian Mullins' Fiat 127 was travelling fairly fast down the Clontarf

Road when he lost control and smashed into a lamppost. It was a Friday night, 27 June 1980. Mullins was 25 years old.

He was at his peak as a footballer.

Before that night and after that night, Brian Mullins was Kevin Heffernan's favourite footballer ever. Bigger and better than Ollie Freaney or anybody Heff had played with on Vincents and Dublin teams in the fifties and sixties. Far bigger and far better than anybody in the seventies.

But that summer night Mullins thought he was going to die. The certain thought was in his head just before he struck the lamppost. And, when he awakened in the back seat of his tiny car, a bone coming through the skin of his right leg, his jaw smashed, eight teeth gone missing, he thought that if he did not move he would die any second when the car burst into flames.

It would be two years before Brian Mullins came back. He had spent much of the time in between trying to talk, to begin with, then trying to walk. He studied in New York, and tended bar in Rosie O'Grady's in the centre of Manhattan.

He came back, and he remained Heff's favourite footballer. But Brian Mullins was never the same footballer again.

He was slower.

Heavier.

He would play for Dublin for three more summers when he came back, and, in the first of those summers, in the All-Ireland semi-final replay in Páirc Uí Chaoimh, in Cork, he gave the most outstanding all-round performance of his life.

If there was one piece of Brian Mullins that Kevin Heffernan favoured over everything else about him, it was the man's heart.

Mullins was more warrior than man.

Though, forever, he would amaze Heff by what he would say and do off the field. Heff was enthralled by his manliness. Also by his courage, and his convictions. At times, Mullins seemed demented.

He was paranoid in the most far-fetched way imaginable when it came to newspapermen. Mullins would have burned all the newspapermen in Ireland even faster than Heff himself.

It came as no great surprise to Heff when he heard that Mullins had given away the last of his All-Ireland medals.

Warriors don't often play with trinkets.

Mullins had given his three All-Ireland medals from the seventies away to the three women in his life, his mother, his wife Helen, and his mother-in-law.

The one All-Ireland medal he won in the eighties was also handed to another on 13 July 1985, after he had watched Bob Geldof's Live Aid concerts at Wembley Stadium in London and the John F. Kennedy Stadium in Philadelphia.

Brian Mullins' fourth, and last, All-Ireland medal, raised £2,500 in the Live Aid auction.

35

'Stop the shots, drive your kickouts as far as you can ... and keep talking to the defenders in front of you.'

KH

Sunday morning, 18 September 1983

Heff told them all to be at the Na Fianna GAA grounds on Mobhi Road by noon. In the hut, the previous Thursday evening, he had been calmer than John O'Leary could remember him being in weeks.

Heff did not raise his voice once.

In the last few days before the 1983 All-Ireland final the last thing Kevin Heffernan wanted to do was to give all the young fellas sitting around him a dose of the heebie-jeebies.

Teams with the heebie-jeebies did not usually win All-Irelands. Teams with the heebie-jeebies nearly always lost them.

Heff was very clear.

He had told them to do everything as normal for the next three days. He told them not to sit around at home, and not to worry. He didn't even want them to think too much about the All-Ireland final.

And Galway?

'We will beat Galway on Sunday,' he asserted.

Dublin teams always beat Galway, or always should beat Galway if everybody does what they are supposed to do, if everybody plays hard from start to finish, if nobody gives Galway an even break, if nobody does anything damned stupid. That was Kevin Heffernan's total view.

He told them they'd meet up at the Na Fianna grounds at noon.

They'd get something to eat together. Maybe take a walk in the Phoenix Park if the day was dry. Then hit into Croke Park.

They'd be out of the place by six o'clock with the Cup.

Heff didn't tell them all that last bit. But that's what he was thinking. There was no possible way that Heff could see Dublin losing to Galway in an All-Ireland final. It would be unnatural.

All wrong.

John O'Leary got more words out of Kevin Heffernan than most footballers. Perhaps it was because he was in goals.

From the very start he thought Heff was God.

And talking to God was big.

It was O'Leary's fourth championship with Heff. The first three ended up with Dublin being swallowed up in Leinster. At last, 1983 was different. Dublin were Leinster champions. Heff could smell an All-Ireland title.

The victory over Cork, in their own backyard, had brought the best out of everyone. Even Kevin Heffernan. John O'Leary had never seen Heff more excited. The trip down to Páirc Uí Chaoimh had given Heff the rare chance to surprise and confound the other team.

John O'Leary had seen another side of Heff.

He'd also got to see Heff as his own personal nurse of sorts. The Dublin goalkeeper had asked for trout for his dinner, when the team settled into their hotel in Blarney the evening before the All-Ireland semi-final replay. Everyone else on the team stuck to their trusted sirloin steaks.

It was a nasty piece of fish.

It zapped its way through John O'Leary's system, and by bed-time he was already throwing up everything and anything that had been in his stomach in the previous twenty-four hours.

When Heff arrived at his bedroom door, to check on his goal-keeper's exact colour of green, he did not come empty-handed.

Heff had a brandy and 7-Up in his hand.

A teetotaller himself, Heff advised his keeper to knock it back.

'Do you think you were to blame for those goals?'

That was the first time Heff had ever spoken to him. It was the spring of 1980, and O'Leary had come through two years with the Dublin minors. He was 19 years old, and had played his first game for Heff's Dublin. It was an O'Byrne Cup game against Kildare.

They had scored two goals.

Heff stood in front of his young keeper and asked him if he thought he was to blame for them. The directness of the question surprised O'Leary.

He was not sure what to say.

But he thought honesty would be best.

'No.'

That was it.

That was his first conversation with Heff.

Paddy Cullen was gone. Finally retired, and Heff had to find a new goalkeeper. He thought John O'Leary was to blame for at least one, maybe both of the Kildare goals. But he didn't need to tell the young fella that.

Three months later, when the championship came around, Heff decided to put one of his defenders in goals. He gave Mick Kennedy the job against Meath, and in the Leinster semi-final Kennedy had conceded a couple of goals against Meath in Navan. Kennedy was no miracle-worker as a goalkeeper. He was meat, potatoes, two veg, and while he definitely would not pull any ball out of the fire, neither would he be some sort of jibbering wreck. Dublin won handily enough, 3–13 to 2–7.

There was no good reason on earth for Kevin Heffernan to decide on taking Mick Kennedy back out of the Dublin goals.

Everybody knew that.

John O'Leary planned to be behind Mick Kennedy, standing up on Hill 16 for the Leinster final against Offaly.

O'Leary was moved down country the summer of his first job, and he found himself working in the Northern Bank in Wexford. He was looking forward to the weekend back home, and going into Croker. On the Friday before the game, however, when O'Leary got home to his parents' house in Balbriggan, he was told a county board official had called.

They wanted him in Parnell Park the next morning.

The next morning, there were three goalkeepers and Mick Kennedy on the field. O'Leary saw that Niall Fitzgerald and Mick O'Brien had also been called in. After training, Heff told the three of them to go down to the other end of the field and start taking kickouts.

John O'Leary knew he had a big, booming kick of the ball. But, in front of Heff, and Donal Colfer and Lorcan Redmond, who were standing there to one side, like God and Two Wise Men, O'Leary didn't do his best.

On his way home, John O'Leary hoped he would be sitting in the Dublin dug-out, with the others, and close to Kevin Heffernan. He'd get to see Heff at work, and that would be amazing in itself.

That was top of his list of hopes on Saturday night.

Heff said he wanted everyone to meet up the next day, two o'clock, at the back of the Nally Stand.

All of the players and substitutes, and those who would not get to tog out, were there at the back of the small stand, but the gates were locked.

Heff was not happy as he went to look for another way into the ground, and brought his team around the back of Hill 16.

The game was an hour away.

John O'Leary sat down in one corner of the dressing-room. They were all there. Some of the greatest footballers that had ever played for Dublin. They all had All-Ireland medals. They were all business, all rigidly locked away in their own routines. John O'Leary was watching them, and did not have a worry in the world.

'You're in today, John!'

Heff had walked over to him and handed him the goalkeeper's jersey. Left it with him without another word, and walked back to the table in the middle of the room and took up the next jersey.

That's all Heff said. It was John O'Leary's second short conversation with Kevin Heffernan, but Heff had spoken and walked away as though the two of them were old friends. He had said it casually, as though they had been talking all of their lives.

The next sentence from Heff was longer.

And more detailed.

'Stop the shots, drive your kickouts as far as you can . . . and keep talking to the defenders in front of you.'

It was a Leinster final.

Dublin had won the previous six Leinster finals with Paddy Cullen in goals. Dublin would lose the 1980 Leinster final.

They'd lose 1–10 to 1–8.

Matt Connor would send one of his very special pile-drivers past John O'Leary. Offaly would win and they would win three Leinster finals in a row, in 1980, '81 and '82.

But Heff had never blamed John O'Leary for anything ever again.

'There were only twelve of them, I was proud of every single one of them . . . and the three fellas sent off.'

KH

Sunday afternoon, 18 September 1983

John O'Leary looked down the field. There seemed to be twice as many maroon jerseys as blue jerseys. In front of him, as he waited to take his kickout, were eleven Dublin footballers.

Looking for them was one problem.

Finding them on a rainy, soggy day in Croke Park, with the wind having the final say in the direction of every second ball, seemed all but impossible. Getting the ball down the field, however, was his first great difficulty. The same wind was close to a full-blooded gale.

And it was blowing straight into Croke Park's Railway End, and into John O'Leary's face.

It was six minutes into the second half of the All-Ireland final.

Dublin had led 1–5 to 0–2 at half-time.

But, amazingly, Galway had staggered at the start of the second half. Just like Dublin had at the very start of the game. It was one thing having a wind at a team's back, but a wind like this con-founded wind? It was capable of fooling anybody, in any colour of jersey, at any time.

A Barney Rock free had increased Dublin's lead, and then Joe McNally got another point.

There were eight points in it.

Heff had told them at half-time to hold on to the ball, and not to give it up to Galway or the wind. He wanted no risky passes. Three times he told them.

'Nothing risky out there . . . you hear me?'

If there was one message Kevin Heffernan wanted to get into the heads of his team, it was that.

There had been a craziness to the first half.

There had been scrapping and wild tackling in the atrocious, far-fetched conditions. Then the digging started, off the ball to begin with. Tempers had been let loose, and were on the rampage long before half-time. The referee, John Gough, had never known a game like it.

No referee had ever been prepared for a game like the 1983 All-Ireland football final. Gough started booking and sending off people. It was mayhem.

In the tunnel at half-time something else had happened.

John O'Leary had been first back to the dressing-room. Dublin had been defending the Canal End goal and when the half-time whistle blew, O'Leary had run off the field at a decent pace. He was the first man back in the room.

Nobody else arrived for a long time.

It felt like a minute.

It may have been only half that long, but O'Leary heard shouting and a whole clatter of yelling as the rest of the team came in through the doorway.

Someone had hit Brian Talty.

The Galway midfielder had gone down in the first half and Brian Mullins had been accused of putting him down.

Mullins was sent off.

Someone in a blue jersey put Talty down in the tunnel as well.

O'Leary was told that, and he heard other bits and pieces of what had happened in the tunnel. Seemed there were a few punches thrown.

Heff had immediately come in and quietened everyone down. He wanted lads to sit down, and clear their heads. He wanted them to listen. He had to roar at the top of his voice to get control of the room, but when Heff had everyone's attention he spelled it out.

Slowly.

He needed calmness.

Dublin were a man down. The referee had sent off Mullins after 27 minutes. John Gough's patience was up. Three minutes later he sent off Ray Hazley and Tomás Tierney, who were involved in one of a dozen or so scuffles that had presented themselves in the first half an hour.

Galway had the extra man, and Heff was telling everyone they needed to funnel back into their own half of the field every time Galway got possession in the second half.

Everyone needed to work harder than they had ever worked in their lives on a football field. They had thirty-five minutes to win an All-Ireland.

To do that, they had to hold the ball.

No risky passes.

He didn't want any ball lost.

He didn't want any ball turned over.

Every ball had to be used, the full length of the field, and every ball had to be a score or it had to go wide.

Either way, Dublin could regroup.

Everyone could get back behind the ball, everyone except Joe McNally. Heff wanted him to stay up front. He needed someone staying up there. And McNally, with the size of him, was the best man on the team at holding on to a ball and protecting it from defenders and all types of nosy parkers.

'Everyone else . . . BACK

'. . . YOU HEAR ME?

'BACK . . . !'

And he told them to counter-attack.

When Dublin got the ball, Heff wanted the ball worked forward fast. He wanted the ball up to Joe McNally. Fast, fast, fast. And he wanted men to support him. He kept telling the fellas that Galway had only one extra man. There weren't four or five extra Galway men out there.

'What's one man?' he asked.

'One man won't win this for them!' insisted Heff.

Five minutes into the second half, between Barney Rock's free-kick and the Joe McNally point that left Dublin eight points clear, Ciaran Duff would become the third Dublin footballer to be tossed out of the All-Ireland final by John Gough. His man, Pat O'Neill, had fallen on the ground. Duff foolishly tipped the side of O'Neill's head with the point of his boot. The referee needed to try, somehow, to control the rest of the game.

Duff was off as well.

Dublin were two men down.

John O'Leary was standing over his goalkick.

He knew it was going to be the longest half an hour he had ever spent on a football field.

In the next four minutes he would take another three goalkicks, and that's how it would be for the remainder of the All-Ireland final. Galway were panicking out the field. They were lashing the ball. Their full-forward line had no chance of winning any ball that was sent in. Each time, wild and hopeless kicks towards the Railway End goalmouth had scampered over John O'Leary's end-line.

Galway needed a goal to begin with.

Heff knew that might cool down their heads.

A goal was his biggest fear.

There were only twenty-five minutes left. Galway had missed with two good goal chances in the first half. Gay McManus had been put through by Val Daly and didn't keep his head. A few minutes after that, Heff saw Barney Rock, of all people, go down on a point-blank shot from Daly and save a certain goal.

But Heff knew Dublin should be leading by more.

McNally should have got them a second goal, instead of a point. Tommy Drumm's pass inside had been inch perfect and McNally was inside the Galway full-back line that had been blown down the field by the wind. He had only their keeper, Padraig Coyne, to beat. But McNally didn't keep his head either. Or else he had been too cool in trying to lob the ball over Coyne's head.

He hit the ball hard into the wind and it ended up going a foot over the crossbar. Heff watched Galway score three points in the next six minutes. Galway also got their goal.

A cross from Brian O'Donnell dribbled across the Dublin small square and Stephen Joyce was fastest off the mark to plant it in the net. On Heff's watch there were nineteen minutes left in the game.

There were only three points in it.

Dublin 1–8, Galway 1–5.

Barry Brennan missed a good chance of a point for Galway. Their third and last substitute, John Tobin, who was a veteran of Galway's defeat by Dublin in 1974, was also wide when he should have scored.

Galway were back wasting chances again.

And they were still kicking the ball wildly, and too long. When more points did not follow Stephen Joyce's goal, the Galway midfielders and defenders had officially lost the plot.

They were playing like a team that was down to its last two or three minutes. But there were twelve or thirteen minutes still to go on Heff's watch.

Michael Brennan kicked a point for Galway.

Seamus McHugh kicked one.

Barry Brennan hit over a free.

Win or lose, Heff was proud of them.

All of them. They were all working harder than he could ever have demanded any group of footballers to work.

All of them, including Joe McNally, all alone at the other end of the field. McNally, who'd had his 19th birthday four days earlier. Four months earlier, nobody even knew he was a footballer.

He was a goalkeeper.

He looked too fat to be a footballer, and certainly one look at him and most football managers would have concluded that he was not made to be a county man.

Certainly not out the field.

In fact, Joe McNally was the Dublin minor goalkeeper the first time Kevin Heffernan laid eyes on him. McNally played for the county minors in 1980 and '81, and even as a minor he managed to fill a good deal of the space between his two posts. Heff gave the boy his chance on 15 March when Dublin played Armagh in the National League. John O'Leary was out injured.

McNally did OK.

He didn't make any mistakes.

Before and after training in Parnell Park, however, Heff kept seeing his sub keeper do some brilliant things whenever he was playing around with the ball. And Heff finally decided to find out something about the extra large boy.

Next time he picked McNally, three months later, he named him at full-forward on the team to play Meath in the first round of the championship. It was a brazen decision by Heff.

And, at the time, it seemed far more brazen than brilliant.

Joe McNally did less than OK. He found Meath full-back, Mick Lyons, impossible, and his only major-sized contribution to the whole afternoon was when he belted the ball across the Meath goalmouth in the middle of the first half and had his shot bounce off the chest of Lyons' corner-back, Phil Smith.

The ball inched over the goal-line.

It was a draw match.

Heff dropped McNally for the replay that Dublin won by two points after thirty minutes of extra-time. He didn't pick him for the Leinster semi-final against Louth either. But against Offaly in the Leinster final, Heff wanted to have another look.

And, whenever Kevin Heffernan wanted to have a proper look at a footballer, then he didn't beat around the bush. McNally was in against the Offaly full-back line, the tightest and meanest full-back line in the country. And that full-back line stood between McNally and the Offaly keeper Martin Furlong, a grizzled relic from a generation past who usually put more fear into forwards than all three men in his own full-back line put together.

If McNally did well, great.

If Joe McNally did not do well, Heff would most likely have left him back sitting on the substitutes' bench, having to patiently wait for John O'Leary to one day retire.

Against Offaly, he scored one goal and two points.

Everybody who was wondering what on earth Kevin Heffernan had been thinking, quickly got on the same wavelength as the Dublin manager that afternoon in Croke Park in July.

Dublin would score two more precious points before the end of the 1983 All-Ireland final. Joe McNally would play a part in both.

From nowhere, Heff had found Dublin a new full-back, and at the other end of the field a target man who surprised everybody. Dublin had also come from nowhere for the second time in Kevin Heffernan's life and amazed the whole country.

For a third time, Heff had also dug into the past.

In 1963 Heff had had a word with Des Ferguson about coming back and helping him out at full-forward. In 1974 he had the self-same conversation with Jimmy Keaveney. The No.14 shirt was once again vacant. In '83 the same chat over the same jersey was re-enacted with Anton O'Toole before he had time to tell Heff that he might be retiring with the rest of the seventies gang.

Dublin 1–10, Galway 1–8.

From zero to All-Ireland champions.

Barney Rock scored from six free-kicks, in true Jimmy Keaveney style. Rock also scored the most sensational, uncanny goal seen in Croke Park in five years. It was styled more on Mikey Sheehy's wizardry than Keaveney's, and Sheehy's remarkable goal scored against Paddy Cullen in the '78 final.

This time around, twelve minutes into the game, Galway keeper Padraig Coyne was off his line. He had come out to the edge of his large square to take a kickout and give it his all into the wind, but in the wretched underfoot conditions Coyne had failed to get his boot through the ball.

It went 35 yards. Straight into the hands of Barney Rock.

Rock didn't hesitate.

One look, and he unleashed a lob of sheer perfection that dipped under the Galway crossbar just before a horrified Coyne arrived back on his line.

No doubt, that act of genius saved Dublin. Rock's genius and

Heff's brilliance had combined to make Dublin All-Ireland champs again.

Heff was closer to Rock than any Galway player.

He was on the field for the goal.

He had raced in to tend to Joe McNally who was sprawled out on the ground after one of the more minor scuffles of the afternoon.

John Gough was ordering Heff off the field.

But, at the same time, the referee had directed Coyne to take the free, and he had turned his attention on the Dublin manager when Rock received the ball. Heff was refusing to take very much direction from the Antrim referee.

His insistence on acting like a fiercely stubborn Florence Nightingale would land Heff in hot water. It was, in fact, the second time in nine months that Heff had turned up on the field un-announced and definitely uninvited.

In December, after Dublin had travelled down to Tralee and prised a one-point victory out of a grey, uninspiring afternoon, Heff had been called before the Games Administration Committee in Croke Park and received a caution for his behaviour. On that occasion Heff had rushed in to see to Charlie Redmond.

More Florence.

The young Dublin forward had been knocked to the ground by Johnny Mulvihill. The few reporters in the ground agreed that when Heff showed up his intentions were not entirely of the nursing kind, and that there was a 'scuffle'. Heff told the bosses in Croke Park that he was looking to get to his player on the ground.

Mulvihill was in his way.

They asked him how Mulvihill had fallen over. Dilly-dallying with the GAA's many disciplinary committees had never interested Kevin Heffernan, not as a player, and never for even half a minute as a manager.

'How had the Kerryman fallen over?' Heff considered to himself.

Heff informed them that it had taken very little.

37

'We were All-Ireland champions . . . they couldn't take that from us.'

KH

Monday, 19 September 1983

The luncheon for the Dublin and Galway teams in Jurys Hotel in Ballsbridge was not going all that well, it had to be said.

Traditionally, as touchy-feely situations go, the GAA normally found the luncheon for the previous day's winners and losers to be a two or three out of ten.

On this occasion, the luncheon was not quite reaching the one mark. Before it was over, both teams were asked to get someone up to sing a song. There was nothing strange in that, it was another long established, and usually hopeless, effort at reaching some primary level of cosiness.

Dublin were first up.

Joe McNally was up on his feet.

Admittedly, he quickly showed everyone amongst the three hundred guests gathered in the hotel ballroom that he had a voice, in addition to having the daintiest feet for such a big man. McNally aired 'The Fields of Athenry'.

Tommy Drumm thought it a good choice.

He felt it might help.

An appropriate note, considered the Dublin captain, with which to end the shouting and roaring and barracking that had immediately followed Dublin's victory.

It was not.

*

Kevin Heffernan, for starters, had never apologized for anything he had ever seen or done on a football field. By himself, or by one of his own, never.

The game was played by men.

Often, and sometimes far too regularly, men on every football team got into a rage and made themselves look right eejits, or raving lunatics.

And when the game was over men shook hands.

Sooner or later.

Sometime.

Eventually, nearly everyone forgave one another.

That was Gaelic football. The game that Heff loved more than any other game in the world, and after a game he never looked for anyone to say sorry to him. Never. And he didn't say sorry either.

Sorry was for softies.

Weaklings.

And if a man was to apologize for his actions he was completely undermining his own standing the next time he had to play against the same crowd.

If everyone was apologizing, nothing would ever get done. There'd be no games played. So, in Heff's book, unless somebody was killed, all apologies were out.

Out of the question.

Galway claimed that Brian Talty had not been able to play in the second half of the All-Ireland final because of the blow he had taken in the tunnel at half-time. Their chairman, Mattie Potter, had his mind on an official protest to the GAA's Central Council. Potter was a very unhappy man.

'It is a sad day for Gaelic football,' he announced. 'We came to play football, but Dublin wanted to win by hook or by crook . . . and they did.'

Dublin chairman Don Cotter was more relaxed. And he found time to add up all of the free-kicks in the game. Galway had received twenty frees. Dublin had received twenty-six. 'I don't understand how we can be accused of rough play,' added Cotter.

Heff, like everyone else in both camps, agreed that it had been a terrible game of football. But Heff had never witnessed a team display of greater courage.

'No team has ever fought as hard.'

The GAA was looking for big apologies.

The president of the association, Paddy Buggy, a Kilkennyman, someone who didn't shy away on the field as a hurler himself, spoke to both teams at their silent luncheon. He didn't spare them.

'The game brought no credit to the association,' declared Buggy. That meant, without doubt, that trouble was about to quickly brew.

It was trouble with an axe.

Within two weeks, after asking Heff and his footballers, and a smaller-sized gang of Galway footballers to come to Croke Park to explain themselves, the axe fell mainly on Dublin.

Ciaran Duff got twelve months.

Ray Hazley and Tomás Tierney got one month each.

The Galway centre-back, Peter Lee, even though he did not get chucked out of the All-Ireland final like the others, also got one month.

Brian Mullins got two months for striking an opponent, but the GAA was not finished at that. Mullins also got three months for running on to the field in the second half. Two months for allegedly striking someone, but three months for walking on to the field and not going near anybody.

'He discredited the association by his unauthorized incursion on to the field after being sent off,' ruled the GAA's top bosses.

And they threw the same line at Heff.

He got three months as well.

Heff and his three footballers were given seven days to lodge an appeal against their suspensions. The GAA held its breath.

But Heff had long before decided to get on with his life.

No apologies.

No excuses.

And no stammering and fumbling around trying to get some GAA committee to go lightly on him. That was worse than an apology in Heff's head.

No hiding either.

Heff would publicly dare the GAA to drop him into more hot water, all over again, by showing up and being seen at Dublin's next game.

And Brian Mullins, like his Vincents and Dublin manager, would line out one month later for Leitrim in the New York football championship and risk a further six-month ban.

Six days after getting his three months, Heff travelled with his team to Navan for the opening game in the National League.

Tony Hanahoe was in charge of Dublin team affairs.

Heff, under the rules of his suspension, was supposed to have absolutely nothing to do with anybody in a blue jersey, not during the week, and most definitely not on the Sunday of the game.

When the time came for Dublin to leave their dressing-room they were clapped on to the field by Seán Boylan and his Meath team.

It was a mild, dry Sunday afternoon, and there were 12,000 people in Páirc Tailteann to see how the All-Ireland champions were after their celebrations, and to see how hard and how often Meath lads would hit them.

'Let's clap them on to the field . . . we have to do that,' midfielder Gerry McEntee had told everyone around him in the Meath dressing-room, '. . . and then let's kick the shite out of them!'

When Heff walked out of the dressing-room, where he was not supposed to be in the first place, he was greeted by an old opponent.

Brian Smyth was Meath chairman, and he was also a man who had captained Meath to their first All-Ireland title in 1949, when Kevin Heffernan was 20 years old and just about finding his feet on the Dublin team that would have to wait nine years for an All-Ireland of their own.

Smyth kindly explained to Heff that it would probably not be wise for him to go into the Dublin dug-out. Smyth added that he had a better seat for him.

Brian Smyth had ordered a chair on the sideline especially for Kevin Heffernan.

'What are you doing?' asked one of Smyth's underlings.

'I'm getting a chair!' Smyth replied.

'For Heffernan?'

'Do you think,' stated Smyth, '. . . do you think I'm going to tell Kevin Heffernan he can't stand or sit on this sideline?'

Smyth had another question.

'That I'm going to tell Kevin Heffernan to go home?'

The Meath chairman had an answer to both.

'I'll do no such thing!'

38

'I'm told Tyrone are warming up in front of the Hill . . . I want you all to go out there . . . go down to the Hill, and show them that that's ours!'

KH

Sunday, 19 August 1984

Des Ferguson had handed over the reins of the Meath team to Seán Boylan. Nobody else wanted them. All of Snitchie's great knowledge and massive enthusiasm for doing things right, which normally meant doing things the very successful Vincents way, was lost on a Meath dressing-room that was too damned dispirited and simply feeling sorry for itself.

The place was also usually half-empty on Tuesday and Thursday evenings, or any evening when Ferguson called training. The disrespect shown to one of the game's true heroes, and the general levels of ignorance in the dressing-room, were fairly astonishing. Heff wouldn't have hung around if he was there. Snitchie gave it two years.

In the late autumn in 1982, the Meath chairman Brian Smyth told Boylan the job was his, if he wanted it. Though Smyth told the herbalist, who had also been a Meath hurler, and who lived close to him in Dunboyne village, that it might not be such a good idea to take it.

Seán Boylan said he'd do it.

But he also said that if anyone better came around the corner and wanted the job, they could have it instead.

In the summer of '83, in his first championship, Boylan's team met future All-Ireland champions Dublin in the first round. There were barely over 20,000 people in Croke Park. Meath led 0–5 to 0–3 at half-time. Dublin scored one lucky goal, and then Meath scored an own goal. The game ended a draw, 2–8 each.

In the replay Dublin scored two luckier goals. They led 2–6 to 0–4 at half-time. It was 2–8 to 0–14 at full-time. After thirty minutes extra-time, Dublin won 3–9 to 0–16. There were a few more people, 24,303 in total, in the ground.

When the two teams met a third time, in the Leinster final in '84, twice as many people paid into Croke Park, 56,051. Meath started without Mick Lyons, who had broken his thumb two weeks before. This time Dublin scored two great goals in the first half. Meath missed a penalty. Dublin had John Caffrey sent off. They led 2–3 to 1–4 at half-time. They won 2–10 to 1–9.

Heff told reporters afterwards that the game came down to 'courage and strength' and that Dublin had enough in both departments.

Heff did not know that Meath were also filling up fast in both of those departments, thanks to their new manager, whom everyone had doubted, but who was personally visiting the homes of every one of his footballers every second week and making sure that they were filling up on self-belief and ambition, in addition to filling up on courage and determination.

Boylan, first of all, had breathed life back into the carcass of the Meath team that had been laid low by Heff in the middle of the seventies. Joe Cassells, Gerry McEntee and Colm O'Rourke were giving it another go, and Seán Boylan was also smartly picking and choosing from clubs all over the country, big and small, footballers and even some men who were Meath hurlers.

Meath would find themselves sitting out the summer of '85 after walking into Tullamore with its chin out, and being k.o.'d by Laois.

But Seán Boylan had a team almost built, and when he finally found himself a free-taker in the summer of '86 Dublin were soon to be in a considerable amount of trouble. Brian Stafford could hit them over the bar as often as Jimmy Keaveney or Barney Rock, all day long.

*

In the summer of '84, Heff had less than eighteen months left in his life as Dublin manager. And, he didn't know it, but he would time his exit to perfection. Six months after Heff left, Dublin would lose their Leinster title to Meath.

Dublin would lose their Leinster title in '86, and Dublin would lose to Meath five summers out of the next six.

Summers that had no championship backdoors.

Summers that were guillotined.

But, in 1984, Dublin were still Leinster champions.

Kerry, Galway and Tyrone were in the last four, and Dublin joined them. Dublin and Kerry were in opposing semi-finals.

Heff was ready to resume the longest war, and the greatest war of his football life. Him and Dwyer.

Him and Kerry.

First there was Tyrone.

They were playing in an All-Ireland semi-final for the first time, but when Croke Park's chief steward, CIÉ bus inspector John Leonard, knocked on their dressing-room door and told them 'two minutes' he was immediately informed that the Ulster champions were ready to go.

Leonard was happily surprised.

He thought getting them out would be like pulling teeth.

'Out you go, then!' said Leonard.

As Heff prepared to have a last word with his fellas in their dressing-room, before sending them on their way, he was told that Tyrone were up to some mischief.

'They're acting the bollox, Heff . . . they're down at our end.

'They're warming up in front of the Hill.'

Heff nodded his head.

He was ready to say what he had to say, and this late piece of news would help. The one thing Heff hated more than softies and weaklings on a football field were bullies. He's met enough of them as a player himself.

He'd seen too many of them.

And he thought they were a waste of time. Mainly because they were cowards. Nearly every bully he ever met or viewed from the sideline was a complete coward at heart. The team were on their feet and forming a circle around him.

'Tyrone coming down here . . . and thinking they'll be bullies?'

Heff said his piece.

He knew it would cause a ruckus, and have everybody talking and giving out for days, but he knew what he wanted to say at the very end of his piece.

'To hell with them!'

He informed his players that Tyrone were on the field, and that they were down at the Hill 16 end.

'That's our end of this ground!' stated Heff.

He looked around him.

Anything he asked them to do, they would now do.

'I want you all to go out there,' roared Heff.

'Go down to the hill, and show them that that's ours!'

Everyone obeyed.

Apart from Mick Holden.

A specialist in innocent mischief, but someone who was also fully prepared to go to any war he was asked to attend by Kevin Heffernan, Mick Holden knew cuckoo orders when he heard them.

The Dublin team battered their way out of the dressing-room and charged down the corridor and out on to the field. They did not stop running until they arrived at the hill. John O'Leary found Tyrone keeper, Adrian Skelton on the goal-line.

O'Leary joined him.

There were nearly fifty players racing about and milling around, and taking pot shots at both goalkeepers. It was a blitzkrieg, and a bit dangerous. Gerry Hargan took a belt of one ball flush on the face and needed some attention.

Everyone else was racing around and waiting for a row to happen.

Meanwhile, back at the Dublin dug-out, Mick Holden was standing with a bottle of water in his hand. Heff arrived and asked him what was wrong.

'Thirsty, Kevin . . . need some of this water.'

Holden's biggest worry that day had been which boots to wear. The Dublin team had been receiving free gear from Puma and Adidas throughout the summer, and both had given boots to the whole squad. Holden was in a quandary. Some players decided on Puma. Others thought Adidas were that bit lighter.

'Why offend anyone?' thought Holden.

As he swigged some more water and spat it out on the ground, Mick Holden stood, one foot in a Puma boot, one foot in an Adidas boot.

It made sense.

What was happening down at Hill 16 made no sense to Mick Holden at all. At times, he thought to himself, Heff was half mad.

When the game finally got under way, Tyrone froze in front of the All-Ireland champions. It took them 28 minutes to get their first score, despite the almost complete dominance of Eugene McKenna in the middle of the field. And that included Frank McGuigan.

McGuigan had become the talk of the championship. In the Ulster final he had scored 11 points against Armagh. All from play, five with each foot, and one with a fist. Gerry Hargan would hold him to just four points, three of them from open play. Rock scored Dublin's first goal. Dublin led 1–6 to 0–2 at half-time. McNally got the second. Afterwards, Tyrone called Dublin childish.

Nobody in Dublin apologized.

Dublin 2–11, Tyrone 0–8.

Mick O'Dwyer had an old team on his hands.

It wasn't like the last time he had gone head-to-head with Kevin Heffernan on the sideline. Then, Heff had elders. Dwyer had youth.

The roles of the two managers with their teams had also reversed. This time it was Dwyer's turn to manage with subtlety and finesse.

In the 1984 All-Ireland final Kerry would have a small handful of boys on a man's team. Tom Spillane, Pat's young brother, was in the centre of the defence, all arms and legs, and raw athleticism.

Tom's minor midfield partner from 1980, Ambrose O'Donovan, was wearing the No.9 jersey alongside Jack O'Shea. In the forward line, Dwyer was trying John Kennedy and Willie Maher out for size.

Ogie Moran and John Egan had been subs in the Munster final, but otherwise the changes from the late seventies were minimal. Dwyer was telling everyone in his dressing-room that it was time to give it another run. Maybe not a five-in-a-row of All-Irelands, but a run nevertheless.

Kerry had been caught in the final minute by a Séamus Darby goal that denied them their 'five' in '82. In the summer of '83, a Tadhg Murphy goal also in the last minute had left them for dead against Cork in Munster.

'Let's get the circus back on the road!'

That was Dwyer's message in 1984.

The circus officially kicked off in Killarney. Kerry were eight points ahead of Cork at half-time, and slowed to a canter in the second half and won by seven. In the All-Ireland semi-final the circus was in full colour and swinging with rich entertainment. Kerry had 11 points to spare over Galway. Sheehy, Liston and Egan were back in the full-forward line.

Just like the old days.

Sheehy scored a goal and four points.

Egan got a goal and two points.

Heff, from the very beginning of the year, had to push and shove to make sure that everyone in his dressing-room knew what they were supposed to be doing. It was so unlike the seventies.

The hut remained the hut.

Everyone in the hut still said what Heff wished to hear. And they were All-Ireland champions, like his fellas in '74, but there the similarities ended.

When news had come through at the beginning of 1984 that Heff might be gone, there was no shock or horror. No feeling amongst the squad that the world was ending, and Heff was getting out first.

That's how it was in '76 when Heff told them he had to go.

Eight years later, when it was announced at the beginning of January that Kevin Heffernan was wanted on an ESB contract in Sudan, and that he was possibly going to be away for nine months, nobody looked like they were about to faint.

In April, Dublin took the hour's journey to Mullingar to play Westmeath in the first round of the Centenary Cup, the special knockout competition that the GAA had introduced to celebrate its first 100 years. For All-Ireland champions, it should have been a doddle. Dublin scored five points.

Westmeath won by two.

When Heff came into the dressing-room to speak with his team, something unusual happened.

He left the door open behind him.

Usually, Heff would announce his arrival with a slammed door. It was one way of shutting everybody up, and getting them to listen. This time the door remained opened wide.

They could all hear shrieking and wild laughter coming from the dressing-room down the corridor. Heff had received more than an earful of the Westmeath celebrations as he talked over the game quickly outside the room with Donal Colfer and Lorcan Redmond. He thought it would be no harm for his players to also hear.

Two months earlier, the big shots sitting all around him had been relegated from Division One of the National League.

Heff didn't say anything.

He stood there glaring.

He just wanted the big shots to know that they had become a laughing matter to some people.

39

'If you don't let in any goals on Sunday . . . we'll win.'

KH

Sunday, 23 September 1984

Heff made his promise to John O'Leary.

No goals.

And Dublin will still be All-Ireland champions.

Kerry 0–14, Dublin 1–6.

O'Leary had kept his part of the bargain, and only found himself needing to be in any way elasticated midway through the first half when Ger Power came in from the right at the Railway End. Power's shot was stopped on the line. Gerry Hargan then swept it out of danger.

Also in the first half, Jack O'Shea worked another opening for a Kerry goal, but he decided at the last second to pass the ball off to Power, and a decent opportunity of really testing O'Leary went astray.

There was no Mikey Sheehy on the field. An Achilles tendon injury had sidelined him for a fortnight, and Dwyer had replaced him with Power.

John O'Leary's day was quieter without having Sheehy around.

But the 1984 All-Ireland final was one-sided. Worse than that, it slightly bored neutral spectators in the packed ground.

The war?

The two best teams in the country, the two teams that had won nine of the previous ten All-Ireland football finals between them.

The war was not resumed. Instead, Kerry's twenty-eighth All-Ireland title, and their sixth All-Ireland since 1975, had been a cakewalk. It left Heff more embarrassed than angry. As usual, when Kerry smashed his dreams with the heel of a big boot, he was more angry with himself.

Dublin had been timid.

He asked himself how reigning All-Ireland champions could, actually, be timid. And he had to wonder if his own state of alarmingly heightened respect for Kerry, which bordered on fear, had spread through his young team.

There had only been one booking in the entire seventy minutes, for Chrissakes! That was Tommy Doyle, one of theirs, and it had been for nothing much whatsoever. Not one Dublin footballer was booked by the referee.

It didn't make sense.

His half-forward line had performed like three blind mice. Duff didn't cause Doyle any problems. Tom Spillane suffocated Tommy Conroy, who was supposed to be Heff's playmaker-in-chief. Rock had scored one goal and five points, but, in open play, he too was kept well in check by Mick Spillane.

They were on top in nearly every square foot of the ground, but Kerry were taking their time. Ten minutes before half-time Brian Mullins gifted them a point, after fielding the ball in his own square and then delivering it straight to Pat Spillane. That made it 0–5 to 0–2.

Conroy kicked Dublin's other point before half-time. It was 0–7 to 0–3 at that stage. With the wind at their backs, Dublin also had a costly sum of three bad wides just before the break. First from Jim Ronayne, and then from Anton O'Toole. Rock was wide with the third from a '50'.

Heff had started with five forwards.

He had John Kearns in the No.13 shirt, but had ordered him to stick around the middle of the field as a third man.

It was a numbers game that was backfiring on Heff. His half-forward line was virtually missing in action, apart from Rock doing his kicking duties with two good frees and two '50's. Inside, O'Toole was coming out the field to get away from Sean Walsh and win some ball. But, one on one in the full-forward line Walsh was the sheriff on duty the whole day.

That left Joe McNally v Páidí Ó Sé.

It was Boy v Man in the first thirty-five minutes.

In truth, it was just such a match-up before the game even started, as when Páidí waited for McNally to join him in the corner of the field between the Canal End and the Cusack Stand he noticed that his opponent was not slowing down his trot as he zeroed in towards his spot.

Páidí had his hand extended towards McNally.

Joe McNally revved up in the last yard or two and smacked into Páidí with his massive right shoulder.

Páidí landed on his rear end.

It was Páidí Ó Sé's first time to play right corner-back for Kerry in an All-Ireland final. New surroundings. And all of a sudden he was on his arse, wondering what had happened.

Retribution was required. Though not instantly, thought Páidí. He got back up on to his feet, and wiped his hands. The national anthem was about to start. And when it did everybody in the ground would be turned to the Tricolour at the opposite end of the ground and above the Nally Stand, their heads in the air, their chins raised, and some people on the field, the linesmen and even one or two of the umpires, would be in full voice.

Everyone was fifteen seconds into the national anthem when Páidí landed a fair kick up Joe McNally's backside.

McNally staggered forward, and turned and looked behind.

He did nothing about it.

Neither did Joe McNally get a score before Heff decided midway through the second half to take him off the field.

Heff headed to the dressing-room with a grave uncertainty of where to start in putting things to right, and where to end. To begin with, he needed to lift them out of it. After that he'd make up his mind.

It was a game he had felt so good about.

He had never feared Kerry less. He still worried about them

every day before the All-Ireland final, but Heff had been so strong in his own mind about both teams' strengths and weaknesses.

He had decided the game would probably turn on a goal.

Winning or losing might come down to a flick of a switch. One opening, one shot. He had fancied McNally to maybe beat Páidí. Or Tommy Conroy to sail inside the youngest Spillane in the centre of the Kerry defence, and cut open the Kerry defence as quickly as he occasionally cut open the Dublin defence in Parnell Park when he took off on one of his spiralling runs.

When the newspapermen came to see Dublin training the week before the final, Heff had been welcoming as usual. It was one night a year in which he knew he had to offer it up. Say hello, say goodbye, and say sweet damn all in between.

Heff had talked to them that evening, however.

He had talked about Dublin and Kerry playing in five finals in ten years, and re-setting standards for everyone else that were higher than ever before.

He talked about himself and Dwyer just a little as well.

'Someone must set standards, and if Mick O'Dwyer and I are doing that, then I believe that is good for the game,' he had asserted.

They knew very well how he felt about Kerry.

'Are you worried, Kevin?' they had asked.

Heff, whenever he saw that question rear its head, had always disappointed the small herd of newspapermen in years gone by.

On this occasion, he should have remained dumb, monosyllabic at a push.

However, for some damned reason, in comparison with his responses over former summers, Heff had almost gushed.

'There's never a match you're not worried about!

'Of course we have worries meeting Kerry,' he continued, '. . . but Dublin are a good team. Let me put it this way . . .

'We have players on our side that I would not want to see opposing me.'

They'd even asked him for a forecast.

And he'd responded.

'No forecast ... except this ... we'll have a good All-Ireland final.'

Heff had to wonder if he had given his own fellas, as well as the newspapermen, a bum steer.

Kerry went five points up four minutes into the second half.

John Kennedy hit a breathtaking pass across the field, finding the Bomber on the far right wing. He looked up and pounded the ball over the bar from 40 yards out. Kerry got a '50'.

Kennedy made it a six-point lead.

There were signs, however, that Dublin were settling, and starting to look like All-Ireland champions. Mick Holden and Mick Kennedy were scooping up possession in each corner of the defence. In front of the pair of them, P. J. Buckley and Pat Canavan were beginning to get forward.

Without further warning, in the 43rd minute, Duff found Conroy. He crossed to Rock, who controlled the ball with one hand and beat Charlie Nelligan with a low, hard drive from ten yards.

Goal.

The goal left it 0–9 to 1–3.

Heff expected the goal to summon forth a super-human effort.

Kerry scored five more points.

Dublin got three.

Heff wondered, deep down, had they given up before they had started.

Ambrose O'Donovan walked up the steps of the Hogan Stand.

Sam Maguire awaited him. The Cup was decked out on either side, its handles covered in bountiful green and gold ribbons. Heff stood with his players in the middle of the field.

It was as hard as ever to watch.

John Dowling.

Pat Spillane.

Ogie Moran.

Tim Kennelly.

And this young pup, O'Donovan.

Five of them, and Sam!
He had watched each of them.
Five Kerrymen looking the happiest five men in Ireland.
The war was twenty-nine years old and it was not for turning.

40

'We are due a really big match, a big performance at our very best . . .
I hope it comes together against Kerry.'

KH

Sunday, 22 September 1985

It was the morning of Kevin Heffernan's last day fighting Kerry.

The end of a very long war was only a few hours away. It was warm, but overcast on the northside of Dublin city. It would be even warmer in Croke Park. There was little or no wind, however. It was not a perfect day on which to call a halt to thirty years of plotting the undoing of Kerry.

But it was close to such a day.

It had all started when Heff was 26 years of age. Before then, of course, as a teenager, he had taken on Kerry in Croke Park, in the GAA's prized and famous no man's land, green and beautifully flat and full of so many promises, and he had lost.

That was a warm-up.

The war had formally commenced in September of 1955.

In Croker!

On the same amazing field.

On a day that was just as close to perfection when the time came for him to walk out his front door that morning.

22 September 1985 was also a day that would end with Heff doing something that he never imagined himself doing in his long and busy life, or even considering for half a second.

He would shoot Brian Mullins.

In full view of 69,389 people jammed into the ground, and with Dublin playing with twice as much pride and heart as they had done twelve months before, he would turn to Donal Colfer and Lorcan Redmond and quickly agree with them.

They had to take Mullins off.

Take him out of the game.

Dump him on the sideline.

Heff made the final decision, and ordered it done.

Brian Mullins.

His lifetime general, and Heff's team captain in 1985.

The one man with whom he would choose to enter any jungle. The first Dublin footballer he would send on to any field crowded with Kerrymen.

Heff took less than a minute to make the decision.

It didn't break his heart.

He'd worry about his heart, and Brian Mullins' heart, afterwards.

'They lacked commitment,' stated Heff, who was absolutely furious.

It was seven months earlier, back in February of '85, and Dublin had lost to Wexford and left their hopes of making it through to the play-off stages of the National League up in smoke.

Wexford 1–5, Dublin 0–7.

They had floundered in Division Two.

He was never as mad with them all, and he had never been as outspoken about his own in front of damned nosy newspapermen.

'They were the same against Roscommon!' Heff accused.

'It's bloody well ridiculous . . . you cannot win matches playing well for a couple of minutes, now and again.'

It was a long spring.

May and June had gone to schedule, though Dublin had Laois in the Leinster final, which was a surprise. No Meath.

Seán Boylan and his team had cantered by Kildare in the first round, but then walked into a Laois haymaker in Tullamore, like Dublin had in the same venue at the beginning of the same decade. Laois beat Meath by double scores.

Laois were looking tricky.

Heff knew he would have to be careful, though he also knew in his heart that if he kept everything steady and nobody did anything stupid, they would win. In a Leinster final, he fully knew that amongst other things Laois would suffer from altitude sickness.

Heff's only real concern, and it was a small enough worry, was about his centre-back. Tommy Drumm had gone off to the Middle East a few months earlier, and had said his thanks and goodbyes to Heff and everybody in the dressing-room. He was not coming back either, for a game of football.

Noel McCaffrey was Heff's new No.6.

Heff liked the cut of him, even though he was on the small side, and was extremely light on his feet. McCaffrey also was more like Drumm in that he did not possess one mean or cruel bone in his body. He was all-footballer.

And he was a doctor. He was smart, and he listened to Heff and did what Heff told him. He held the middle in his first Leinster final, but also sallied forward whenever he had the ball and saw nothing but space in front of him. There was a real bounce to Noel McCaffrey's stride.

Though Dublin were only one point up at half-time. It had spilled down all day, and it was 0–4 to 0–3 at half-time. Dublin would also go a long and weary sixteen minutes without a score in the second half. And John O'Leary foiled Laois when they found themselves with three great chances of goals.

Air to the brain was the biggest problem for Laois, as Heff had expected.

Dublin 0–10, Laois 0–4.

The All-Ireland semi-finals again separated Dublin and Kerry. The reigning champs had shown no lack of hunger against Cork in the Munster final. They took everything Cork threw at them, on and off the ball. They'd also lost their former captain, Ambrose O'Donovan, who was carted off the field on a stretcher by the end, blood flowing from a wound on his face. Kerry did not have their shooting boots on. They had sixteen wides, but Eoin Bomber Liston and Mikey Sheehy scored the goals that made all the difference in a 2–11 to 0–11 win.

Kerry had Monaghan in their semi-final.

Dublin had Mayo.

Both games would end in draws. It was the first such occurrence in GAA history in thirty years, since 1955, when Heff had made it to an All-Ireland final for the first adult battle with Kerry.

There were fireworks before Kerry got the better of Monaghan in their two games in the month of August. The Bomber had had enough of Monaghan full-back Gerry McCarville, after their first encounter on the edge of the square, and fifteen minutes into the replay he had levelled his man. The Bomber was sent straight to the line. The punch seemed to get everybody on the Kerry team in the correct mood, and they were all business thereafter, winning by five points.

Dublin 1–13, Mayo 1–13.

Heff told Brian Mullins to play with the wind in the first half of the first meeting between Mayo and Dublin, and it was 1–10 to 1–4 when the time came to change ends. Mayo never gave up, and Billy Fitzpatrick and T. J. Kilgallon scored two points in the final forty-five seconds to earn themselves a second chance.

But, there were also fireworks between Dublin and Mayo.

Unlike Kerry and Monaghan, this time things became overheated in the first meeting of the teams. These were also real fireworks, the kind that would continue for over two months, right up to the first week of November.

On the Tuesday morning after their drawn semi-final, Heff was told that Mayo were not happy. Their left half-back, John Finn, was out of the replay. In fact, his football life and his working life were both left in a total wreckage by what had happened in the game.

That was a surprise.

Finn had received a blow to the face in the game, but he had finished it to the end. That evening, however, unbeknownst to Kevin

Heffernan or his team, or more importantly the Dublin footballer who had punched Finn on the side of the face, it was discovered in hospital that a substantial amount of damage had been done.

Finn's jaw had been broken in two places.

He had also lost a tooth. While he was lying on the sideline after receiving the punch, he had seven stitches inserted in a wound on the side of his chin.

The GAA's best brains were unable to re-fix the semi-final for three weeks, so John Finn and his family had time to ask for some justice.

Dublin said nothing.

Heff said nothing.

'It simply isn't good enough that one player can break another player's jaw, and get away with it,' stated Finn. 'There has to be some punishment . . . and the Dublin county board should be punished as well.'

On the Tuesday before the All-Ireland semi-final replay, Mayo were informed that an inquiry was finally being instigated.

Two days before the replay the GAA's Games Administration Committee discussed what had allegedly happened.

In October, the GAC and the Dublin county board refused to name the Dublin footballer who had been asked to attend Croke Park for questioning. In November the investigation was closed. The GAC said it had conflicting evidence and that it was not possible to take any disciplinary action whatsoever.

Dublin 2–12, Mayo 1–7.

John Finn had to get on with life.

So too Mayo, who made a small charge in the opening half of the All-Ireland semi-final replay, and then went into reverse, and seemed to accept their fate. They had come close to getting to the final for the first time since 1951, but not close enough.

Two goals from Ciaran Duff made them understand it was not going to be their day or time in GAA history, and that Dublin were heading into their sixth All-Ireland final against Kerry in eleven years.

Duff scored his first goal nine minutes into the second half at a time when Mayo were two points up. His second goal left Dublin six points in front.

'I didn't think at any stage that we would lose,' stated Heff afterwards, already spoiling for the All-Ireland final that would be coming around the corner faster than ever before due to the drawn matches.

Two weeks.

No long, drawn out month of distraction and foolish, unnecessary talking. It was all systems go.

The difference between the average ages of the teams had narrowed in the preceding twelve months. Coming into the final in '85, Kerry's average age was 27.5 years. Contributing heavily to that number were Páidí Ó Sé, Ger Power, Ogie Moran, Pat Spillane and Mikey Sheehy, who were sitting on six All-Ireland medals each, and needed just one more to equal the record of the legendary Kerins O'Rahillys net minder, Danno O'Keeffe.

Dublin were averaging 24.5 years.

Heff decided on four changes from the team that had been wholly defeated twelve months before.

Two of those were forced on him. Anton O'Toole had decided to join Tommy Drumm in retirement. Heff instead had Ray Hazley back from a long injury, and he also had Noel McCaffrey and Dave Synnott in defence. Up front, the new boy was Charlie Redmond.

Dwyer had only lost one man to retirement. John Egan had called it a day, and Timmy O'Dowd had stepped into the Kerry starting fifteen. But while Heff and Dwyer had some new blood in defence and attack, both men knew that the All-Ireland final would be largely won or lost in the middle of the field.

There, Dublin were struggling. They had been outplayed twice in the middle by Mayo, and Heff knew that, like '84, he would have to think up something smart and surprising on this occasion.

Three men had not been enough to get on top of Jack O'Shea and Ambrose O'Donovan a year earlier.

Heff had two weeks to make full use of his best thinking cap.

They flew by.

The last battle in Heff's long war commenced.

The ball was thrown into the air.

Twenty seconds: Ambrose O'Donovan passed off to Tom Spillane. Jack O'Shea had galloped into space. Point to Kerry.

Two minutes: Páidí Ó Sé grabbed the ball, but his clearance was atrocious. The ball went directly to Dave Synnott. He was pulled down. Barney Rock struck the free cleanly. Point to Dublin.

Ten minutes: Eoin Liston found O'Donovan charging forward into space. O'Donovan parted to his midfield partner Jack O'Shea. Point to Kerry.

Eleven minutes: Ray Hazley lost possession of the ball 40 yards from his own goals. Timmy O'Dowd gathered. He passed to Eoin Liston. The Bomber gave it to Ger Power. He was clean through. He was knocked to the ground inside the large square by Pat Canavan. The referee, Paddy Kavanagh from Meath, blew for a penalty. Jack O'Shea smacked the penalty kick. Goal to Kerry.

Twelve minutes: Mikey Sheehy got the ball, twisted once. Tommy Doyle had left his own half-back line and found space for a shot. Point to Kerry.

Fourteen minutes: Liston found O'Shea again, with all the time in the world. O'Shea kicked the ball high. Point to Kerry.

Kerry 1–4, Dublin 0–1.

Dublin were being murdered in the middle of the field. Kerry were winning everything in the air, and on the ground they were first to claim the ball as well. Brian Mullins could not get close to his oldest and greatest opponent, Jack O'Shea.

Time and bad luck had left Mullins looking ten years older, and three or four stones heavier. It was, all of a sudden, no contest between the two midfield giants of the decade.

Jim Ronayne was not helping Mullins much. He simply didn't

have the speed to match either O'Shea or O'Donovan in the manic opening fifteen minutes.

Worse still.

The Kerry half-back line was also on the offensive. Tommy Doyle, Tom Spillane and Ger Lynch were repeatedly crossing into the Dublin half of the field, and breaking through tackles.

The Dublin defence was being overrun.

Heff had never imagined it happening so blatantly.

Or so quickly.

The Bomber was absolutely destroying Gerry Hargan in the Dublin full-back line. He was being delivered the best ball of his life in a Kerry jersey. It was being served up for the Bomber. Left. And right.

The Bomber had one of his huge hands in every Kerry score.

Heff had problems everywhere.

Those problems that needed immediate fixing covered three-quarters of the field. He had never encountered so many problems before in an All-Ireland final.

Eighteen minutes: Sheehy kicked a free. Point for Kerry.

Twenty-four minutes: Sheehy kicked another free. Point for Kerry.

Twenty-seven minutes: Liston found Power in space, and he set up Ogie Moran with an easy opportunity. Point for Kerry.

Twenty-eight minutes: Pat Spillane wildly cleared the ball from his own goalmouth. The ball passed in front of the Kerry posts and left Tom Carr with a straightforward opportunity. Point for Dublin.

Thirty-one minutes: the Kerry midfield was still on the loose. O'Donovan placed O'Shea, who set up Pat Spillane. Point for Kerry.

Kerry 1–8, Dublin 0–2.

In his dressing-room Heff, like never before, had so much to say.

He could not do everything. He needed to talk his team into doing it for themselves out on the field.

But, at the same time, changes would need to be made.

He looked at Brian Mullins.

His complete and total blue warrior looked old, and shaken. The spirit was still there. He could see it in Mullins' face. His eyes.

Heff knew that it was possibly all over for Brian Mullins.

But Heff would wait.

There were only three men doing what Heff believed they would do in the All-Ireland final. That was Synnott, who had fought back the rampaging Kerry attacks better than anyone. McCaffrey was also in the front line of what was happening out on the field. He too was battling for every inch.

And John O'Leary was cool and strong, and looked as steady as he had ever looked in Heff's eyes. But everywhere else there were little and big disasters.

Heff could have taken off twelve players.

He had to think.

Think smart, and not raise a white flag by making a ridiculous number of changes. There could be no sign of panic.

Against Kerry, that would be the very end.

Heff picked out John Kearns and told him to move into the middle and work there as a straight, traditional midfielder. No more wandering.

Into the middle.

Do the job there with Jim Ronayne.

He then walked over to his captain, to Mullins.

'Brian . . . you're going into the right corner for the second half!'

Right corner-forward.

It would be the first time Mullins had played there in over twenty years. He would have to make the best of it.

Dublin, also, would have to make their best of Brian Mullins.

A back injury had him struggling in training for the fortnight before the All-Ireland final, but Heff expected Mullins to overcome it. Forget all about it once he found himself on the field with Kerry.

Heff decided to give the greatest footballer he had ever known a little bit more time. They needed goals. Maybe Mullins could break down the ball, knock people over. He decided to give Mullins one more chance.

*

Thirty-six minutes: Synnott raced forward once again, and passed the ball off to Tom Carr. He found Tommy Conroy. Point for Dublin.

Forty-two minutes: McCaffrey broke through the Kerry midfield, and off-loaded the ball to Conroy. Point for Dublin.

Forty-seven minutes: Kearns caught the kickout from Charlie Nelligan, and immediately planted the ball over the bar from over 50 yards. Point for Dublin.

Kerry 1–8, Dublin 0–5.

Three points in twelve minutes!

Forty-eight minutes: O'Donovan grabbed the ball, and laid it off to Ger Lynch. He travelled almost 50 yards with the ball. Lynch lobbed the ball into the path of O'Dowd, who had screeched through the middle of the Dublin defence. O'Dowd gave O'Leary no real chance. Goal for Kerry.

Seventeen minutes into the second half, Kevin Heffernan found himself doing the deed that he could not possibly have imagined.

He told P. J. Buckley he was going on.

He told Buckley that Brian Mullins was being taken off.

The time had come and gone.

He had waited too long.

Heff knew he should have taken Mullins off the field at half-time. Not call him off in the middle of a game. And have him walk off the field like a defeated, broken man.

It took Mullins a long time to reach the dug-out.

Fifty-two minutes: Sean Walsh for once misjudged the flight of the ball. Kearns had again kicked it long. Walsh was too far under it. The ball fell to Joe McNally. McNally drilled it home. Goal for Dublin.

Fifty-five minutes: A breaking ball was claimed by Ciaran Duff.

He made ground, and came crashing down. Rock stabbed at the free as usual. Point for Dublin.

Sixty minutes: Carr passed the ball to Kearns. He took one quick look up at the posts, and from the sideline struck another screaming kick over the bar. Point for Dublin.

Kerry 2–8, Dublin 1–7.

Dublin were outrunning Kerry. In the middle of the field, Kearns and Ronayne had managed to completely turn the tables on O'Donovan and O'Shea.

Kerry had scored once in the second half.

Once in twenty-five minutes.

And their wait for a second score would continue.

Sixty-four minutes: Kearns caught another ball and soloed forward. He sent the ball high into the Kerry goalmouth. McNally got up high, and stayed there. He got his hand to the ball before Walsh. Goal for Dublin.

Kerry 2–8, Dublin 2–7.

There were six minutes left.

Heff saw nothing stopping them.

Kerry had backed off at half-time. They had stopped playing, and waited for Dublin. Heff had watched his team destroy Kerry, and almost catch up in half an hour. Dublin were still on the move.

Heff waited for Dublin to pass Kerry by, and take the lead. He expected it. Everyone was playing well. Dublin were dominating almost everywhere.

Liston had come out of the square and was now working around the middle of the field, trying to dig Kerry out of their frozen state.

The Bomber was in the middle of the field, far away from John O'Leary and the Dublin goalmouth. And Jack O'Shea was further back, now in the thick of his own defence. He was fighting to win the game for Kerry in his own full-back line.

The Bomber and Jacko were exactly where Heff wished them to be with the 1985 All-Ireland final ready to be won or lost by either team.

Sixty-five minutes: Lynch came out of his own defence with the ball. O'Shea carried it forward. Ogie had the ball, and was stupidly fouled. The ball was moved forward for arguing by two Dublin players. Sheehy struck the free-kick perfectly. Point for Kerry.

Kerry 2–9, Dublin 2–7.

Sixty-five and a half minutes: Duff gathered the ball at the other end. He was foolishly upended. Rock calmed himself before striking the ball. Perfectly. Point for Dublin.

Kerry 2–9, Dublin 2–8.

Sixty-eight minutes: Lynch again. He raced forward and found Pat Spillane, who took a few short solos. Spillane then unleashed a massive kick. Point for Kerry.

Sixty-nine minutes: Sheehy chipped the ball into O'Dowd's path. O'Dowd had too much pace. He tried to lob the ball over O'Leary's head. No goal. Point for Kerry.

Kerry 2–11, Dublin 2–8.

Seventy minutes: John Kennedy had too much space. The Dublin defence had flagged. He kicked a point from the left wing. Point for Kerry.

Kerry 2–12, Dublin 2–8.

He didn't know it.

But Kevin Heffernan's private war was over.

His long war with Kerry was lost.

He would not meet them in Croke Park, or anywhere else for that matter, ever again.

Dublin had not fought hard enough, for long enough. And they had also fought against bad luck. In the maddening second-half onslaught on the Kerry goal they might have had a penalty.

Jack O'Shea had picked the ball up off the ground with both hands. The referee didn't see it, or saw it and gave the Kerry midfielder the huge benefit of a doubt. They could have had two penalties.

Tom Spillane had also carelessly knocked over Duff. The referee didn't appear to care on that occasion.

It didn't matter.

A long war was lost.

Dublin had beaten Kerry in one All-Ireland final.

Dublin had beaten Kerry in Heff's absence in an All-Ireland semi-final. But three All-Ireland semi-finals had been lost.

And five All-Ireland finals.

All lost.

John Dowling.

Pat Spillane.

Ogie Moran.

Tim Kennelly.

Ambrose O'Donovan.

And Páidí Ó Sé.

Heff stood in front of the dug-out as Kerry supporters invaded the field from all directions. He had imagined, despite himself, and always ridding himself of the image when it landed in his head, seeing Brian Mullins climbing the steps of the Hogan Stand.

Mullins lifting Sam high.

But, Brian Mullins was wearing a tracksuit top and he was bunched amongst the group of Dublin footballers who were in the middle of the field, surrounded by wild men and wilder women in green and gold.

There was nowhere for Mullins to go.

His prepared speech would never be heard halfway up the Hogan Stand. Or in homes all over the country!

Mullins would have made a big speech.

It would have been one of the few classics.

Páidí Ó Sé, instead, was about to accept the Sam Maguire.

Páidí was waiting, his hands on his hips.

A last Kerryman.

But one of the truest Kerrymen, the youngest son of Tommy and Beatrice Ó Sé from Ard an Bhóthair in Ventry.

As Kerry as a Kerry footballer could get.

When Páidí was born, Tommy and Beatrice's two older boys had begged their parents to call the new baby in the family after a famous Kerry footballer.

Tommy and Beatrice Ó Sé decided to call their baby after Paudie Sheehy.

They'd call their last boy Páidí.

Four months before Kevin Heffernan's war with Paudie Sheehy's Kerry started with a defeat in the 1955 All-Ireland final, Páidí Ó Sé had been born.

Heff stood and watched.

Páidí Ó Sé lifted Sam over his head.

Part Six

A Life in the Shadows

41

'I write to advise you of a decision by Donal Colfer, Lorcan Redmond, Tony Hanahoe and myself to opt out of our positions with the county senior football team. We have been considering the question over a period, and the beginning of a new year and a new county board management seems an appropriate time for all concerned.'

KH

Tuesday, 14 January 1986

The letter in his hand, as he walked down by Mountjoy Square, was his 'long, long goodbye' to Dublin. He would never manage a Dublin football team again, but it would take twenty-seven years before his goodbye was fully completed. Before, finally, he had nothing more to do for the team.

He was meeting Jim King at the Dublin GAA headquarters on Belvedere Place. The letter was for the county secretary. It said very little, and explained nothing much at all to him.

But the letter, signed by Heff, marked the end of twelve spell-binding years. He said hello to King, and explained what the letter meant. He did not stay very long. He had not gone to the county board offices for a conversation.

Heff just wished to formally announce that it was over.

There was nothing more to discuss. The Dublin GAA public was left to make up its own mind about what had just happened. The Dublin football team was left equally unenlightened. Heff did not call one single player.

He always believed, for managers and players alike, there was only one way to go. That was in silence, and almost always Dublin footballers learned of their demotion from the team or, worse still, removal from the panel, in perfect silence as they sipped a cup of tea and read their morning newspapers.

It was the easiest way to do an always difficult, gut-wrenching piece of football business. Clearest too. Of course it was not courageous or in any way decent to deliver the message through a third party but no conversation meant no tears, no tantrums, and no possibility of any grey area.

Black and white. You're either in the dressing-room!

Or . . . you're not!

Himself, Donal Colfer, Lorcan Redmond and Tony Hanahoe were leaving the Dublin team in the middle of a new football year, four games into the National League, deep in Division Two. But nobody was mad at their sudden decision. Officers of the Dublin board informed the media that the letter was not one of resignation.

Retirement, they felt, was a more appropriate word.

Heff, however, already had another job on his hands. Shortly before Christmas, he had been appointed manager of the Irish team to play Australia in 'Round Two' of the Compromise Rules series.

That was one good reason why Heff might have wished to retire. Another good reason was that Dublin had been beaten by Kerry, soundly, and soundly again, in successive All-Ireland finals in 1984 and '85. A third possible reason was the election, two days before Heff drove to Belvedere Place to hand in his letter, of Phil Markey as the new Dublin chairman.

Once upon a time, in the earliest seventies, when St Vincents and UCD ruled the county and fought with every muscle to rule one another in the Dublin championship, Markey had fallen out with Heff and mostly everyone in Vincents.

Phil Markey had called it as he saw it.

The rivalry was not pretty, and Phil Markey said it was not pretty to watch, though he chose his own collection of words to describe what was happening. Markey was not kindly spoken about

Vincents. He rightly sickened people in Vincents with what he had to say.

What was happening was that Vincents and the students were battering the living daylights out of one another and also occasionally playing some outstanding football in championship games. To a great many people in the GAA, words such as Markey's, over the years, would have been as forgettable as water poured over the back of a duck far too busy and successful to take any notice whatsoever.

But, to a great many people in St Vincents GAA club, Markey's words were damaging. They were filled with acid. They decided that Markey's words could never be forgotten, or removed.

Kevin Heffernan was amongst that number.

In the autumn of 1984, Kevin Heffernan had been playing golf in Clontarf Golf Club at the same time as 8,000 people took their seats in Páirc Uí Chaoimh to witness Ireland and Australia meet in 'Round One' of what was about to become one of the most violent and wholly absorbing experiments in the great and bountiful history of the Gaelic Athletic Association.

The first test between the countries was two minutes old when Mick Lyons was k.o.'d. A man by the name of Mark Lee had clattered into the Irish full-back. That same year he won the 'Best and Fairest' award with his club Richmond, and at the end of his footy career he would become a senior constable with the Victoria police force.

Lee was six feet and six inches tall.

He weighed in at 17 stones.

Lee was five inches taller than Lyons and fully three stones heavier. In Cork, that grey, dripping Sunday, Lyons was soon being carried off the field, out cold, with no more worries about Mark Lee.

Lyons being stretchered off the field did two things.

It encouraged the rest of the Australian party to pack the early minutes of the game with extra physicality and artillery and, at the same time, it left every man jack on the Irish team in a state of shock at seeing Meath's indestructible full-back pole-axed, and stretchered out of sight, before anyone had worked up an early sweat.

After that . . .

MAYHEM.

Australia won that first test 70–57. In Croke Park, one week later, Ireland levelled the series with an 80–76 win. The Aussies finished off the Irish another week later with a whole series of shemozzles over the littlest and daftest things in the last test, back in Croker. They won the third and decisive test 76–71.

In fifteen days, the best group of Gaelic footballers in the country had been knocked off their feet, had shakily got back up, and had been knocked back down. In the crowd of just over 32,000 who paid in to view the third test at first hand was Kevin Heffernan.

The Australians were led in 1984 by a man with a hawkish nose, and an everlasting grin that spelled out, alternatively, at different times during the three-week tour, either a level of snideness or a degree of smugness. It was always hard to tell. Neither went down well in Ireland.

His name was John Todd.

He became the GAA's first ever 'Public Enemy No.1'.

The Irish team had been co-managed in 1984 by Liam Sammon, the genial former Galway star from the sixties and seventies, and by Peter McDermott, the elderly and gentlemanly Meath star from the forties and fifties.

The pair of them had been surprised by Todd.

They had been outmanoeuvred in three 'warm-up' games before the first test, when the Australians had not lifted a finger and, instead, allowed the Irish teams to put on a full and thorough exhibition of their skills. The Irish management duo had also been out-fought. And out-talked.

John Todd had done the full number on Irish soil.

The question remained who the GAA would send out to Australia two years later, in 1986, if not quite to put some manners on the Aussie team boss, then to try to shut him up for a little while at least. Winning on the field was also an ambition.

It was going to need someone with tough skin.

Someone who did not believe in the over-use of terms such as 'excuse me' or 'sorry about this', and a man who had said, not once, but one hundred and one times in private and in public, that he would have no mercy for his own mother if she stood between him and the winning or losing of a game of football.

Heff always said he'd have dropped May Heffernan in a heartbeat.

It helped in the appointment of Heff that he had evidently taken a particular dislike, before he even left this country, for Mr Todd.

42

'I want it to be understood that we are not picking a Gaelic football team. There are fundamental differences between Gaelic and the game we'll be playing in Australia.'

KH

Sunday, 12 October 1986

Heff did not know that he had already started on his last great act, in four fast weeks, as a football manager.

But, Christ, he certainly was acting like it.

He was livid.

All of the players he had brought with him, the whole sorry 12,000 miles from Dublin airport, seventeen and a half hours in the air, with just a one-hour refuelling stop in Bombay, were now seeing Heff up close for the first time. Really up close.

They had set off eleven days earlier.

At a press conference, before leaving home, he had told all of the Irish journalists that he had picked footballers who were durable, adaptable and fast. He now stood before them in the team hotel in Perth. It was the morning after the night before. The first test had been played under lights in the Western Australia Cricket Oval. The Irish had scored five easy 'goals', which were worth six points each in the hybrid game of football.

The Australians had scored just one goal.

But the Aussies had beaten the Irish 14–5 in 'overs' that were worth three points each, and they had also beaten the visitors 16–12 in 'behinds' or 'wides' that were valued at a single point each.

That's what sickened Heff the most. The Australians, who could barely kick the ball 30 or 40 yards with any degree of accuracy, had even beaten his team when the damned wides were added up.

At the end of it all, the scoreboard read 64–57.

John Todd was one up.

Todd was also doing nearly all of the talking, for each of those eleven days, and it had gotten right up Heff's nose.

In the team hotel, ten o'clock the next morning, Heff laid into his players. He never raised his voice. That was not his style.

He spoke slowly. Calmly, but he was viciously condescending, hissing with thinly veiled insults, and by the time he left them to it the meeting was into a fourth hour. Heff had spoken about every single footballer on the field. He now wanted every footballer to speak to one another. He wanted them to analyse what had happened out there. He wanted them to come back to him with feedback. He wanted them to tell him how the Aussies had gone about the business of winning the game.

They should know.

They were out there, not him.

By lunchtime, every footballer in the room, including team captain Jack O'Shea, was re-checking his sense of manhood. Re-checking, and verifying to one another the men they believed themselves to be.

Without a second's thought, Jack O'Shea had accepted the captaincy of the Irish team when Kevin Heffernan had called him up one evening at home. Pat Spillane, the most spectacular points scorer of all on the Mick O'Dwyer teams that had come up against Dublin, was also on board.

Others were not.

The Bomber had said a definite no straight away. It was a decision he would publicly regret when his career was over, when he admitted that having Heff as his manager would have been a greater experience than getting to travel every inch of Australia, but he said sorry to Heff in one phone call, said he could not do it. His loyalty to Mick O'Dwyer was not for bending, not even for the trip of a lifetime, the opportunity of living the life of a professional footballer for a full month.

Other Kerry players also felt that their man had been wronged.

He had won more All-Irelands than anybody else.

He was manager of the reigning All-Ireland champions.

Christ, four-in-a-row All-Ireland champs in the seventies, and three-in-a-row All-Ireland champs when the job of deciding the Irish manager was under way.

If anyone bothered to count . . .

It was clear as day to them that Mick O'Dwyer did not get the job of managing the first Irish team on foreign ground simply because the GAA bosses in Croke Park did not believe that he had tipped his cap often enough.

Dwyer was a Kerryman and was considered an unhappy GAA man.

Heff was a Dublin man and was considered a happy GAA man.

That was the Kerry vote.

Nevertheless, Heff had three Kerrymen.

Jacko, and Pat and Tom Spillane. Though Jack O'Shea, who would build a friendship with Heff that would last for the next quarter of a century, never quite fathomed why the Irish manager only ever called him 'Johnno' all through the tour in 1986 and for ever more.

Johnno O'Shea never sought an explanation.

As Heff had warned everybody in the GAA at the very beginning, he wasn't picking men based on their county of birth, and neither was he picking men on what they had achieved on a football field.

There were a lot of men out there, all over the country, and he wanted to find the kind he thought he needed for this very different task at hand.

Peter Quinn was counting money in a back room, under the stand in St Tiernach's Park in Clones, when Kevin Heffernan walked in. Five years later Quinn would be president of the Gaelic Athletic Association, but that afternoon, halfway through the 1986 Ulster final, in which Tyrone and Down were arguing it out as fiercely as ever, Peter Quinn was counting the day's takings.

Heff had been led into the room by a couple of officials he'd never met before who'd absolutely insisted, and wouldn't take no for an answer, on getting him a cup of tea. The last thing Heff wanted was a cup of stale tea. He'd miss the start of the second half, but he didn't mind too much. He'd already seen enough.

There were four names written down on the inside of the cigarette packet that he had finished that morning, when he was leaving home. He'd broken apart the packet and flattened it out, just like he had broken apart and flattened out many hundreds, no thousands, of cigarette packets before it.

It was not the tea that would detain him from the game's restart. It was the information. Peter Quinn had some good information.

'Any good fella I haven't seen?' he'd asked Quinn.

'Out there?' replied Quinn. 'There's a few good lads out there, rightly enough, you could do with in Australia, Kevin.'

Heff agreed. There might be one . . . or two.

'Anywhere else up here . . . anyone I should look at, do ye think?'

Nobody came to Peter Quinn's mind, initially, but he wondered. He'd been to a game of hurling the week before, between Derry and Fermanagh. He'd just wandered into it.

'There's a lad . . . a big red-haired lad in Derry,' said Quinn.

Heff took a last mouthful of tea.

It was time to be getting back out to his seat. The crowd were working themselves up again outside. The second half was five minutes in, and Heff put the cup down and thanked his tea-makers.

'Where's he play?' asked Heff.

'In the middle of the field . . . or the centre of the defence,' replied Quinn, who had started back to counting the cash, thinking that Heff had not paid too much notice to his suggestion.

'He's a hurler now . . . but he's a right good footballer too, I hear. And you should see him run through lads . . . he's as strong as a horse . . . I've never seen a stronger man in a long time!'

Heff asked for a name, and wrote 'McGilligan' on the blank side of his cigarette packet.

'We don't know what to expect. The Australian Rules game has norms different from Gaelic football, as we saw last week. There is also a cultural difference. With the best will in the world, we could have a few hiccups.'

KH

Tuesday, 14 October 1986

Mick Lyons was in Heffo's sights from the foyer of the team hotel. Lyons was alone, his hands in his pockets, slowly ambling through the car park.

Heff walked out the side door.

He surprised Lyons. The two men had not spoken more than a handful of words in almost two weeks. In the first test, Heff had gone with Brian McGilligan as the 'big man' on his team selection. It was a role that Mick Lyons had fitted into perfectly, and exactly, with Meath for several years.

Lyons had been the Allstar full-back in 1984, and by the end of '86 he would win his second Allstar award. Lyons, officially, without a doubt in the world, was the greatest living full-back in Ireland. Like everyone else in the Irish party, Lyons had never heard of McGilligan, but the Derryman was strong.

Everyone told everyone else, normally with a big smile bursting out on their faces, just how strong McGilligan was.

'Fuck . . . he's even stronger than O'Byrne!' everyone agreed.

Pat O'Byrne, another red-haired giant of a man from Wicklow, was the second 'big man' on the Irish team. He also got the nod over Mick Lyons when Heff started filling in the names on his team selection for the first test.

Though Heff thought the world of Lyons.

Lyons was everything Heff admired, and secretly loved, in a footballer. Fearless, for starters. But, after that, Mick Lyons filled so many other boxes. He was quiet. There was no nonsense out of him. Never talked for the sake of it, and never made big promises.

Lyons did it.

He performed.

And, after he did the job, Lyons still said absolutely nothing. Not to journalists, and not even in the bar or in the relaxed company of other footballers by the pool, could Lyons be heard from a distance of more than two or three feet.

But, in Australia, Heff had still not put his absolute faith in Mick Lyons. He hoped that time would come.

'Well, Mick!' said Heff, when he met him outside the team hotel.

Lyons still had his hands in his pockets.

The night before some of the Irish players had lingered a little longer than Heff thought they might in a local bar. Different times on their return had been given to him by some of his 'friends' and personal allies within the Irish party. Amongst others, Heff had Paddy Moriarty, head of the ESB, and also Paschal Taggart, one of Ireland's most astute financiers and future chairman of Bord na gCon, to chat with about the Australians and discuss strategy.

Heff didn't care all that much about the late night.

But he wanted to use the night to his advantage.

'I didn't think you'd be with that crowd last night, Mick!'

That's all Heff said, and then he turned and walked back into the cool of the hotel, leaving Mick Lyons feeling a little bit more like a small boy than he had ever felt in well over twenty years.

That's how Heff wished him to feel.

Heff now knew that Lyons would do anything he was asked to do, and would be desperate to wipe away the disappointment that he felt in him. Lyons didn't know that Heff was happy.

Happy that Lyons had been out with the gang, and happy that he had been able to bring the night to Lyons' immediate attention.

Lyons was now back in the centre of Heff's planning.

*

The Irish team had flown into Melbourne the previous morning. A new city had meant it was time for some of the players to have a little adventure, and break out of Heff's tough grind of twice-daily training sessions and endless team meetings and video sessions. The video sessions could start out harmless enough but could last for three hours all on their own.

Hence, the 'group therapy' on the Monday night.

In the first test in Perth, however, the Australians had indulged themselves in some of the rough stuff more than the Irish. Five players were sent off. Pat O'Byrne and Tom Spillane were dismissed. And three Aussies joined them, though the single and most industrious architect of the many rows breaking out all over the field seemed, as usual, to be the squat, grandly moustached figure of Robert Di Pierdomenico.

The local sports writers called him 'the Dipper'. The Irish two years earlier, and again in 1986, called him 'the Bollox'.

There was very definite information about the new game that the Irish players had to get their heads around. The games were being played on rectangular pitches, not oval pitches preferred by Aussie Rules, measuring 145 metres long and 90 metres wide. Games were of eighty minutes duration, broken into four quarters. There were two normal goalposts with a net, and then there were two outer posts called 'behind' posts on either side of the goalposts. There were two referees, one Irish and one Australian, on the field at all times.

That was the technical stuff.

More important was that there was a lean, angular man called 'Todd', and a fattened and younger man called 'the Dipper'.

Officially, both were 'bolloxes' in Irish eyes.

Todd was insulting the Irish team every day he was asked to open that thin little mouth of his.

It was war.

Clearly, thus far, this was Todd's war.

Heff wasn't one to read up on a man. One good look, usually, told him close to everything he wished to know. That included managers and footballers. One look at Todd, and Heff knew that he was merciless, that Todd too would drop his own mother in a heartbeat.

Todd's career had made him into such a man. In 1955, when Heff entered his first All-Ireland final and left the field feeling nothing but overwhelming shame after losing to Kerry, John Todd was a 17-year-old winning his first individual 'medal', something that's a big deal in Aussie Rules. But that same year Todd messed up his knee, and messed it up for good, leaving him a bit of a wreck for the rest of his footy career. A torn anterior cruciate ligament was often the end of a man's career in the fifties and sixties. Todd, however, was leaving the field for nobody.

Todd kept going on the field, with his knee stuck together with bandages and tape, and finally a leg brace, for another eleven years, and he played 132 games for the Bulldogs, 13 for Western Australia, and, in 1961, he was named an All-Australian. He was a mean, tough, son of a bitch on the field, and even meaner on the sideline coaching a Premiership-winning East Freemantle in '74, the same year Heff managed Dublin to their first All-Ireland win.

Todd coached five more winning teams to Premierships after that, and would not stop coaching until he had seen his way through 721 footy games. He quit in 2002, sixteen years after Heff had quit on Dublin, and upon hearing the news the Parliament of Western Australia suspended its standing orders in order to pass a motion of congratulations to John Herbert Todd for his splendid contribution to Australian Rules football.

Todd was deeply annoying.

But, Todd was no fool of a man.

He was a worthy, dangerous opponent.

Heff knew he had no room for sentiment, error, loyalty, or touristy foolishness, as he waited for the second test. He already knew, pretty much, exactly how he was going to beat Australia, and damn Todd in front of his own people.

That would be exceptionally sweet.

But, he had to get his selection perfect for VFL Park the following Sunday. Moving the names of players he didn't want to the left and players he wanted to the right was tricky, especially as he did not immediately have enough players in the bundle on the right. He had brought fourteen men from the 1984 Irish squad with him in his official tour party of twenty-eight footballers. The majority of them were in the bundle on the left, unfortunately.

Heff had nineteen players to name for each test. He would have to make a third bundle of players in the middle and wait and see, and then decide on who might have it in him to make that extra bit of difference when things got interesting out there on the field.

His instinct had been to build a whole new team, and he now realized that it might have been even smarter to build a whole new travelling party. There were exceptions, naturally, like Jack O'Shea, his captain, but his vice-captain, Plunkett Donaghy, the hard-working blond midfielder from Tyrone, was omitted for the first test and was left out in the cold for the rest of the tour. Also in Heff's left-hand bundle, surprisingly, and staying there were Colm O'Rourke, Pat Spillane and Mick Holden.

It was a waste of time to try to guess how Heff was working it all out in that brilliant mind of his.

O'Rourke was Ireland's top scorer two years before, totting up a cool 45 points while skin and hair were flying all around him in three games, and there was nobody faster and nobody capable of winning a high ball in the forward line better than the Meath corner-forward.

Spillane was Spillane. Meticulous, and nobody on the Irish squad was as serious about what had to be done as Pat Spillane.

And Holden? He was *only* Kevin Heffernan's most loved Dublin footballer since Jimmy Keaveney and Brian Mullins.

Heff's mind was impregnable.

Mick Lyons heard Heff call his name.

He stood up and threw off his tracksuit top. The second test in VFL Park that Ireland would eventually win by a clearcut margin, beating the Aussies 3–1 in 'goals', drawing with them 10–10 in 'overs' and beating them 14–10 in 'behinds', making it a final handsome victory tally of 62–46, had entered the second quarter.

There were only 10,800 people filling up much less than one-sixth of the amazing oval arena, so it was not hard for a man on the Irish bench to hear the Irish team manager.

Mick Lyons stood beside Heff.

Out on the field, the game did not look all that different to the first test in Perth, though the Australians were quieter and better behaved. Heff knew that that might do for Todd, who'd be quite happy to sneak a win after a bit of a non-event of a game, and close down the three-game series early with an overall victory.

Heff needed more from his team, and he mostly needed his team to turn the tables on Todd's team. Todd knew the Irish did not start rows. The Irish would be there for the end of most of the rows, but they didn't make up their minds to start them.

Not the Irish.

Heff wanted a row on the field.

He wanted a row straight away.

'Mick . . . I want you to go out there and hit that fella over there!'

Heff pointed in the direction of the Dipper.

'. . . the fella with the moustache, Mick . . . Give him a thump!'

Mick Lyons did not say anything.

Heff did not say anything more.

Then, ten seconds later, Heff shouted.

'Go in!'

Mick Lyons ran on to the field and ran straight to Robert Di Pierdomenico, the toughest, baddest man that John Todd had on the field.

And Mick Lyons gave him a thump.

It was the first great row that an Irish team had ever started with Australia and, in the middle of it, with two dozen players scuffling in five or six different places on the field, and no end in sight after thirty seconds, and then forty seconds, and with the Dipper holding Lyons around the neck, a little chink of diplomatic negotiation commenced.

'Let's stop this . . . and get up to the other end, mate,' the Aussie suggested to Mick Lyons. 'Or we're going to be in trouble . . . you and me. Right . . . mate?'

Mick Lyons agreed to the Dipper's terms.

'I could go down now to the front door of the hotel and stop the first man passing by and ask him, "What if I asked you to play next Friday night? What would you do for me?" And he would say the same thing to me.

'Go away now, and think about it and we'll talk again tomorrow.'

KH

Friday, 24 October 1986

There was no controlling Teddy McCarthy.

Twenty-one years old, in Australia for the first time in his life and, basically, inviting the biggest, square-jawed footballers in Australia to form an orderly queue in the Football Park in Adelaide so that he could hit them.

Teddy had been warned by one of the referees five minutes earlier, as was his marker, but John Todd immediately sent a fresh man in Teddy's direction with orders to rough him up, and get a reaction. Get him out of the game. It was a standard procedure in the psyche of every Australian Rules coach.

Teddy's new marker started giving him lip. Then they started pushing and shoving one another, and then Teddy gave him a belt.

He was ordered to the line, but as Teddy was walking in Heff's direction one of the Australian interchange players started telling the young Cork footballer and hurler what he would like to do to him.

Teddy made a beeline for Aussie No.3. The only problem was another big Aussie, employed as a cameraman for local TV was in the way. It looked on television sets back in Ireland as though Teddy

327

McCarthy was taking on every male over 18 on the whole frigging continent.

When it was all over, in the privacy of the Irish dressing-room, Teddy earned himself a hand on the shoulder from Kevin Heffernan.

A rare medal of honour.

And a rarer moment still, of intimacy and endearment, between Heff and any footballer.

Teddy McCarthy was at the very end of a crash course in getting to know and understand Kevin Heffernan. It began back in Melbourne, six days earlier, in the hotel bar where the Irish team was celebrating its victory. The series was tied 1–1, and Heff told the fellas to go out and enjoy themselves, as usual with the addendum of not to even think of coming to him crying the next morning.

The fellas were finished with the beer. It was eleven o'clock, and vodka and orange seemed a far better idea. Next, Teddy was informed by his new Dublin buddy, Joe McNally, that Southern Comfort was a sure fire winner.

'It's yer only man,' Joe swore to him.

Teddy McCarthy saw Kevin Heffernan walk into the bar, and sit down with Mick Holden and Niall Cahalane for a few minutes. Heff then walked over to where Teddy and Joe were standing.

Heff turned directly to Teddy and asked him what he had thought of the game. And Teddy told him it was great, 'It was super!' Teddy thought that might be the end of Heff's polite conversation. After all, he hadn't picked Teddy in his panel of nineteen for the game, and the closest he got to the nineteen during the first test was when he ran on and off the field with water bottles. Entering the last week of the tour, Teddy had every right to presume he could keep his feet up.

Between the first and second tests, Teddy was also named as one of the team's official ambassadors, alongside Colm O'Rourke and Pat Spillane, which meant photocalls and receptions, and lots of wine and cheese, as the playing squad got an early night for themselves back in the team hotel. Teddy felt he had acquitted himself admirably in that role.

'What if I asked you to play next Friday night?' said Heff. 'What would you do for me?'

Teddy had no idea whatsoever what to say.

Finally, Teddy promised Heff he'd do his best. He could think of nothing else to say. He had no idea what Heff wanted him to say.

'I'll see you in my room at midnight,' replied Heff, adding with a touch of a rasp, '. . . see if you can come up with a better reply.'

The only player who had spent time with the manager in his room all through the tour had been the team captain, Jack O'Shea. Heff made sure to run every team selection by Jacko. He was not just rewarding the Kerryman for standing by him when the call went out to 'stand by Dwyer', he also wanted Jacko to fully represent him on the field when things descended into madness.

Teddy was only the second player to get a royal summons.

Joe McNally was chuckling. Teddy emptied the last of his Southern Comfort, and announced he wanted no more for the rest of the night. McNally was no help when Teddy sought counselling before getting into the elevator and heading for the manager's room. Gerry Hargan also thought it was hilarious. Mick Holden took the situation more seriously but had no ready-made solution. Three of Heff's former Dublin fellas were actually clueless.

At five minutes to midnight, Teddy McCarthy knocked on Kevin Heffernan's bedroom door. Heff was lying back on his bed. Teddy sat down on a chair by the window, but he need not have bothered, because the conversation was short.

Teddy was asked, had he thought about what was said in the bar? And Teddy said he had, and then Teddy gave the same answer, give or take a few words, that he had given Heff half an hour or so earlier.

'Teddy,' Heff commenced. 'I could go down now to the front door of the hotel and stop the first man passing by and ask him, "What if I ask you to play next Friday night? What would you do for me?" And he would say the same thing to me.

'Go away now, and think about it and we'll talk again in the morning,' Heff concluded.

*

At the breakfast table, there was no sign of Heff. There was no sign of him either when Teddy was walking towards the team bus that was taking everyone to the ten o'clock training session. And then, like a flash, Heff stood in front of him.

'What's your answer?'

'Fucking hell, Kevin,' said Teddy, desperate for escape, for any words that might free him. 'All I can say is that I will run 'til I drop.'

'That's what I wanted to hear,' replied Heff.

The tables had been turned for the third test.

Not just one table, but all of them. Heff knew that as soon as he heard that John Todd had sounded real nasty and angry in his press conference immediately after the second test.

The Aussie coach called Heff's fellas a 'bunch of bloody wimps'. When he heard the exact choice of words used by Todd, Heff did more than chuff. He was fairly ecstatic.

'They are not tough enough to handle a real game,' fumed Todd. '. . . Whether that is ice hockey or marbles, it's all the same.

'We in Australia don't complain . . . we don't have cream cakes at ten o'clock in the morning . . . we've been brought up in a tough school.'

Heff could not have asked Todd for greater help. He could not have written the Australian coach's replies himself and made them any more valuable.

It was a nice little dollop of extra incentive to have the Australian camp calling the Irish camp names. However, that's all it was. With one game to go, Heff's team was now the aggressor and Heff's team had fully come to terms with a winning tactical approach, and, on top of that, as it had been at the very start of the tour, Heff's team were still twice as skilful as their hosts.

All the tables, indeed, had turned.

Heff had his players pushing the Aussies around the place. He had them playing the ball on the ground, and kicking anything that moved on the ground, including Australian hands which were about to pick up the ball. The home team was incensed by this particular form of barbaric behaviour. Heff refused to step back, and reminded his fellas that every loose ball on the ground was there to be pulled on, any time they felt like it.

Heff now had the full measure of Todd in getting maximum value from all of his interchange players. He also had Todd's most skilful ball players identified, and double-teamed.

Heff even had a blackboard.

He outlined everything. Black and white, with names inserted for good measure in case some of his fellas were completely stupid. The choicest nugget, illustrated on the board, was how the Aussie corner-forwards were running the Irish corner-backs around the place, without going anywhere near the ball, and how Todd would then throw on two fresh pairs of legs to take immediate advantage of any back who looked three-quarters banjaxed.

Heff called a halt to that little trick of the trade.

He had Todd's number.

John Todd had nowhere to turn.

The victory was in sight. It didn't matter much that John O'Leary had a hairline fracture of his little finger. Joe McNally could do just the job in goals if necessary. It didn't matter unduly that Jack O'Shea had a broken nose, or that two of the real playmakers on the team, Val Daly and Greg Blaney, had bruised ribs and a torn calf muscle respectively. Heff felt in complete control.

He even threatened, for good measure, to pull his team out of the third test if the refereeing by the Aussie-appointed official, Rowan Sawers, did not come up to scratch. Heff thought it worth a try to put some manners on everyone ... the Aussie Rules bosses, the Aussie Rules officials, and the Aussie Rules team.

He told everyone he didn't want any more trouble, and reminded the Irish and Australian journalists that his team would be trying their very best to play football. 'But,' added Heff, knowing for sure that the Australians were not going to be as fast at kicking off big rows as they were at the beginning of the month, '... if mêlées are to develop, we will not be found standing out on the road.'

*

It was relatively easy in the end.

Ireland beat Australia in Football Park in Adelaide 4–0 in 'goals', 8–7 in 'overs', and lost only 7–11 in 'behinds'.

The final scoreline on a wet and soaking evening read 55–32.

There were stars, obvious ones like Jacko, and Cork's breezy Jimmy Kerrigan, and Derry's muscular young running-man Dermot McNicholl. Far more of the stars on the Irish team, however, were fellas who would never have been on the plane of any other Irish manager, fellas like Brian McGilligan from Derry, Pat O'Byrne from Wicklow, Michael 'Spike' Fagan from Westmeath, and an 18-year-old kid from Cork called John O'Driscoll, who twisted and turned Aussie defenders, rose higher than anyone to pluck clean possession in the third test and, finally, beat Colm O'Rourke's points haul from 1984 by an impressive enough margin.

John O'Driscoll, with just two championship games with Cork under his belt, was the top scorer in the 1986 Compromise Rules series with 49 points.

The journey home was long, and fuelled with alcohol for everyone but the Irish team manager, who remained stone-cold sober the whole thirty-hour trip from Sydney to Melbourne, then Perth to Singapore to Muscat, then to London and into Dublin. Twice over the Mediterranean the passengers were told to extinguish their cigarettes and put on oxygen masks. Each time the captain subsequently explained it was a false alarm but, each time, more alert than his tired and drowsy team, Heff was quick to completely ruin two new fags.

Heff's last great act on a 'national' stage had the sort of triumphant procession at the end of it that the man had always avoided by hiding himself somewhere, anywhere, it didn't matter. During Dublin's emotional parade through the streets of Dublin, after claiming Sam Maguire in 1974, Heff had nursed his way into the thick of the thousands of supporters who applauded his team as they stood on a rostrum in front of the GPO. It was Robbie Kelleher who spotted his manager's face, almost lost in a sea of delirious faces down on O'Connell Street.

It was harder to hide on a plane.

The Artane Boys Band awaited Heff and his team in the VIP car park in Dublin airport. There were triumphant banners,

WELCOME HOME, WIMPS

HEFFO'S SECOND ARMY

Before he knew it, Heff was hoisted in the air by Jacko and his own players and paraded through the airport. Photographers massed around them from every side. Jacko was soon up in the air beside him.

'Johnno . . .!' said Heff, surprised to see Jacko.

'I'm getting out of here fast,' Kevin Heffernan then announced, as he was lowered towards ground level, laughing.

'I'm going to have nothing more to do with you lot!'

He meant it too.

Epilogue

'No defeat as a manager ever hit me like 1955. That was the first time. It was Kerry. I had great hopes. That formed a large part of what I became as a person.'

KH

Wednesday, 3 November 2004

He was in rare company.

He was also in the company of a man who once, and only once, admitted that Kevin Heffernan had 'defined his life'.

Mick O'Dwyer spoke those words in public.

The pair of them, Heffernan and O'Dwyer, were never friends. They never hugged one another, or grabbed each other by their shoulders and formally acknowledged one another in Croke Park. It wasn't their style. Certainly, it wasn't in the emotional armoury of Kevin Heffernan to lower his own defences very much at any point in his life.

But it always appeared such a great shame to everyone else who watched in awe that, for almost the full dozen years, two of the greatest men in the history of Irish sport, two men who fought it out all that time like two outrageously skilful swordsmen, never once gave up, and gave in, and fell into each other's embrace.

Once . . . just once . . .

That's all that would have been needed to complete the most gripping duel perhaps that this country has ever seen enacted.

The closest Heff and O'Dwyer came to it was in 2004. For one day, in the grounds of UCD, and on a great stage, they were brothers in arms.

If not arm-in-arm, they nevertheless walked together and posed for the cameras wearing two fluffed-up mortar boards perched on their heads, and each man resembled the other in their purple and red cloaks, and their purple and green neckwear.

Mick O'Dwyer did most of the talking, resembling more of a Cheshire cat than his new best friend for a day. Kevin Heffernan responded to O'Dwyer. He laughed too, and in full glare of the Irish public he had never looked quite so relaxed. Each man received an Honorary Degree of Doctorate of Laws. They were joined by seventeen others who also received Honorary Degrees, including a man as quick on his feet as Michael Flatley, and a man who did his business slowly and powerfully like Willie John McBride. They were joined by scientists and industrialists, sculptors and politicians, but this particular day in University College Dublin's 150th year of celebration was owned by the pair of them.

'We didn't talk very much, hardly at all, in fact,' O'Dwyer reflected in the days after Heff's death. 'But we both knew what was going on in the other fella's mind.'

In some things in life, they were also of the same mind.

O'Dwyer never did get to manage an Irish team, far away from home, or on Irish soil. He was named as one of eight men under consideration for the Irish manager's job, for the return trip by Australia in 1987, but decided to withdraw his name from a race that looked a little unseemly to him. Heff's name was also on the list. After all he had achieved in Australia in 1986, he was also informed that he would have to line up with seven others.

Heff soon said he was also out.

Heff stayed in St Vincents thereafter.

There, he coached important teams and unimportant teams, slow teams like the junior 4 footballers, and young teams like the Under-15 hurlers. Both won their championships under Heff.

He also stayed in the shadows within the county.

For the twenty-seven years after his 'retirement' as Dublin manager he had no direct role in the appointment of anyone else to the job which, because of Heff himself, had become the toughest and highest-profile piece of work in the Gaelic Athletic Association. But there was never a Dublin manager appointed in all of that time without someone whispering that someone else had whispered to them that Kevin Heffernan had been consulted, that he'd had his say.

A whisper that Heff had nodded his head.

Or had not done so.

In the 1990s, his once young friend Mickey Whelan was appointed Dublin team manager. Whelan had been 'adopted' by St Vincents as an older footballer. Heff minded him at the start, and then they became resolute friends. They would go to the cinema together the night before the bigger games, to the Savoy or the Carlton at the bottom of O'Connell Street. Whenever they asked one another for help, it was a request that could never be declined.

In 1969 Whelan had emigrated to the US and qualified as something of a 'genius' in physically preparing football teams. When Whelan came back home four years later, Heff asked him to devise the training regime that would make Dublin, in 1974, the fittest team there had ever been in Gaelic football.

When a Vincents man asked, another Vincents man could never say no. That was one of the 'unbreakables' in the life and times of St Vincents GAA club.

Twenty-two years later, Mickey Whelan was manager of the Dublin team that was setting out in the Leinster championship, in the defence of the All-Ireland title so hard-won by Pat O'Neill in September of 1995. That defence opened against Westmeath. The game was in Navan, which meant the Dublin team boarding a bus for a change.

When the players climbed up the steps of the bus each man, in turn, was surprised to see Kevin Heffernan, sitting there, two seats behind the driver. Nobody was told what Heff was doing there.

Heff just said hello to the fellas.

They didn't see him in the dressing-room in Páirc Tailteann

before the game. Westmeath were beaten by ten points, and two weeks later the players boarded the same bus. Dublin were on the road again, back to Navan to play Louth in the Leinster semi-final. Heff was seated in the same seat as before.

Again, he said hello to the fellas, some of whom, like team captain John O'Leary, had been brought on to the Dublin team and managed by him for half a dozen years. Heff did not explain to anybody what he was doing on the team bus.

When O'Leary asked why Heff was hanging around the team, he was told little or nothing. He was actually informed that Kevin Heffernan had no lift to the two matches, and that Mickey Whelan had told his old friend that he could hop on the team bus if he liked.

O'Leary knew that was a child's answer.

Dublin would lose to Meath in the 1996 Leinster final, forfeiting their All-Ireland crown before the summer was half over.

After 'retiring' in 1986 Heff had never been seen in the company of the Dublin football team before that summer. And, after '96, he was never seen up so close to the team ever again.

They came to him.

His face did appear on a postage stamp.

For a man who valued his privacy, and made its protection a rabidly intense mission throughout his adult life, to the point that he really lacked only a guard dog at work day and night, it was a particularly beguiling day, the day Heff received into his hands a page of stamps with his face on every one of them.

But Heff knew when to oblige.

Those were mainly days when he had no bloody choice.

In 1984 Kevin Heffernan was named at left corner-forward on the GAA's Football Team of the Century. Sixteen years later, he was again named in the No.15 shirt on the Team of the Millennium. He was the only Dublin footballer on either team and, each time, he had six Kerrymen for teammates.

On each occasion, there were dinners and speeches, and a great big fuss was made for an entire afternoon in Croke Park. Worse still, the postage stamps, presenting coloured drawings of the faces of each man on the Team of the Millennium, were in public use for the next twelve months.

Kevin Heffernan had never gone out of his way to look for glory, at work or play. Almost all of his daily working life had been consumed by the Electricity Supply Board. He had joined in 1950, in central stores, and after graduating from Trinity College with a Bachelor of Commerce degree he moved to the ESB's head office, where he spent twenty years moving through ranks, working in accounts, then finance, becoming an assistant accountant in Sligo, then coming back to Dublin to move into the research and audit departments. In 1970 he was appointed to the personnel department, where he took up the job as manager of industrial relations. He was a consultant on ESB projects in Saudi Arabia and Sudan but, after thirty-six years of service, he left on early retirement in 1985.

Bertie Ahern, the Minister for Labour, wanted Kevin Heffernan to become chairman of the Labour Court. And Heff was duly appointed, and served in the role until August 1994 with the steadiest hand, even though Ahern's predecessor in office, Labour's Ruarí Quinn had initially criticized the appointment as a retrograde step that broke with the tradition of impartiality and fair play. Heff had been nominated to the position by the Federated Union of Employers. Ruarí Quinn thought it quite like 'making Heffo referee between Dublin and Kerry and expecting him to be impartial at all times'.

Heff got stuck into being the best he could possibly be at the job.

That was the most supreme quality to his nature as a man. At the Labour Court, and with Bord na gCon, where he was chairman until 1995, and where a decade later he was asked to chair a new body built to police greyhound racing for doping offences, Heff mostly did a quiet and stunningly effective job of work.

He loved his dogs.

He liked human beings more, especially those who played football and hurling, but Heff made many more appearances in Shelbourne Park than he ever did in Croke Park. In neither place did he like to mingle with royalty. The riff-raff and the cheap seats were more to his liking.

As chairman of the greyhound board he had helped in overviewing the building of Shelbourne Park into a magnificent home for the sport, where people could dine in considerable style, and drink at polished wooden counters. And watch the dogs through a vast expanse of glass, not having to even think of budging from their seats if they wished to place a few bob on the backside of one of the mutts.

Heff loved his dogs all right, and he owned and co-owned a few down through his adult years, and once owned a small part of a horse, but in Shelbourne Park anyone wishing to find him knew they would do so on ground level underneath the fancy new stand.

Heff did not have a fine seat at a great height.

Instead, he had his usual 'spot'.

Heff stepped into the limelight only when there was no other way out, and, on 17 May 2004, he prepared himself for such a day.

He was conferred a Freeman of Dublin.

He admitted to feeling 'very chuffed'.

He also told journalists that he knew the honour meant that he could graze his sheep, if he decided to purchase any in the future, in places like College Green and St Stephen's Green.

'I know when you are dead they fly the flags at half mast,' he added, before he signed the necessary papers which put him in the same company as Isaac Butt, the great political leader who was the first to be honoured by the city, in 1876. Heff, suddenly, was in the company of the most exalted and highest order.

John McCormack, George Bernard Shaw, John F. Kennedy and Eamonn de Valera, Noel Purcell, Maureen Potter and Bono and all of U2, including the band's manager Paul McGuinness, had been conferred before him on days such as Kevin Heffernan's big day in the centre of his home city.

None of them, however, apart from Ulysses S. Grant, who accepted his 'freedom' when he was on an around-the-world trip with his wife Julia in 1879, and definitely not Mother Teresa nor Bob

Geldof, would really have been made of the right stuff to enact the requirements carried in the small print of the conferring.

Heff, and the American Civil War general, no doubt would have been up to defending the city from attack, as the 'Freedom' could have called upon either man to defend the city and join its militia at short notice.

And each Freeman and Freewoman, as nailed down by law in 1465, has, at that time, to provide themselves with a longbow, and twelve arrows, made of yew, witch-hazel or ash.

For such a fight, Heff would turn up.

However, whether Kevin Heffernan would listen to Ulysses S. Grant, or have some ideas of his own written down on the flattened insides of a packet of cigarettes, would have remained unknown.

Notes on Sources

As explained at the beginning of this book, I first met Kevin Heffernan in the early 1980s. From my first meeting, I found him to be less fierce and far less daunting as a character to sit down with, and to chat with informally, than I had ever imagined. Heffo could be scary all right, but away from GAA fields, one on one, he was usually welcoming and kindly, and for a young man like myself starting out my adult life as a footballer and a journalist, it was always an especially rewarding experience to spend time with him.

I was lucky enough to do so on many occasions, and the last time we spoke, in May of 2011, whether it was because of my ill health, or Heffo's pending ill health, we spoke intimately about a great many football men and football games.

The quotes from Heffo which introduce each of the chapters in this book come from a wide number of sources, but a great many of them are also taken from our own conversations, and that last conversation.

In these notes, I am offering the sources from which I read, for the first time, a great many of Kevin Heffernan's thoughts on GAA life, and winning and losing. If some of these same quotes originated elsewhere – and were first offered by Heffo to other journalists – then I would like to take this opportunity to fully acknowledge those sources and to express my thanks and, where any oversight or omission may occur, I would like to offer my apologies in advance.

Chapters 1 and 2

The opening quote to Chapter 1 was said to me by Heffo in our last meeting. The opening quote to Chapter 2 is taken from *Football Captains: the All-Ireland Winners*, a superb body of work undertaken by RTÉ's Brian Carthy in 1993 and published by Wolfhound Press.

As a personal rule, I do not attend funerals, unless the deceased is a family member or a close friend. Therefore I did not attend the Church of St Vincent de Paul when Kevin Heffernan's remains were brought to his home parish in the final week of January 2013, nor did I attend his funeral mass the next day.

Details of Kevin Heffernan's last journeys were taken from contemporary newspaper reports, as were the words of those who spoke from the altar (including Fr John Fitzpatrick, Tony Hanahoe and Pat Gilroy).

Also the words spoken by Mickey Whelan ('they did him proud') outside the church were reported by John Fogarty in the *Irish Examiner*.

Details on the deaths of Heffo's friends and opponents, including Des and Lar Foley, Ollie Freaney, Noel Drumgoole, Mick Holden, Tim Kennelly, John Egan and Páidí Ó Sé were taken from contemporary newspaper reports.

I also spoke to several of Heffo's friends and teammates who attended the church on both days.

Chapter 3

The opening quote to Chapter 3 appeared in an interview given to Tom Humphries of the *Irish Times* in 2006.

The biographical details of the Right Reverend Monsignor William Fitzpatrick, the co-founder of St Vincents GAA club, appeared in the club's silver jubilee history, which was published in 1981.

The story of 'Doc' Fitzpatrick's car carrying up to fourteen boys to games in the Phoenix Park was retold to me by Dessie Ferguson.

Information on the creation of Marino parish, which appears in Chapters 3, 4, 5 and 6 in particular, was obtained from a variety of sources including St Vincents club history, and the following websites: www.marinoparish.ie; www.theirishstory.com (Rhona McCord, 'A Garden City – the Dublin Corporation Housing Scheme at Marino, 1924'); www.ucd.ie (Ruth McManus, 'Public Utility Societies, Dublin Corporation and the Development of Dublin, 1920–1940').

Chapter 4

The opening quote to Chapter 4 appeared in Brian Carthy's *Football Captains: the All-Ireland Winners*.

The biographical details of Reverend Brother Ernest Fitzgerald, who co-founded St Vincents GAA club with the 'Doc' Fitzpatrick, appeared in the club's silver jubilee history.

Chapter 5

The account of how Kevin Heffernan, Jimmy Lavin, Joe Duffy, Dessie Ferguson and two of their friends from Civil Service GAA club, decided to purchase and build their houses as one 'building project' was recounted to me by Dessie Ferguson.

Chapter 6

The opening quote to Chapter 6 first appeared in David Walsh's seminal work 'Back to the Hill', which included interviews with Heffo and all of his team, and was published in *Magill* magazine in 1989.

The story of 'the Kerry Medals' and the subsequent meeting between Scoil Mhuire, Marino and Westland Row appeared in St Vincents GAA club history.

Chapter 8

The opening quote to Chapter 8 appeared in Tom Humphries' book, *Dublin v Kerry: the Story of the Epic Rivalry that Changed Irish Sport*, which was published by Penguin Ireland in 2006.

Chapter 9

St Vincents' defeat in the 1951 Dublin senior hurling final, and the injuries suffered by Seán Óg Ó Ceallacháin of Eoghan Ruadh in that game, were honestly recounted in St Vincents GAA club's jubilee history, in which the club also expressed its regret for its role in that violent encounter.

Sean McDermott's rivalry with St Vincents was recounted to me in 2012 by Paddy 'Hands' O'Brien, when he also spoke of his subsequent memories of playing against Kevin Heffernan, in particular the famous 1955 Leinster final (see Chapter 10) when Meath, as All-Ireland champions, were taken apart and left baffled by the running tactics of the Dublin team.

Chapter 10

The quote introducing Chapter 10 was published in Brian Carthy's *Football Captains: the All-Ireland Winners*.

The biographical details of the legendary Kerry trainer, Dr Eamonn O'Sullivan, appeared in Weeshie Fogarty's expertly detailed www.terracetalk.com.

Chapter 11

The opening quote to Chapter 11 appeared in Tom Humphries' *Dublin v Kerry: the Story of the Epic Rivalry that Changed Irish Sport*.

The account of how Kerry captain John Dowling appeared on the field on his own before the 1955 All-Ireland final has been adapted from the interview with the player conducted by Brian Carthy in *Football Captains: the All-Ireland Winners*.

The full story of the 1955 All-Ireland final was probably most dramatically recounted by Mick Dunne in the *Irish Press* in the two days following Dublin's defeat to Kerry, and certainly Dunne's writings helped me greatly in re-enacting the two most traumatic defeats in Kevin Heffernan's football career (the second defeat, re-enacted in Chapter 12, was the 1957 Leinster final loss to Louth).

Chapter 12

The opening quote to Chapter 12 appeared in Brian Carthy's *Football Captains: the All-Ireland Winners*.

Chapter 14

The legendary story of how a recently retired Kevin Heffernan drove to north Meath and talked Dessie Ferguson into ending his own retirement and famously playing for Dublin the next day against Kildare, in the Leinster championship, was recounted in brilliant detail for me by Dessie Ferguson in the same family home in which Heffo suddenly appeared that Saturday morning.

Chapter 16

The opening quote to Chapter 16 appeared in an interview given to Tom Humphries of the *Irish Times* in 2006.

The fiercesomeness of the meetings between St Vincents and UCD in the seventies have been recounted on many occasions, but some of these games and, in particular, the dual role of Pat O'Neill as a 'footballer and a medical doctor' quickly became folklore – and often 'grew and grew' with the telling as footballers sought to impress one another with what they had heard. The stories of these games (and their entrails) were handed down to me as an impressionable young footballer by UCD students and my later Meath colleagues, Gerry McEntee and Colm O'Rourke.

Chapter 17

The opening quote to Chapter 17 first appeared in David Walsh's 'Back to the Hill' in *Magill* magazine in 1989.

I relied on Bernard Brogan (the senior!) for guidance when recounting the early days of Heffo's managerial reign in 1973–74. Bernard was also generous and honest in detailing the staggered start of his own brilliant career – as well as its sudden conclusion.

Kevin Heffernan's encounter with the legendary Kilkenny county secretary, Paddy Grace, before one 'underwhelming' meeting between Kilkenny and Dublin in December of 1973 in Division Two of the National League, has been documented in a number of different publications (the game preceding Kilkenny and Dublin has different participants and is a different grade, in most!). I took guidance from them all, and adapted this meeting in Nowlan Park on this occasion.

Chapter 18

The opening quote to Chapter 18 first appeared in David Walsh's 'Back to the Hill' in *Magill* magazine in 1989.

Heffo's surprise conversation with a young Terry Jennings has also appeared in many other publications, and the exact exchange between the Dublin manager and the boy about Jimmy Keaveney vary in detail. Once again, I have adapted this conversation on this occasion.

Chapter 19

The conversation between Jimmy Keaveney and his Cork friends, Frank Cogan and Billy Morgan, has appeared in a number of publications. I have adapted the exchange on this occasion.

Kevin Heffernan's performances on the golf course in 1974 – in the Lord Mayor's Cup and in winning the Clontarf Golf Club Captain's Prize – are taken from contemporary newspaper reports.

After Heffo's death, Dermot Gileece penned a tribute in the *Irish Independent* to the man's skills as a golfer, which also gave an insight to Heff's peculiarities when he spent time in his beloved golf club.

Chapter 20

The opening quote to Chapter 20 appeared in *The Sunday Times* in 2013.

The plotting of the Kerry full-forward line to get a 'hit' on Dublin goalkeeper, Paddy Cullen – and the advice of Páidí Ó Sé – has been written about in many publications, though I chose to rely on Páidí's own account of this exchange which was published in his autobiography, *Páidí: the Life of Gaelic Football Legend Páidí Ó Sé*, as told to Seán Potts, which was published by Townhouse in 2011.

Chapter 21

Mick O'Dwyer's attendance in 1975 at a GAA coaching course in Gormanston College that was being presented by Kevin Heffernan and Down star Joe Lennon has been written about in many publications. Equally, there have been different versions of how O'Dwyer was coerced into taking up the job as manager of the Kerry football team. In both of these cases I chose to be guided in the main, though not entirely, by Mick O'Dwyer's autobiography, *Blessed and Obsessed: Official Autobiography of Mick O'Dwyer*, with Martin Breheny, which was published by Blackwater Press in 2007.

Mick O'Dwyer's thoughts in the autumn of 1975 on the evolution of Gaelic football and his frustration with same ('If that's the way Gaelic football was going then the GAA should change the blessed rule, and let everyone throw it. Get rid of the fisted pass and the handpass altogether') were taken from interviews O'Dwyer gave to newspapermen before the '75 All-Ireland final.

Chapter 22

The opening quote to Chapter 22 appeared in David Walsh's 'Back to the Hill' in *Magill* magazine in 1989.

The manner in which Kevin Heffernan used the old Nissen hut in Parnell Park for team meetings, and the effect this had on almost all of his players, has been documented in many publications over the decades since the early seventies, though because of the extraordinary nature of the conversations, what transpired and what was said by individuals in 'the hut' varies between many of these same publications. I also spoke to Heffo about the importance of those team meetings, and how he controlled the emotions of his players before major championship games and, therefore, in Chapter 22, and subsequent chapters, I give a freshly constructed and intimate account of life in 'the hut' (which in most other publications is referred to as 'the shed').

Chapter 23
The opening quote to Chapter 23 appeared in Brian Carthy's *Football Captains: the All-Ireland Winners.*

Páidí Ó Sé's arrival in Dublin, on the train with the rest of the Kerry team before the 1975 All-Ireland final, is based on his own account of that early day which was published in his autobiography, *Páidí: the Life of Gaelic Football Legend Páidí Ó Sé*, as told to Seán Potts. Also, the dressing-room conversation before the 1975 Munster final between the late Páidí and the late Kerry legend Joe Keohane first appeared in the same publication.

Chapter 25
The opening quote to Chapter 25 appeared in the *Irish Press* in 1976.

Chapter 27
The opening quote to Chapter 27 appeared in Tom Humphries' *Dublin v Kerry: the Story of the Epic Rivalry that Changed Irish Sport.*

The interaction and conversation between Kevin Heffernan and Bobby Doyle in the hours and minutes before the 1976 All-Ireland final have been recounted in a wide number of publications. I have adapted their exchanges in this chapter.

Croke Park groundsman Con O'Leary's work before the 1976 All-Ireland final, and his view on the condition of his beloved pitch, appeared in contemporary newspaper reports.

Chapter 28
The opening quote to Chapter 28 appeared in the *Irish Independent* in 1976.

Chapter 30
The biographical profile of Tony Hanahoe was built, in particular, on the writings of David Walsh, Brian Carthy and Tom Humphries.

Chapter 31
The opening quote to Chapter 31 appeared in *The Sunday Times* in 2013.

Chapter 32
The opening quote to Chapter 32 appeared in the *Irish Times* in 2006.

The quick conversation between Mick O'Dwyer and Eoin Liston

midway through the first half of the 1978 All-Ireland final – when Liston complained to O'Dwyer of being injured – is sourced from Mick O'Dwyer's autobiography, *Blessed and Obsessed: Official Autobiography of Mick O'Dwyer*, with Martin Breheny.

Chapter 33

Mick Holden's elaborate excuse for being late to a Dublin training session is sourced from Tom Humphries' *Dublin v Kerry: the Story of the Epic Rivalry that Changed Irish Sport*, though the late Mick Holden also recounted the same conversation to me. I have recounted the conversation as it appeared in Humphries' book.

Chapter 34

The opening quote to Chapter 34 appeared in the *Irish Press* in 1984.

Kevin Heffernan's brief, angry conversation with Barney Rock late in the first All-Ireland semi-final between Dublin and Cork in 1983 was sourced from a tribute article penned by Rock in the *Irish Daily Mail* in 2013.

Brian Mullins' near tragic car crash in 1980, and his thoughts and emotions, are sourced from several publications, but, in particular, the writings of David Walsh and Tom Humphries.

Chapter 35

The opening quote to Chapter 35 appeared in John O'Leary's autobiography, *Back to the Hill: John O'Leary, the Official Biography*, with Martin Breheny, which was pubished by Blackwater Press in 1997.

John O'Leary's illness, and the 'medication' he received from Kevin Heffernan, before the 1983 All-Ireland final replay between Dublin and Cork was sourced from the same book.

Chapter 36

The opening quote to Chapter 36 appeared in the *Irish Press* in 1983.

Kevin Heffernan's instructions in the Dublin dressing-room at half-time in the 1983 All-Ireland final were adapted from contemporary newspaper reports and private conversations I had with several of the Dublin players when we were selected on Leinster teams together in the years that followed.

Chapter 38
Kevin Heffernan's final words to the Dublin team, when he ordered them to 'reclaim' the Hill 16 end of Croke Park from the Tyrone team that was warming up there, is taken from contemporary newspaper reports, and my own private conversations with Dublin players.

Chapter 39
The opening quote to Chapter 39 appeared in John O'Leary's autobiography, *Back to the Hill: John O'Leary, the Official Biography*, with Martin Breheny.

Páidí Ó Sé's physical exchange with Joe McNally prior to and during the playing of the national anthem before the 1984 All-Ireland final between Dublin and Kerry has been reported in several publications but I have adapted the incident from Páidí's 2001 autobiography, *Páidí: the Life of Gaelic Football Legend Páidí Ó Sé*, as told to Seán Potts.

Chapter 40
The opening quote to Chapter 40 appeared in the *Irish Independent* in 1985.

Chapter 41
The opening quote to Chapter 41 appeared in the *Irish Press* in 1986.

Chapter 42
The opening quote to Chapter 42 appeared in the *Irish Press* in 1986.

Jack O'Shea explained in *The Sunday Times* in 2013, in a tribute penned on Kevin Heffernan's life and times, that Heffo, for some reason, always called him 'Johnno' during the Irish tour of Australia in 1986.

Peter Quinn's conversation with Heffo, at half-time during the Ulster final in 1986, was recounted to me by Peter, and has been adapted in this instance.

Chapter 43
The opening quote to Chapter 43 appeared in the *Irish Independent* in 1986.

Kevin Heffernan's conversation with Mick Lyons and his subsequent order, when he dispatched Lyons to start a fight with the Australian Robert Di Pierdomenico ('the Dipper') during the second test between Ireland

and Australia in 1986, was recounted to me by Heffo in our last conversation. It has been adapted in this instance. 'The Dipper's' brief conversation with Mick Lyons as the fight was nearing a conclusion was recounted to me by Mick Lyons.

Chapter 44

The opening quote to Chapter 44 appeared in Teddy McCarthy's autobiography, *Teddy Boy: the Teddy McCarthy Autobiography*, with Donal Keenan, published by Irish Sports Publishing in 2012.

Kevin Heffernan's conversations with Teddy McCarthy before the third test between Ireland and Australia in 1986 were recounted to me by Teddy in the first instance, and later appeared in Teddy's autobiography.

Epilogue

The opening quote to the Epilogue appeared in *The Sunday Times* in 2013.

Kevin Heffernan's appearance on the Dublin team coach, on the two occasions in 1996 when he joined the team and management on their way to Leinster championship games, was sourced from John O'Leary's autobiography, *Back to the Hill: John O'Leary, the Official Biography*, with Martin Breheny. The explanation given to O'Leary for Heffo's presence each day was also sourced from the same book.

Bibliography

Books and Magazines

Teddy Boy: the Teddy McCarthy Autobiography, Teddy McCarthy and Donal Keenan, Irish Sports Publishing, 2012

Princes of Pigskin: a Century of Kerry Footballers, Joe Ó Muircheartaigh and TJ Flynn, The Collins Press, 2008

Blessed and Obsessed, Mick O'Dwyer and Martin Breheny, Blackwater Press, 2007

Dublin v Kerry, Tom Humphries, Penguin, 2006

Páidí: the Life of Gaelic football Legend Páidí Ó Sé, Páidí Ó Sé and Sean Potts, Townhouse, 2001

The Final Whistle: the Colm O'Rourke Autobiography, Colm O'Rourke, Hero Books, 1996

Back to the Hill: the Official Biography of John O'Leary, Martin Breheny, Blackwater Press, 1997

Football Captains: the All-Ireland Winners, Brian Carthy, Wolfhound Press, 1993

'Back to the Hill', David Walsh, *Magill* magazine, January 1989

St Vincents GAA Club: a History, 1931–1981

Newspapers

'For Heffo, it was always about the team', *Irish Examiner*, 30 January 2013

'GAA Icon Heffo begins his final journey home', *Irish Independent*, 29 January 2013

'Dub's spiritual director "Humble Heffo" gets final round of applause', *Irish Independent*, 30 January 2013

'Farewell to a Legend', *Irish Daily Mail*, 30 January 2013

'Heffernan was before his time', *The Sunday Times*, 27 January 2013

'King of the Hill', *The Sunday Times*, 27 January 2013

'We listened to Heffo more than anyone in the game', *Irish Daily Mail*, 26 January 2013

'Micko: there was always a huge respect between the two of us', *Irish Independent*, 26 January 2013

'Kerry pioneers the kings of the urban-rural frontier', the *Irish Times*, 17 September 2011

'From Dublin to the wilds of north Meath unscathed', the *Meath Chronicle*, 15 December 2010

'Mickey Whelan: more than a simple purist', the *Irish Times*, 22 April 2009

'Friends pen tribute to Dubs legend Joe', *Evening Herald*, 4 February 2009

'Blue bloods keeping it in the family', the *Irish Times*, 25 August 2007

'Hanahoe hopes for capital gain', the *Irish Times*, 24 August 2007

'Yank Murray – a star on the GAA fields of Fingal', *Fingal Independent*, 1 February 2006

'Death of Noel Drumgoole', the *Irish Times*, 11 January 2005

'Ned Roche, "The Exile", had an indestructible presence', the *Kerryman*, 24 October 2004

'Todd garners gathering of greats', Australianrules.com.au, 2004

'The John Todd story', wafootyforum.yuku.com, 26 February 2004

'GAA mourns sudden death of Lar Foley', *Irish Independent*, 5 May 2003

'Celebrating the footballing achievements of Kerry's Ned Roche and Eddie Walsh', the *Kerryman*, 28 March 2002

'Pioneers run rules over the Rules', the *Irish Times*, 10 October 1998

'New rinse for the blue brigade', the *Irish Times*, 8 June 1996

'Foley a great dual player', *Irish Press*, 7 February 1995

'The shooting star who fell to earth and had a second meteoric rise', the *Irish Times*, 18 September 1993

'Death of Ollie Freaney', the *Irish Times*, 28 September 1991

'Kevin Heffernan named Labour Court chairman', *Irish Press*, 8 April 1989

'O'Shea appointed captain of Ireland team for tour', *Irish Press*, 26 September 1986

'Heffernan's voyage into the unknown', the *Irish Times*, 1 October 1986

'Dublin's brave fightback is halted in remarkable final', the *Irish Times*, 23 September 1985

'Too close for Dublin's comfort', *Irish Press*, 9 September 1985

'Commando-style raids gain Dublin success', the *Irish Times*, 9 September 1985

'John Finn calls for inquiry', *Irish Press*, 30 August 1985

'Liston sent off, Kerry crush feeble Monaghan', *Irish Press*, 26 August 1985

'Injury to Finn will make him miss replay', *Irish Independent*, 22 August 1985

'Smiles all round as Brogan inspires Mayo to a draw', the *Irish Times*, 19 August 1985

'Brilliant Laois backs make Dublin work all the way for victory', *Irish Independent*, 29 July 1985

'No problems expected for Dublin selectors', *Irish Independent*, 23 July 1985

'Ragged Dublin could not withstand Kerry spirit', the *Irish Times*, 24 September 1984

'O'Shea brilliance may not suffice for Kerrymen', the *Irish Times*, 22 September 1984

'Mick Holden – the joker in the Dublin pack', the *Irish Times*, 21 September 1984

'Formidable opponents says Heffernan', *Irish Independent*, 20 September 1984

'Dublin bandwagon keeps rolling but a bit out of tune', the *Irish Times*, 20 August 1984

'Memorable for all the wrong reasons', the *Irish Times*, 20 August 1984

'O'Shea-inspired Kerry make it another day of woe for Galway', the *Irish Times*, 13 August 1984

'14-Man Dublin hold on tight with Meath', *Irish Independent*, 23 July 1984

'Blow to Dublin as Heffernan leaves for Sudan', *Irish Independent*, 21 January 1984

'Match brought no credit to the GAA', *Irish Independent*, 20 September 1983

'Galway protest following interval incident', the *Irish Times*, 19 September 1983

'Four sent to the line in unsavoury final,' the *Irish Times*, 19 September 1983

'McNally's rapid promotion,' the *Irish Times*, 15 September 1983

'Dublin victory margin astonishes', the *Irish Times*, 30 August 1983

'Cork left to regret moment of slackness', the *Irish Times*, 22 August 1983

'Improved Dublin surprise champions in exciting final', *Irish Press*, 1 August 1983

'Dublin just beat Meath in test of spirit and stamina', the *Irish Times*, 4 July 1984

'Meath and Dublin provide few thrills', *Irish Independent*, 13 June 1983

'Heffernan receives a caution', *Irish Press*, 6 December 1982

'Heffernan to explain Tralee incident', *Irish Press*, 4 December 1982

'Leading the Dubs out of the desert', the *Irish Times*, 2 December 1981

'Heffernan still Dublin adviser', *Irish Press*, 2 October 1979

'Heffernan plays an active role in Dublin training', *Irish Independent*, 6 July 1979

'Dublin's supremacy never threatened', the *Irish Times*, 26 September 1977

'Hanahoe makes own mark as Dublin chief', *Irish Independent*, 22 September 1977

'Heffernan heads jobs team', *Irish Press*, 6 September 1977

'Kerry attack should win keen tactical battle', the *Irish Times*, 20 August 1977

'Special meeting to seek Heffernan's successor', *Irish Independent*, 21 October 1976

'Dublin quintet receive unique Trinity tribute', the *Irish Times*, 13 October 1976

'Heffernan will decide in week's time', *Irish Independent*, 12 October 1976

'The thoughts of Heffo', the *Irish Times*, 25 September 1976

'Croke Park is prepared come hell or high water', *Irish Independent*, 25 September 1976

'O'Reilly out of favour in half-back line', *Irish Press*, 25 August 1976

'Meath take 1974 O'Byrne Cup with late score', the *Irish Times*, 22 March 1976

'St Vincents worth much bigger victory', *Irish Independent*, 23 February 1976

'Heffernan takes charge of Leinster team', *Irish Independent*, 10 February 1976

'Uncertainty of last year is replaced by the confidence of kings', the *Irish Times*, 25 September 1975

'Derry show resolution and skill but lack the team work of the champions', the *Irish Times*, 25 August 1975

'Kildare deeply humiliated despite numerous glaring Dublin misses', *Irish Press*, 28 July 1975

'O'Connell still a key figure in Derry's bid', the *Irish Times*, 22 August 1975

'Heffo's fans take over the festivities', *Irish Press*, 24 September 1974

'Lord Mayor's Cup: Heffernan has double date', *Irish Press*, 8 August 1974

'Lord Mayor's Cup: Heffernan continues forward march', *Irish Press*, 14 August 1974

'Lord Mayor's Cup: Heffernan goes out to Corkman Condon', *Irish Press*, 16 August 1974

'St Vincents regain Dublin title', *Irish Press*, 16 July 1966

'Champions rarely had full team available', *Irish Press*, 24 September 1963

'Heffernan may play in crisis', the *Irish Times*, 17 September 1963

'Dublin through to final – superb comeback by Des Ferguson', the *Irish Times*, 24 June 1963

'St Vincents still Dublin champions', *Irish Press*, 12 November 1962

'St Vincents complete a notable double', *Irish Press*, 19 September 1960

'Five-goal Joyce led massacre at Mullingar', *Irish Press*, 30 May 1960

'It's that old Kerry magic', *Irish Press*, 17 August 1959

'It's Dublin–Kerry', *Irish Press*, 3 August 1959

'Dublin make no mistake', *Irish Press*, 27 July 1959

'Last minute point earns draw', *Irish Press*, 6 July 1958

'Heffernan's help wins O'Byrne Cup', *Irish Press*, 6 April 1959

'Dublin's victory – exiles did not avail of chances', *Irish Press*, 6 October 1958

'Jubilant Dublin fans greet their teams', *Irish Press*, 30 September 1958

'The penalty that never was: Derry content after their gallant bid', *Irish Press*, 30 September 1958

'Dublin's Day – lightning goal puts paid to Ulster rally', *Irish Press*, 29 September 1958

'Superb forward line breach dauntless Derry defence', *Irish Press*, 29 September 1958

'Dublin's last kick a winner', *Irish Press*, 18 August 1958

'Louth flattered by final score', the *Irish Times*, 21 July 1958

'Dublin recapture Leinster crown', *Irish Press*, 21 July 1958

'Doubt over Dubs attacking movement', the *Sunday Press*, 20 July 1958

'Carlow's selectors gave Dublin every chance', *Irish Press*, 23 June 1958

'Resurgent Dublin's great win', *Irish Press*, 2 June 1958

'Fitter Dublin advance – Mayo meet faster masters', *Irish Press*, 21 April 1958

'Dublin steamroll: champions' hope of double vanishes', *Irish Press*, 24 March 1958

'Louth win Leinster – Dublin fail to last the pace', *Irish Press*, 8 July 1957

'Dublin coast to Leinster final', *Irish Press*, 24 June 1957

'GAA denial of rough play in American games', the *Irish Times*, 14 June 1956

'Another football title for Kerry; narrow victory over Dublin's injury-hit side', the *Irish Times*, 26 September 1955

'The kingdom wins 18th title', *Irish Press*, 26 September 1955

'Dublin in final at last', *Irish Press*, 12 September 1955

'Challengers great play routed Meath', *Irish Press*, 25 July 1955

'St Vincents hurlers for senior ranks', *Evening Herald*, 18 December 1941

Websites

www.terracetalk.com (Dr Eamonn O'Sullivan's son writes about his father – the legendary Kerry trainer)

www.terracetalk.com (Dr Eamonn O'Sullivan, a man before his time, by Weeshie Fogarty)

www.marinoparish.ie

www.theirishstory.com (Rhona McCord, 'A Garden City – the Dublin Corporation Housing Scheme at Marino, 1924')

www.ucd.ie (Ruth McManus, 'Public Utility Societies, Dublin Corporation and the Development of Dublin, 1920–1940')

www.dublinheritage.ie

www.ucd.ie (UCD's rich footballing history)

www.independent.ie (Sporting allrounder transformed ailing fortunes of GAA in Dublin, January 27, 2013)

Picture Acknowledgements

Page 1

A young Kevin Heffernan at the beginning of his Dublin career: © *Independent News and Media* PL335879; Heffernan poses at the start of his 'long war': © *Independent News and Media* PL1845992; Dublin team, 1955 All-Ireland final: © Connolly Collection/Sportsfile 745217.jpg.

Page 2

1955 All-Ireland final: © *Independent News and Media* PL1915585; Dessie 'Snitchie' Ferguson with the Dublin team: © *Independent News and Media* PL1955630; the Dublin team in the 1965 National Legue semi-final: © Connolly Collection/Sportsfile PL1507566.

Page 3

The Dublin team before the 1974 All-Ireland final: © Connolly Collection/Sportsfile 415039.jpg; Heff keeps a close eye on proceedings: © *Independent News and Media* PL1695980; Mickey Ned O'Sullivan leads the Kerry team on the pre-match parade: © Connolly Collection/Sportsfile 047461.jpg.

Page 4

Heff and Tony Hanahoe: © *Independent News and Media* PL1696692; Sean Doherty, 1977 All-Ireland semi-final: © Connolly Collection/Sportsfile 745227.jpg; Eoin 'the Bomber' Liston beats Mick Holden in the air, 1979 All-Ireland final: © Connolly Collection/Sportsfile 284490.jpg.

Page 5
Jimmy Keaveney against Kerry in 1981: © Ray McManus/Sportsfile 028091.jpg; Mícheál O'Hehir and Heff: © Ray McManus/Sportsfile 018206.jpg; Heff and David Hickey: © *Independent News and Media* PL1916090

Page 6
John Gough sends Brian Mullins to the line: © Ray McManus/Sportsfile 019842.jpg; Brian Mullins leads the Dublin team in the pre-match parade before the All-Ireland final against Kerry in 1985: © Ray McManus/Sportsfile 190042.jpg; Páidi Ó Sé lifts the Sam Maguire Cup: © Ray McManus/Sportsfile 190039.jpg.

Page 7
Mick O'Dwyer, 1986 All-Ireland final: © Ray McManus/Sportsfile 190003.jpg; Heff congratulates Jack O'Shea: © Sportsfile 709674.jpg; Kevin Heffernan sits amongst his Irish squad, 1986: © The Peter McDermott Collection/GAA c1987003.

Page 8
Team of the Millennium: Heff stands between Pat Spillane and Mick O'Connell: © Ray McManus/Sportsfile 031572.jpg; the surviving members of the Dublin team that captured the National League title in 1953 regrouped in 2012: © Sportsfile 625967.jpg.

Index

Note: KH in the index refers to Kevin Heffernan.

ABOUT THE AUTHOR

Liam Hayes was a midfielder on the successful Meath football team that won All-Ireland titles in 1987 and 1988, and captained the Royals in their legendary four-game saga against Dublin in the Leinster Championship in 1991 before being defeated in the All-Ireland final by Down.

He began his career in journalism at the *Meath Chronicle* before joining the *Sunday Press* as Chief Sports Features Writer in 1985. He is a former Sportswriter of the Year in 1986 for his writings on boxing and golf. His bestselling memoir of his years as a Meath footballer, *Out of Our Skins*, was first published in 1992 and reprinted in 2011.

He was the founder of *The Title* sports newspaper in 1996, and founding editor of *Ireland on Sunday* in 1997. In 2004 he founded Gazette Group Newspapers.